Berlitz HANDBO

AUSTRALIA

Contents

FAMILY FRIENDLY SYMBOL 👪

This symbol is used throughout the Handbook to indicate a sight, hotel, restaurant or activity that is suitable for families with children.

Top **25** Attractions

1 Uluru-Kata Tjuta National Park
Home to two of the Northern Territory's major draws: Uluru (Ayers Rock) and Kata Tjuta (The Olgas) (see p.149)

2 The Great Barrier Reef
Queensland's number one tourist attraction is as extraordinary as the brochures claim (see p.22)

3 The Great Ocean Road
International car companies regularly shoot their television commercials on Victoria's stupendously scenic coastal drive (see p.185)

4 **South Australian Wine Regions**
Wine, dine and visit the cellar doors
of world-class wineries *(see p.202)*

5 **Daintree EcoLodge & Spa** Bask
in a rainforest environment at this
Queensland eco-lodge *(see p.143)*

6 **Australia Zoo** The Queensland rep-
tile park that was home to 'Crocodile
Hunter' Steve Irwin *(see p.128)*

7 **Sovereign Hill** Victoria's heritage
park re-creates Ballarat during the
1850s goldrush *(see p.187)*

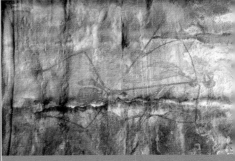

8 **Kakadu National Park** Ancient rock
art and incredible flora and fauna
southeast of Darwin *(see p.158)*

9 **National Gallery of Australia** The most impressive of Canberra's many museums and galleries *(see p.111)*

10 **The Manly Ferry** Sydney's famous ferry, from Circular Quay through the harbour to Manly *(see p.69)*

12 **Litchfield National Park** One of the Northern Territory's amazing national parks *(see p.161)*

11 **Wilson's Promontory National Park** Set up camp in Victoria's beloved 'Prom *(see p.183)*

13 **Ningaloo Reef** Coral, fish and dolphins galore in a Western Australian marine reserve *(see p.229)*

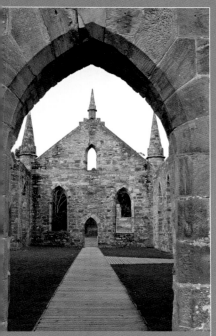

15 **Byron Bay** A sybaritic and wonderfully scenic seaside town in northern NSW (see p.85)

14 **Port Arthur** This colonial penal settlement on Tasmania's Tasman Peninsula offers a spooky ghost tour every evening (see p.244)

16 **Margaret River** Drink, eat or catch a concert in Western Australia's premier wine district (see p.223)

17 **Wilpena Pound** The remote Flinders Ranges region of South Australia is home to this natural phenomenon (see p.210)

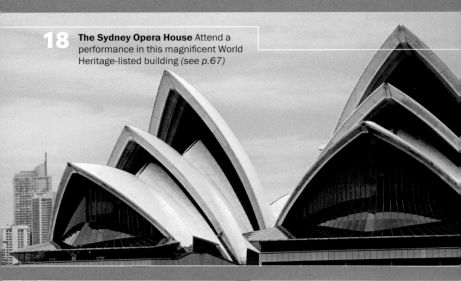

18 **The Sydney Opera House** Attend a performance in this magnificent World Heritage-listed building *(see p.67)*

19 **Mindil Beach Sunset Market** Feel the pulse of tropical Darwin while eating, drinking and shopping at this outdoor market *(see p.160)*

20 **The Eastern Beaches Coastal Walk** Spectacular coastal views and swimming opportunities on Sydney's favourite walk *(see p.76)*

21 **Cable Beach** Ride a camel along a magnificent stretch of sand in Western Australia *(see p.231)*

22 **Icebergs Dining Room** Enjoy a leisurely lunch and view the pageant on Bondi Beach *(see p.102)*

23 **Moorilla Estate** Great river views, food and art at this Hobart vineyard *(see pp.243 and 255)*

24 **Berardo's** Dine amongst socialites at this slick restaurant on Queensland's Sunshine Coast *(see p.146)*

25 **The Overland Track** An iconic bushwalk traversing the Tasmanian Wilderness *(see p.52)*

Australia Fact File

Australia is the world's sixth-largest country by area, and encompasses landscapes and climates ranging from desert to rainforest, mountains to plains. Most Australians live in cities along the eastern seaboard. New South Wales, Victoria and Queensland are the three most populous states (where around 77 percent of Australians live), and their capitals (Sydney, Melbourne and Brisbane) are home to over 10 million people, nearly half of the country's overall population.

 BASICS
Population: 22 million
Area: 7,702,491 sq km
(2,973,948 sq miles)
Official language: English
Capital city: Canberra
National anthem: Advance
Australia Fair
National colours: Green and gold
Main airline carrier: Qantas
National flag:

CURRENCY
Australian dollar (A$)
A$1 = 100 cents (c)

The following figures are approximate:
£1 = A$1.52
€1 = A$1.34
US$1 = A$0.94

KEY TELEPHONE NUMBERS
Country code: +61
International calls:
0011 + country code + number
Police: 000
Ambulance: 000
Fire: 000

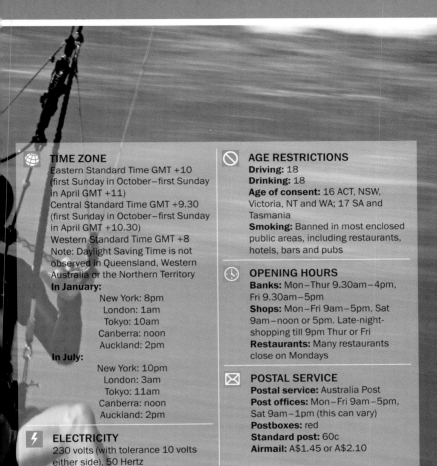

TIME ZONE

Eastern Standard Time GMT +10
(first Sunday in October–first Sunday
in April GMT +11)
Central Standard Time GMT +9.30
(first Sunday in October–first Sunday
in April GMT +10.30)
Western Standard Time GMT +8
Note: Daylight Saving Time is not
observed in Queensland, Western
Australia or the Northern Territory
In January:

New York: 8pm
London: 1am
Tokyo: 10am
Canberra: noon
Auckland: 2pm

In July:

New York: 10pm
London: 3am
Tokyo: 11am
Canberra: noon
Auckland: 2pm

ELECTRICITY

230 volts (with tolerance 10 volts
either side), 50 Hertz
Three-pin flat plug

AGE RESTRICTIONS

Driving: 18
Drinking: 18
Age of consent: 16 ACT, NSW,
Victoria, NT and WA; 17 SA and
Tasmania
Smoking: Banned in most enclosed
public areas, including restaurants,
hotels, bars and pubs

OPENING HOURS

Banks: Mon–Thur 9.30am–4pm,
Fri 9.30am–5pm
Shops: Mon–Fri 9am–5pm, Sat
9am–noon or 5pm. Late-night-
shopping till 9pm Thur or Fri
Restaurants: Many restaurants
close on Mondays

POSTAL SERVICE

Postal service: Australia Post
Post offices: Mon–Fri 9am–5pm,
Sat 9am–1pm (this can vary)
Postboxes: red
Standard post: 60c
Airmail: A$1.45 or A$2.10

Trip Planner

WHEN TO GO

Climate

The seasons in Australia are the reverse of the northern hemisphere's, and the best time to travel will depend on your destination.

In the tropical zone north of the Tropic of Capricorn (aka the Top End) around Darwin, near Cairns and in the far north of Western Australia, there are only two seasons: the Dry (approximately April–October) and the Wet (November–March). In the Dry, there are warm days, clear blue skies and cool nights. In the Wet, heavy rain alternates with sunny hot weather. On the Great Barrier Reef most rain falls in January and February.

In the southern temperate zone seasons are more distinct. Winter days in Sydney are usually sunny with a maximum of 15°C (60°F), while humid summer temperatures can regularly hit 30°C (90°F) and higher. Snow falls on the southern

Public Holidays	
1 January	New Year's Day
26 January	Australia Day
25 April	Anzac Day
25 December	Christmas Day
26 December	Boxing Day
Moveable dates	Good Friday, Easter, Easter Monday, Queen's Birthday

Additional public holidays are celebrated only in certain states. For details, go to http://australia.gov.au/topics/australian-facts-and-figures/public-holidays. Government offices, post offices and banks close on public holidays. Shops, supermarkets, cafés, museums and restaurants stay open for most holidays – the usual exceptions are Good Friday, Easter Sunday and Christmas Day.

A rainy day in Sydney

mountain ranges, but not in the cities (except Hobart).

Melbourne is best in spring and autumn – summer can be oppressively hot, and winter grey and miserable. Summers are by far the best time to visit Tasmania, as its winters can be damp and depressing.

South Australia and Western Australia have Mediterranean climates: summers are hot and dry, with highs above 40°C (105°F) not uncommon.

In central Australia, summer temperatures are generally too high for comfort. In winter, the nights may be cool, with clear warm days.

An Australian summer isn't complete without regular trips to the beach

High/Low Season

The tourist seasons are dictated by the weather and by when Australian school holidays fall.

In popular tourist destinations such as the Top End, the Great Barrier Reef, the Gold Coast and Central Australia you will pay a premium for accommodation during these times, and you'll also need to book well in advance.

During Australian school holiday periods, holiday accommodation options and domestic flights are heavily booked. Beach destinations and premium campsites are booked solidly during the summer school holiday period (Christmas day to the end of January) and over Easter. Sydney's hotels are also booked in advance (and prices can skyrocket) over the New Year period.

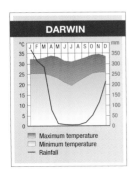

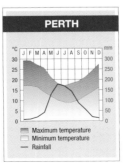

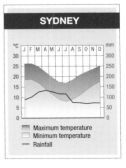

ESSENTIAL EVENTS

The Australian Open is a key event in the sporting calendar

January

Australian Open, Melbourne
The hugely popular Asian-Pacific Tennis Grand Slam.

Sydney Festival
Three weeks of music, dance, theatre and the visual arts.

Country Music Festival, Tamworth, New South Wales
Australia's major festival of country and western music.

February

Adelaide Fringe
World-renowned international arts festival in February–March showcasing independent artists.

Perth International Arts Festival
Month-long festival covering all aspects of the arts.

Sydney Gay and Lesbian Mardi Gras
Famous street parade, dance parties and associated events over two weeks in February and March.

Adelaide Festival
Three weeks of opera, ballet, theatre, art and literature, usually late February–March in even-numbered years.

March–April

WOMAdelaide, Adelaide
Four days of world music, early March.

Melbourne Food and Wine Festival
Australia's most famous food festival, in early March.

Australian Formula One Grand Prix, Melbourne
Petrol-heads converge on the Albert Park circuit in late March.

Ten Days on the Island, Tasmania
Island-dwellers from around the world celebrate their identity with art, music and drama, March–April in odd-numbered years.

May

Biennale of Sydney
International visual arts festival,
May–August in even-numbered
years.

June

Darwin Beer Can Regatta
Picnic race featuring boats constructed of used beer cans.

August

Birdsville Races, Queensland
Weekend of horse racing and revelry
held to raise money for the Royal
Flying Doctor Service.
**Henley-on-Todd Regatta, Alice
Springs, NT**
Dry-land bottomless boat race.

September

AFL Grand Final, Melbourne
Two Aussie Rules football teams
vie for the ultimate prize at the Melbourne Cricket Ground.

Floriade, Canberra
Australia's biggest flower show.
Spring Racing Carnival, Melbourne
50 days of horse racing kicks off in
September and culminates in the
world-famous Melbourne Cup.

October

**Melbourne International
Arts Festival**
A showcase of local and interna-
tional visual and performing arts.

December

Boxing Day Test, Melbourne
The Aussie team plays at the Melbourne Cricket Ground.
**New Year's Eve Celebrations, vari-
ous capital cities**
Fireworks displays – the most spectacular is on Sydney Harbour.
Sydney–Hobart Yacht Race
Competitors in one of the world's
toughest yacht races are farewelled
in Sydney and welcomed in Hobart.

15

Trip Planner

Sydney Gay and Lesbian Mardi Gras

ITINERARIES

There's a lot of terrain to cover if you want to experience the country's highlights. Distances between towns, cities and states are often huge, entailing flights or long road or train trips. To cover the entire coastline (where most settlements are) and take a couple of Outback detours, you really need six months if you are travelling by land. Travelling by air and land and concentrating on large cities and towns, you would need at least two months. In one month (the average-length holiday for most international visitors) you could tour the east coast from Melbourne to Cairns by car, or explore the country's highlights by air and land.

Two Week Whistle-Stop Highlight Tour

Days 1–3: **Sydney.** Climb aboard a few ferries, take the Eastern Beaches Coastal Walk, explore The Rocks and marvel at Circular Quay.
Day 4: Day trip to the Blue Mountains or Hunter Valley.
Days 5–7: **Whitsunday Islands.** Sail around this idyllic stretch of the Great Barrier Reef or relax at an island resort.
Days 8–10: **Far North Queensland.** Base yourself in Cairns or Port Douglas to explore tropical rainforest and the reef.
Days 11–12: **Darwin.** Visit Kakadu and Litchfield National Parks.
Days 13–14: **Uluru-Kata Tjuta National Park.** Explore this extraordinary pocket of central Australia by foot, four-wheel-drive or helicopter.

Three Week East Coast Escape

Days 1–2: **Melbourne.** Wine, dine and gallery-hop in this cultural city.
Days 3–5: Make your way north along Highway 1, visiting Wilson's Promontory National Park, the Sapphire Coast and Jervis Bay en route.
Days 6–8: **Sydney.** Spend a few days exploring Australia's most exciting city.
Days 9–11: Continue north, stopping at Port Stephens, Bellingen and Byron Bay along the way.
Day 12: **Brisbane.** Spend the day in Queensland's major city or head to nearby North Stradbroke Island for some whale or dolphin viewing.

The Rocks are a Sydney highlight

Be sure to visit Uluru-Kata Tjuta National Park while you're in Australia

Days 13–16: Stay on Highway 1, visiting the Sunshine, Fraser, Capricorn and Whitsunday Coasts before arriving at Mackay, gateway to the Great Barrier Reef.

Days 17–21: The Great Barrier Reef. Spend time swimming, snorkelling and sunbathing on one or two islands before ending your road trip in Townsville, from where you can fly to your next destination.

One Month 'Best of Australia' Tour

Days 1–3: Sydney. Experience the city's highlights.

Days 4–8: The Pacific Highway. Drive from Sydney to Brisbane, stopping in laid-back coastal towns including Byron Bay en route.

Days 9–11: Whitsunday Islands. Three days of sailing the Great Barrier Reef or relaxing at an island resort.

Days 12–15: Cairns. From here,

take day trips to the Atherton Tablelands, Daintree Rainforest and Cape Tribulation.

Days 16–18: Darwin. Visit Nitmiluk and Litchfield National Parks.

Days 19–21: Alice Springs. Base yourself here to explore Uluru-Kata Tjuta, Nitmiluk (Katherine Gorge) and Watarrka National Parks.

Days 22–25: Tasmania. Take a driving tour of colonial towns and penal colonies, marvelling at spectacular scenery along the way.

Day 26: Melbourne. Admire the CBD's 19th-century architecture.

Days 27–28: The Great Ocean Road. Drive one of the world's most spectacular highways, visiting the Werribee Park mansion on the way.

Day 29: Ballarat. Soak up history in this magnificent goldrush-era town.

Day 30: Melbourne. Enjoy the great shopping and even better food.

BEFORE YOU LEAVE

Visas and Entry Requirements

Foreign nationals entering Australia must have a passport valid for the entire period of their stay and must have obtained a visa before leaving home (except for New Zealand citizens, who are issued with a visa on arrival in Australia).

The Electronic Transfer Authority (ETA) visa is available to citizens of over 30 countries and can be obtained online or from travel agents or airline offices for a fee of A$20. ETA visas are generally valid for 12 months; single stays must not exceed three months, but return visits within the 12-month period are allowed.

Most EU citizens are eligible for an eVisitor visa, which is free and can be obtained online. Like the ETA visa, these are generally valid for 12 months; single stays must not exceed three months, but return visits within the 12-month period are allowed.

Tourist visas are available for citizens of all countries for continuous

Nationality	Visa Required
Canada	ETA visa
Ireland	eVisitor visa
New Zealand	✗
South Africa	Tourist (subclass 676) visa
UK	eVisitor visa
US	ETA visa

stays of three, six or 12 months. Apply online or through an Australian High Commission office; a charge may be levied whether or not your application is successful.

Visitors travelling on ETAs, eVisitor visas and Tourist visas are not permitted to work while in Australia. For more information and to apply for visas online, go to www.immi.gov.au.

Australian High Commissions

Canada: 175 Bloor Street East, Suite 1100 – South Tower, Toronto, Ontario M4W 3R8; tel: 416-323 3909.
Ireland: 7th Floor, Fitzwilton House, Wilton Terrace, Dublin 2; tel: 1-664 5300.
New Zealand: 72–76 Hobson Street, Thorndon, Wellington, New Zealand; tel: 04-473 6411.
South Africa: 292 Orient Street, Arcadia 12, Pretoria 0083; tel: 12-423 6000.
UK: The Strand, London WC2B 4LA; tel: 020-7379 4334.
US: 1601 Massachusetts Ave, NW, Washington DC, 20036-2273; tel: 202-797 3000.
For more details and for a list of other high commissions, see www.embassy.gov.au.

Australia House is the UK home of the Australian High Commission

Booking in Advance

If you wish to attend a major sporting event or festival during your visit, book tickets and accommodation well in advance. If you are planning to camp near the beach in January or in any popular destination around Easter, you will need to book your campsite(s) up to one year in advance.

Tourist Information

Tourism Australia can supply comprehensive information about visiting Australia. Check its website (www.australia.com), contact its Australian head office (Level 18, Darling Park, Tower 2, 201 Sussex Street, Sydney NSW 2000; tel: 02-9360 1111), or contact one of its overseas offices:

Canada: 111 Peter Street, Suite 630 Toronto, Ontario M5V 2H1; tel: 416-408 0549

New Zealand: Level 3, 125 The Strand, Parnell, Auckland 1; tel: 09-915 2826

UK & Ireland: Australia Centre, Australia House, 6th Floor, Melbourne Place, The Strand, London; tel: 020-7438 4601

US: 6100 Center Drive, Los Angeles CA 90045; tel: 310-695 3200.

Maps and Books

Tourist information centres usually have free local maps. Most car-hire companies supply customers with free road maps, and the various state motoring associations and good bookshops stock Australian road atlases.

To get a feel for Australian culture, read the following novels by contemporary award-winning writers:

Cloudstreet by Tim Winton. This much-loved story is set in Perth.

Eucalyptus by Murray Bail. Modern-day fairy tale and love story set on an Outback property.

My Place by Sally Morgan. A WA writer recounts her quest to uncover her Aboriginal heritage.

The Secret River by Kate Grenville. Vivid re-creation of early settler life on NSW's Hawkesbury River.

Oscar and Lucinda by Peter Carey. Comic love story about 19th-century gamblers set in NSW.

Also look out for novels by Alex Miller (*The Ancestor Game*), David Malouf (*The Great World*) and Peter Temple (*The Broken Shore*).

Websites

www.bom.gov.au – weather
www.deh.gov.au – department of Environment, Water, Heritage and Arts
www.environment.gov.au – parks and heritage sites
www.nationaltrust.org.au
www.newspapers.com.au – news
www.visitcanberra.com.au
www.visitnsw.com.au
http://en.travelnt.com
www.queenslandholidays.com
www.southaustralia.com
www.discovertasmania.com.au
www.visitvictoria.com
www.westernaustralia.com

Packing List

- Sunhat, sunblock and sunglasses
- Insect repellent
- Sturdy walking shoes
- Swimming costume and beach towel
- Detailed driving maps (if applicable)
- At least one pullover (sweater)

UNIQUE EXPERIENCES

The Great Barrier Reef

Just below the surface of the Coral Sea is one of the world's undisputed natural wonders: the Great Barrier Reef. This huge ecosystem is home to more than 2,300km (1,430 miles) of submerged subtropical gardens full of marine life. The only way to appreciate its diversity, grandeur and beauty is to take to its waters equipped with snorkelling or diving gear.

Here, off the northeastern coast of Australia, many millions of minuscule cells multiply relentlessly in fantastic shapes, growing into an infinite variety of brightly coloured forms to create the world's largest living phenomenon. The Great Barrier Reef is home to 400 different types of coral and a seemingly infinite array of luridly coloured marine creatures.

Proclaimed a marine park by the Australian Government in 1975, the Reef was placed on the World Heritage list in 1981, becoming the biggest World Heritage area in existence. It is now managed by the Great Barrier Reef Marine Park Authority (www. gbrmpa.gov.au).

There are many ways of appreciating the coral and its fishy visitors. You can stay dry in a glass-bottom boat, join a brief cruise aboard a semi-submarine or sign up for a snorkelling or diving adventure.

Hundreds of islands are scattered across the protected waters between the coral barrier and the mainland, and more than a dozen have been developed into resorts. These have facilities ranging from spartan to sybaritic, but only two – Heron and Green – are on the Reef itself. From all the others you have to travel by sea or air. Day visits to the Reef can also be made

The Great Barrier Reef is home to a vast array of vivid marine life

from mainland centres such as Shute Harbour/Airlie Beach, Townsville, Mission Beach, Cairns and Port Douglas.

The floods of 2011 washed a mixture of fresh water, sediments, pesticides and other contaminents onto the reef with some deleterious effects. Similarly, initial estimates suggested that Cyclone Yasi damaged around 13 percent of the coral in its path when it hit Cardwell, Tully and Mission Beach in February 2011. The area around Cairns and Port Douglas escaped largely unscathed but do check with dive and tour operators for updates on reef conditions before booking excursions.

The Reef Islands

The 25 or so resort islands inside the Great Barrier Reef Marine Park offer many attractions and a huge variety of accommodation options. They include (listed from south to north):

Lady Elliot Island A coral isle (www.ladyelliot.com.au) situated south of the Tropic of Capricorn and accessed via air from Bundaberg and Hervey Bay. Activities centre on diving, swimming and windsurfing.

Heron Island A small coral island right on the Reef that is adored by divers. The island resort (www.heron island.com) accommodates up to 250 people; no day trips and no camping. Access by boat from Gladstone.

Great Keppel Island Large resort island with a variety of accommodation including a holiday village (www.greatkeppel.com.au/great-keppel-village) with tents, dorm beds, cabins and houses. The Reef is 70km (44 miles) away, but there's good local coral and an underwater observatory. Access via ferry from Rosslyn Bay or air from Rockhampton.

Brampton Island Luxury resort (www.brampton-island.com) closed for redevelopment until 2012 and accessed by air or sea from Mackay.

Lindeman Island The most southerly of the islands in the Whitsunday archipelago, with a Club Med resort

The tranquil Hamilton Island resort

(www.clubmed.com.au) and some campsites (www.epa.qld.gov.au). Access via boat from Shute Harbour.

Hamilton Island A huge resort (www.hamiltonisland.com.au) offering hotel rooms, apartments and bungalows for all budgets. Access via boat from Shute Harbour.

Long Island Close to the mainland and far from the Reef, with three resorts (www.greatbarrierreef.org/

When To Visit

The best time to visit the Reef is between April and October, when the clear skies and moderate breezes offer perfect conditions for coral viewing, diving, swimming and sunning. In November the first signs of the approaching 'Wet' appear: variable winds, increasing cloud and showers. This is also when the venomous box jellyfish appears, staying around until March. By January it rains at least once most days and can be very windy. And when the winds are up and the waters are stirred, visibility in and under the water diminishes.

Great Barrier Reef

islands_Long.php). Accessed by boat from Shute Harbour.

South Molle Island Mainly national park, plus a resort that was under renovation at the time of research. The Reef is about 60km (37 miles) away but coral reefs exist nearby.

Daydream Island The tiniest of all the Barrier Reef resort islands, accessed from Airlie Beach by boat. The resort (www.daydreamisland.com) has a spa.

Hook Island The second-largest island in the Whitsundays, with budget camping, dorm rooms and cabins (www.hookislandresort.com). Accessed via boat from Airlie Beach.

Hayman Island The most northerly of the Whitsunday group is home to a luxury resort (www.hayman.com.au).

Magnetic Island This busy day-trip

The brightly coloured Australian Minor Notodoris nudibranch

destination is virtually a suburb of Townsville, with many of the island's permanent residents commuting to work on the mainland by ferry. There's a wide range of accommodation options.

Orpheus Island National Park and a small and secluded resort (www.orpheus.com.au). Day-trippers are banned. Flights from Townsville and Cairns.

Hinchinbrook Island A continental rather than coral island, but only 5km (3 miles) from the Reef. Home to a national park. There are a couple of campsites (www.derm.qld.gov.au) and an eco-resort (www.hinchinbrook lodge.com.au). Access is via ferry from Cardwell or Lucinda.

Bedarra Island Exclusive resort (www.bedarra.com.au) in the Family Islands group, accessible via neighbouring Dunk Island, although, like that island, it was badly damaged by 2011's Cyclone Yasi and is closed until 2012.

Dunk Island Part of the Family Islands National Park, with one resort (www.dunk-island.com) and a few campsites (www.derm.qld.gov.au). Reached by ferry from Clump Point at Mission Beach. Dunk, too, reopens in 2012.

Fitzroy Island Only 6km (4 miles) offshore and easily reached on day excursions by boat from Cairns. Totally surrounded by coral reef, so a great place for diving and fishing.

Green Island Right on the Reef and popular with day-trippers from Cairns, who get here by boat. Luxury accommodation only (www.green islandresort.com.au).

Lizard Island Favoured by millionaires and celebrities, who stay at the

A spectacular sunset over Hinchinbrook Island

exclusive and pricey Lizard Island Resort (www.lizardisland.com.au). The only other alternative is at the other end of the price scale: a very basic campsite (www.derm.qld.gov.au). Reached by air from Cairns.

Diving and Snorkelling

The best way to experience the Reef is to do as its marine population does and take to the waters. If you are based at an island resort, there are always options on offer to snorkel and dive. But it's just as easy to take a day trip from Airlie Beach, Cairns or Port Douglas. Every morning dozens of fully equipped diveboats and catamarans head out from the three centres to various pre-selected sites on the Reef.

Because the water is so shallow, snorkelling is perfectly satisfactory for seeing the marine life (in fact, many people prefer it to scuba diving).

The Great Barrier Reef

Even so, most boats offer tanks for experienced divers and introductory courses for people who have never dived before. Above the waves, the turquoise void might be broken only by a sand cay crowded with sea birds, but as soon as you poke your mask underwater, the world erupts. It's almost sensory overload: there are vast forests of staghorn coral, whose tips glow purple like electric Christmas-tree lights; brilliant blue clumps of mushroom coral; layers of pink plate coral; and bulbous green brain coral. Tropical fish with exotic names slip about as if showing off their fluorescent patterns: painted flutemouth, long-finned batfish, crimson squirrelfish, hump-headed Maori wrasse and cornflower sergeant-major.

Many of the Reef trips follow a similar format. There's a morning dive or snorkel, followed by a buffet lunch; then, assuming you haven't eaten too much or had too much free beer, an afternoon dive. There should be a marine biologist on board to explain the Reef's ecology. Before you book,

ask how many passengers the boat takes: they vary from several hundred on the Quicksilver and FantaSea fleets to fewer than a dozen on smaller craft.

In general, the further out the boat heads, the more pristine the diving. But don't be conned by hype about the 'Outer Reef' – as the edge of the continental shelf it may be the 'real' Reef, but it looks exactly the same as other parts.

Among the reputable eco-certified operators are:

Aristocat (tel: 07-4099 4727; www.aristocat.com.au) This Port Douglas-based operator offers daily snorkelling and escorted scuba-diving tours, including introductory dives.

Big Cat Green Island (tel: 07-4051 0444; www.greenisland.com.au) Full- and half-day cruises from Cairns to Green Island, where you can snorkel, view coral from a semi-submarine or glass-bottomed boat, dive and parasail.

Cairns Dive Centre (tel: 07-4051 0294; www.cairnsdive.com.au) Offering live-aboard or day cruises for snorkellers or divers, as well as learn-

A diver gets up close to the coral

to-dive courses through all levels from Open Water to Instructors.

Calypso Reef Cruises (tel: 07-4099 6999; www.calypsoreefcruises.com) Reef tours and dive trips from Port Douglas that are suitable for all ages.

FantaSea Adventure Cruising (tel: 07-4967 5455; www.fantasea.com.au) Based in the Whitsundays, this outfit offers everything from a 'Great Barrier Reef Experience' leaving from Airlie Beach and offering snorkelling, semi-submarine coral-viewing, diving and scenic helicopter rides, to a night aboard a floating pontoon on Hardy Reef.

OzSail (tel: 07-4946 6877; www.ozsail.com.au) Operates fully crewed sailing holidays in the Whitsundays with an on-board diving instructor.

Poseidon Reef Cruises (tel: 07-4099 4072; www.poseidon-cruises.com.au) Daily trips from Port Douglas catering for snorkellers as well as introductory and certified divers.

ProDive Cairns (tel: 07-4031 5255; www.prodivecairns.com) Day and live-aboard dive trips from Cairns. Also offers PADI open water learn-to-dive courses.

Quicksilver (tel: 07-4087 2100; www.quicksilver-cruises.com) Huge catamarans take passengers from Port Douglas to Agincourt Reef, where they can snorkel, view coral in a semi-submarine, dive or take a scenic helicopter ride.

Wavelength (tel: 07-4099 5031; www.wavelength.com.au) This well-regarded eco-tourism operator offers small-group snorkelling tours from Port Douglas.

Responsible Reef Tourism

Nearly 2 million tourists and 4.9 million recreational visitors visit the Great Barrier Reef each year, placing enormous pressure on its fragile ecosystem. The Great Barrier Reef Marine Park Authority (GBRMPA) supports sustainable tourism and recreation in the park and encourages the 800-odd tourism operators and 1,700 tourism vessels working here to undergo a comprehensive eco-assessment process and obtain certification with Ecotourism Australia (www.ecotourism.org.au). To obtain certification, operators must maintain high standards in fields including environmental management and contribution to conservation. To access a list of operators with this accreditation, go to www.gbrmpa.gov.au. When you are snorkelling and diving in the Reef, be aware you can cause significant damage to coral if you brush against it or touch it. And never discard rubbish in the water.

27

The Great Barrier Reef

Fabulous Wine and Food Trails

Forget the sunbronzed surfer and weatherbeaten Outback farmer — these days, the stereotypical Aussie is more likely to be a city-based devotee of gourmet food and fine wine. At weekends, these epicurean adventurers decamp to the countryside for tipsy tours of terroir or gastronomic forays into farmers' markets and regional restaurants.

Australia's size means it possesses huge variations in terrain and climate. The result is a profusion of food- and wine-producing regions, all with distinct characters and specialities. Recently, an urban appetite for gourmet and organic produce has combined with the development of a locavore-leaning sensibility to make food and wine from regional Australia as fashionable as it is fantastic. Areas such as the Yarra Valley and Mornington Peninsula in Victoria, Tamar Valley in Tasmania, Hunter Valley in New South Wales, Margaret River in Western Australia, and Barossa Valley and Coonawarra in South Australia have built international reputations for the excellence of their produce and gastro-tourism industries.

The country's Shiraz (Syrah), Cabernet Sauvignon, Pinot Noir, Chardonnay and Semillon are particularly impressive, but there are also vintages of everything from Merlot to Mourvèdre. The best way to garner an understanding and appreciation of the local tipple is to embark on tours of cellar doors in specific regions. While you do this, be sure to look out for local food produce, too.

Visitors can tour these regions under their own steam or on organised tours, book into cooking or wine-discovery classes, attend a vineyard concert, relax in gourmet retreats or even sign up for hard yakka (Aussie slang for hard work) picking grapes or fruit. The only hard-and-fast rules are to bring a good appetite and thirst and to always stay within the legal alcohol limit of 0.5mg per litre of blood if you are driving.

Early morning at the Hunter Valley vineyards

A barrel cellar in the Hunter Valley

Hunter Valley

Australia's oldest wine region is known for its golden-hued Semillon and tannin-laden Shiraz wines, and is an easy day trip from Sydney. Cellar doors well worth a visit include **Audrey Wilkinson Vineyard** ('Oakdale', De Beyers Road, Pokolbin; tel: 02-4998 7411; www.audreywilkinson.com. au; daily 9.30am–5pm), **Brokenwood** (410–427 McDonald's Road, Pokolbin; tel: 02-4998 7559; www.broken wood.com.au; daily 9.30am–5pm), **Keith Tulloch Wine** (Hunter Ridge Winery, Hermitage Road, Pokolbin; tel: 02-4998 7500; www.keithtulloch wine.com.au; Wed–Sun 10am–5pm), **McWilliam's Mt Pleasant** (401 Marrowbone Road, Pokolbin; tel: 02-4998 7505; www.mountpleasantwines.com. au; daily 10am–5pm), **Tulloch** ('Glen Elgin', 638 De Beyers Road, Pokolbin; tel: 02-4998 7580; www.tulloch.com.

Music Among the Vines

In the warmer months, you can enjoy a picnic and a bottle of wine while listening to orchestras, musicians and singers performing at the following vineyards:

- **Leeuwin Estate**, Margaret River, WA (Leeuwin Concert Series, www. leeuwinestate.com.au)
- **Peter Lehmann Wines**, Barossa Valley, SA (A Day on the Green, www. adayonthegreen.com.au)
- **Rochford Wines**, Yarra Valley, Vic (A Day on the Green, www. adayonthegreen.com.au)
- **Tyrrell's**, Hunter Valley, NSW (Jazz in the Vines, www.jazzinthevines.com.au)

au; daily 10am–5pm) and **Tyrrell's** (Broke Road, Pokolbin; tel: 02-4993 7000; www.tyrrells.com.au; daily 8.30am–5pm).

Hunter Valley produce is also highly regarded. The local olives and olive oils are celebrated every year in the Feast of the Olive, an event held in the last week of September. The **Hunter Valley Cheese Co** (McGuigan's Complex, McDonald's Road, Pokolbin; tel: 02-4998-7744; www.huntervalley cheese.com.au; daily 9am–5.30pm) is one of a number of factories producing speciality handmade cheeses.

Recommended eateries include the Firestick Café and Rock Restaurant at **Poole's Rock Winery** (576 Debeyers Rd, Pokolbin; tel: 02-4998 6968; www. rockrestaurant.com.au) and **Muse Restaurant and Café** (1 Broke Rd, Pokolbin; tel: 02-4998 6777; www. musedining.com.au).

The Yarra Valley

This scenic region on the eastern edge of Melbourne is famed for intense and concentrated Chardonnay, elegant

Fabulous Wine and Food Trails

Pinot Noir and delicate sparkling wine. Try them at **De Bortoli** (Pinnacle Lane, Dixons Creek; tel: 03-5965 2271; www.debortoli.com.au; daily 10am–5pm), **Domaine Chandon** (Green Point, Maroondah Highway, Coldstream; tel: 03-9738 9200; http://domainechandon.com.au; daily 10.30am–4.30pm), **Tarrawarra Estate** (Healesville Road, Yarra Glen; tel: 03-5962 331; www.tarrawarra.com.au; daily 11am–5pm), **Yarrabank** (38 Melba Highway, Yarra Glen; tel: 03-9730 0100; www.yering.com; daily 10am–5pm) and **Yering Station** (38 Melba Highway, Yarra Glen; tel 03-9730 0100; www.yering.com; daily 10am–5pm).

Devotees of goat's cheese need go no further than these rolling hills. Producers include the **Yarra Valley Dairy** (McMeikans Road, Yering; tel: 03-9739 0023; www.yvd.com.au; daily 10.30am–5pm) and famed cheesemaker Richard Thomas at De Bortoli winery. For other local produce, try **Kitchen and Butcher** (258 Maroondah Hwy; tel: 03-5962 2866; www.yarravalleyharvest.com.au), an artisanal providore in the small township of Healesville.

To enjoy fruits of the local harvest, eat at **Bella Vedere** (874 Maroondah Hwy, Coldstream; tel: 03-5962 6161; www.badgersbrook.com.au) or at the restaurants at Domaine Chandon, Yering Station or Tarrawarra Estate. Bella Vedere also runs renowned cooking courses.

The Mornington Peninsula

A string of gorgeous beaches and attractive, Mediterranean-style landscape endow the Mornington Peninsula with rock-solid tourism credentials.

The sea spray does wonders for the Chardonnay and Pinot Noir grapes that this region one hour southeast of Melbourne is known for, and there is a cornucopia of local produce to sample, including berries, cherries and olives.

Notable vineyards with cellar doors include **Moorooduc Estate** (501 Derril Road, Moorooduc; tel: 03-5971 8506; www.moorooducestate.com.au; Sat–Sun 11am–5pm), **Paringa Estate** (44 Paringa Road, Red Hill South; tel: 03-5989 2669; www.paringaestate.com.au; daily 11am–5pm), **Port Phillip Estate** (263 Red Hill Road, Red Hill South; tel: 03-5989 2708; www.portphillip.net; daily 11am–5pm), **Red Hill Estate** (53 Shoreham Road, Red Hill South; tel: 03-5989 2838; www.redhillestate.

Local cuisine and a glass of sparkling wine in the Yarra Valley

Unique Experiences

com.au; daily 11am–5pm) and **Stonier Wines** (Corner Thompson's Lane/Frankston-Flinders Road, Merricks; tel: 03-5989 8300; www.stoniers.com.au; daily 11am–5pm).

For a meal to accompany your wine tasting, try the restaurants at the **Willow Creek Vineyard** (166 Balnarring Road, Merricks North; tel: 03-5989 7640; www.willow-creek.com.au), **Montaldo Estate** (33 Shoreham Road, Red Hill South; tel: 03-5989 8412; www.montaldo.com.au) and **Ten Minutes by Tractor Vineyard** (1333 Mornington-Flinders Road, Main Ridge; tel: 03-5989 6080; www.tenminutesbytractor.com.au).

A wine chateau in the Barossa Valley

Barossa Valley

This is the big daddy of them all. Home to over 700 wine growers, 150 wineries and 73 cellar doors, the Barossa has a long history as a food and wine nirvana. Home to Henschke, makers of the world-famous Hill of Grace Shiraz, and a slew of top-notch Shiraz and Cabernet Sauvignon producers, it's also blessed with abundant seasonal produce and speciality food products, including artisan cheese and breads, poultry, hare, yabbies (freshwater crustaceans), and smoked and cured meats.

Among the many excellent wineries in this region, visit **Henschke** (Henschke Road, Keyneton; tel: 08-8564 8223; www.henschke.com.au; Mon–Fri 9am–4.30pm, Sat 9am–noon), **Penfolds** (Tanunda Road, Nuriootpa; tel: 08-8568 9408; www.penfolds.com; daily 10am–5pm), **Grant Burge** (Jacobs Creek; tel: 08-8563 3700; www.grantburgewines.com.au; daily 10am–5pm), **Peter Lehmann** (Para Road, Tanunda;

Fabulous Wine and Food Trails

tel: 08-8563 2100; www.peterlehmann wines.com; Mon–Fri 9.30am–5pm, Sat–Sun 10.30am–4.30pm) and **Rockford** (Krondorf Road, Tanunda; tel: 08-8563 2720; www.rockfordwines.com.au; daily 11am–5pm).

Maggie Beer's Farm Shop (Pheasant Farm Road, Nuriootpa; tel: 08-8562 4477; daily 10.30am–5pm), owned by the celebrity chef and Barossa resident,

Regional Wine Festivals

- **April** Barossa Vintage Festival (www.barossavintagefestival.com.au); Margaret River Wine Region Festival (www.margaretriverfestival.com)
- **May** Hunter Valley Harvest Festival (www.harvest.hvva.com.au)
- **June** Winter Wine Weekend, Mornington Peninsula (www.mpva.com.au)
- **October** Mornington Peninsula Pinot Week (www.mpva.com.au)

is an essential stop for foodies – drop by at 2pm, when there's a daily cooking demonstration. The **Barossa Farmers Market** (www.barossafarmersmarket.com), held every Saturday morning in the historic Vintners Sheds near Angaston, is another tasty temptation.

Appellation Restaurant (The Louise, corner Seppeltsfield and Stonewell Roads, Marananga; tel: 08-8562 4144; www.appellation.com.au), located in a posh vineyard retreat, is high on the gourmet's agenda, and there are also good eateries at the Grant Burge and Peter Lehmann vineyards.

Coonawarra

Love Cabernet Sauvignon? If so, you'll be crazy about the Coonawarra, 440km (273 miles) south of Adelaide. Its secret lies in a marriage of rich red terra rossa

The Coonawarra is famed for its delectable Cabernet Sauvignon

soil, limestone, pure underground water and a long cool ripening season for the grapes. To sample the result of this amazing alchemy, make the pilgrimage to **Bowen Estate** (Riddoch Highway, Coonawarra; tel: 08-8737 2229; www.bowenestate.com.au; daily 10am–5pm), **Penley Estate** (McLeans Road, Coonawarra; tel: 08 8736 3211; www.penley.com.au; daily 10am–4pm), **Petaluma** (Mt Barker Road, Bridgewater; tel: 08-8339 9200; www.petaluma.com.au; daily 10am–5pm) and **Wynns Coonawarra Estate** (Memorial Drive, Coonawarra; tel: 08-8736 2225; www.wynns.com.au; daily 10am–5pm).

Wine is the focus here, but impressive dining options include **Pipers of Penola** (58 Riddoch Street, Penola; tel: 08-8737 3999; www.pipersofpenola.com.au) and the restaurant at Petaluma.

Margaret River

A three-hour drive south of Perth is magical Margaret River. Known primarily for its Cabernet Sauvignon, also produces great Chardonnay, Sauvignon Blanc, Semillon and Shiraz. For top-notch tasting, make your way to **Cape Mentelle** (Wallcliffe Road, Margaret River; tel: 08-9757 0888; www.capementelle.com.au; daily 10am–4.30pm), **Cullen Wines** (Caves Road, Cowaramup; tel: 08-9755 5277; www.cullenwines.com.au; daily 10am–4pm), **Leeuwin Estate** (Stevens Road, Margaret River; tel: 08-9759 0000; www.leeuwinestate.com.au; daily 10am–5pm), **Vasse Felix** (Corner Caves and Harmans Road South, Cowaramup; tel: 08-9756 5000; www.vassefelix.com.au; daily 10am–5pm), **Voyager Estate** (Lot 1, Stevens Road, Margaret River;

Adinfern Estate Gnaraba

Eagle Vale

THE
CAPES
LONG
LUNCH

A Sumptuous Day
@ 5 Wineries / brewery
Dine your way around
a gourmet feast...

the Ginger Fine Foods

Redgate Wines

Margaret River is Western Australia's
premier wine-growing region

Tamar Valley

The popular Tamar Valley Wine Route meanders 58km (36 miles) between the city of Launceston and Bass Strait, passing scenic vineyards, apple orchards and quaint villages along the way. The cool climate perfectly suits Chardonnay, Riesling, Pinot Noir and sparkling wines, and these varietals are produced by highly regarded wineries including **Bay of Fires** (40 Baxters Road, Pipers River; tel: 03-6382 7666; www.bayoffireswines.com.au; daily 10am–4pm), **Piper's Brook** (1216 Pipers Brook Rd, Pipers Brook; tel: 03-6382 7527; www.kreglingerwineestates.com; daily 10am–5pm) and **Tamar Ridge** (Auburn Road, Kayena; tel: 03-6394 111; www.winecompanion.com.au; daily 10am–5pm).

The Tamar's top-notch local produce is showcased at impressive eateries such as **Daniel Alps at Strathlynn** (95 Rosevears Drive, Rosevears; tel: 03-6330 2388) in the Ninth Mile Winery complex, and at **Stillwater** (Ritchies Mill, Paterson Street, Launceston; tel: 03-6331 4153; www.stillwater.net.au).

tel: 08-9757 6354; www.voyagerestate.com.au; daily 10am–5pm) and **Xanadu Estate** (Boodjidup Road, Margaret River; tel: 08-9758 9531; www.xanaduwines.com; daily 10am–5pm).

Of the many local speciality foodstuffs, marron (a crustacean) is possibly the most prized. It is often served at celebrated local restaurants, including **Lamont's** (Gunyulgup Valley Drive, Yallingup; tel: 08-9755 2434; www.lamonts.com.au) and the Vasse Felix, Cullen Wines, and Xanadu wineries.

Further Information

- **Barossa Visitor Information Centre** (tel: 08-8563 0600; www.barossa.com)
- **Coonawarra Vignerons Association** (tel: 08-8737 2392; www.coonawarra.org)
- **Hunter Valley Tourism** (tel: 02-4990 0900; www.winecountry.com.au)
- **James Halliday Australian Wine Companion** (www.winecompanion.com.au)
- **Launceston Travel & Information Centre** (tel: 1800 651 827; www.visitlauncestontamar.com.au)
- **Margaret River Visitor Centre** (tel: 08-9780 5911; www.margaretriver.com)
- **Mornington Peninsula Tourism** (tel: 03-5987 3078; www.visitmorningtonpeninsula.org)
- **Yarra Valley Visitor Information Centre** (tel: 03-5962 2600; www.visityarravalley.com.au)

World Heritage Landscapes

Australia is often referred to as the 'Lucky Country', and this accolade certainly applies when it comes to its natural attractions. In fact, the Land Down Under has more World Heritage-listed natural landscapes than any other country, with 15 appearing on Unesco's list.

The Great Outdoors, as it's sometimes called, is as varied as it is magnificent. Many of Australia's natural landscapes are scientifically unique, populated by species of flora and fauna seen nowhere else on earth.

Unesco's list covers the breadth of the continent, and even extends into Australia's external territory in the Southern Ocean. There are three landscapes in Queensland: the Great Barrier Reef, Fraser Island and the Wet Tropics. The Northern Territory has two – Kakadu National Park and Uluru-Kata Tjuta National Park – and New South Wales has the same number, with the Willandra Lakes region and the Greater Blue Mountains area. So too does Western Australia, home to Shark Bay and the Purnululu National Park.

Some landscapes incorporate more than one state: the Gondwana Rainforests spread from Queensland to New South Wales, and there are Fossil Mammal Sites at Riversleigh in Queensland and Naracoorte in South Australia. Tasmania is the location of just one listed landscape, the Tasmanian Wilderness.

The remaining listings are islands – the Lord Howe Island Group in the South Pacific, and Heard, Macquarie and McDonald Islands in the Southern Ocean.

Being World Heritage-listed doesn't preclude these landscapes from offering vibrant programmes of visitor activities and top-notch tourist infrastructure. This caters not only for foreign visitors, but for locals, whose love of the Great Outdoors is pretty well bred in the bone. So whichever of these landscapes you choose to visit (with the exception of the inaccessible Southern Ocean

Kakadu National Park is home to varied and beautiful landscapes

islands), you will find yourself among native nature-lovers whose pride in this country's extraordinary natural landscapes is only equalled by their enthusiasm to explore them.

We have chosen to feature six of the landscapes here. For more information about exploring the Great Barrier Reef, *see p.22*; for the Blue Mountains, *see p.78*; for Shark Bay, *see p.46*; and for information about Uluru Kata-Tjuta National Park, see *p.149*.

Outback Landscapes

The Aussie Outback is a place of myth and magnificence, where Dreamtime legends take a physical form and where the terrain, flora and fauna are truly unique. It can be hard work exploring these desert landscapes, but one thing is sure – the rewards far outweigh the logistical challenges and perspiration involved.

Kakadu National Park

This unique archaeological and ethnological reserve (www.environment.gov.au/parks/kakadu) has been inhabited continuously for more than 40,000 years. Its cave paintings, rock carvings and archaeological sites record the skills and way of life of both the hunter-gatherers of prehistoric times and the Aboriginal people whose traditional land it is.

The landscape at **Kakadu** ranges from stone country to savannah woodland to billabongs and floodplains. Within it are habitats for a wide range of rare or endemic species of plants and animals, including the elusive black wallaroo, rare white-throated grass-wren,

Aboriginal rock art is a highlight of a trip to Kakadu

spectacular blue-and-orange leichhardt grasshopper, blue-winged kookaburra, agile wallaby, sugar glider, brush-tailed phascogale, antilopine wallaroo, northern quoll, rough knob-tail gecko, the Oenpelli water python, pig-nosed turtle and both the freshwater and estuarine (saltwater) crocodile.

Wildlife and bird spotting is particularly good in the Wet season (Nov–Mar), when the streams and rivers rise and floodplains are inundated. At this time you may encounter over 40 species of migratory birds, thousands of species of insect and about 25 species of frog.

Rock art is extremely important to the Aboriginal owners of Kakadu. The art is an outstanding example of people's interaction with the natural environment, and is an important historic and scientific record of human occupations of the region. There are two main rock art sites: **Ubirr** and **Nourlangie/Nanguluwur**.

Park rangers offer visitors an opportunity to connect with the culture and traditions of the indigenous Bininj/Mungguy people through daily art site talks, walks and cultural activities during the Dry season (Apr–Oct). Contact the park's **Bowali Visitor Centre** on 08-8938 1120 for more information. Other walking tours focusing on rock art, wildlife and bush tucker include the **Wurrgeng Cultural Walk** (tel: 08-8979 0145; reservations@gagudju lodgecooinda.com.au); the **Animal Tracks Safari** (tel: 08-8979 0145; www.animaltracks.com.au); and **Ayal Aboriginal Tours** (tel: 0429 470 384; www.ayalkakadu.com.au).

Boat tours of the park's wetlands and the East Alligator River offer a unique opportunity to experience the park's diversity and wildlife. Operators include **Yellow Water**

Cruises (tel: 08-8979 0145; www.gagudju-dreaming.com); the **Kakadu Culture Camp** (tel: 1800 811 633; www.kakaduculturecamp.com); and **Guluyambi** on the East Alligator (tel: 08-89792411; www.guluyambi.com.au).

Commercial four-wheel-drive tours are available to explore the park and neighbouring Arnhem Land in the Dry season. Contact **Gagudju Adventure Tours** (tel: 08-8979 0145; www.gagudju-dreaming.com).

A number of companies offer flights providing a bird's-eye view of Kakadu. During the Wet season, passengers see the spectacular Jim Jim Falls in full flood. Contact **Kakadu Air** (http://kakaduair.com.au), which offers fixed-wing and helicopter flights from Jabiru East and Cooinda Airstrips; or **North Australian Helicopters** (tel: 08-8972 1666; www.northaustralianhelicopters.com.au), which schedules helicopter flights from Katherine.

Purnululu National Park's Bungle Bungle range is an extraordinary natural phenomenon

The semi-arid Willandra Lakes Region viewed from above

park is only open between April and 15 December. The best time to visit is in early May, at the beginning of the Dry season.

Scenic flight operators include **Alligator Airways** (tel: 08-9168 1333; www.alligatorairways.com.au) and **Slingair Heliwork WA** (tel: 08-9169 1300; www.slingair.com.au). Both offer two-hour flights and full-day fly, drive and walk experiences departing from the regional centre of Kununurra.

Purnululu National Park

The huge **Purnululu National Park** (www.kununurratourism.com) is located in Western Australia's Kimberley region and is one of the most remote of all Outback experiences. In the Kija Aboriginal language purnululu means sandstone, and the park is best known as the home of the **Bungle Bungle Range**, quartz sandstone eroded over a period of 20 million years into a series of distinctively coloured beehive-shaped towers or cones. The best way to appreciate the range is by air; you will see orange-and-black stripes across the mounds and a hidden world of gorges and pools surrounding them.

More than 130 bird species are found here, including rainbow bee-eaters and flocks of budgerigars. The nailtail wallaby and euro live around the massif.

The heat can be extremely oppressive at Purnululu, and as a result the

Willandra Lakes Region

The **Willandra Lakes Region** (www.environment.gov.au/heritage/places/world/willandra) covers 2,400 sqkm (930 sq miles) of a semi-arid landscape mosaic in the Murray Basin area of far southwestern New South

World Heritage Landscapes

Wildlife Watching

Keep these tips in mind when wildlife spotting in the Australian landscape:

- Early morning and sunset are good times to see wildlife
- Use a torch at night to look for nocturnal animals but be careful not to shine strong spotlights onto sleeping roosting birds
- Waterholes along creeklines attract animals – sit quietly to avoid disturbing them
- Walk in small quiet groups
- Do not approach, disturb or feed wildlife
- In the Top End, always obey crocodile warning signs

Wales. It contains a system of ancient lakes formed over the last two million years, most of which are fringed by a crescent-shaped dune or lunette formed by the prevailing winds.

Aboriginal people have lived in this region for at least 50,000 years. Excavations have uncovered the cremated 40,000-year-old remains of 'Mungo Lady' in the dunes of Lake Mungo, as well as an ochred skeleton known as 'Mungo Man', also believed to be 40,000 years old.

Today, the lake beds are flat plains vegetated by salt-tolerant low bushes and grasses. Part of the site is gazetted as the **Mungo National Park** (www.environment.nsw.gov.au/nationalparks), which covers about two-thirds of Lake Mungo and includes the spectacular parts of the Walls of China lunette.

Twenty-two species of mammal are found in the region, as well as many reptiles and amphibians. Parrots, cockatoos and finches are the most conspicuous of the 137 recorded species of bird.

Mutawintji Eco Tours (tel: 08-8088 2389; www.mutawintjiecotours.com.au) is one of a number of companies offering four-wheel-drive tours of the Willandra Lakes Region. Other companies include **Sunraysia Discovery Tours** (tel: 03-5023 5937; www.sunraysiadiscoverytours.com.au); **Tri State Safaris** (tel: 08-8088 2389; www.tristate.com.au); and **Great Divide Tours** (tel: 02-9913 1395; www.greatdividetours.com.au). Some of these companies employ Aboriginal guides and also provide birdwatching tours.

The inviting water around Fraser Island is a swimmer's paradise

Aboriginal-owned **Harry Nanya Tours** (tel: 03-5027 2076; www.harrynanyatours.com.au) provides walking tours of Lake Mungo with a Paakantyi guide who explains all the significant sites.

Island and Reef Landscapes

Australia's beaches vie with the Outback for the title of the most iconic national landscape. In reality, both deserve to share the honour.

Fraser Island

Lying just off the east coast of Australia, this 122km (76-mile) -long island (www.fraserisland.net) is the largest sand island in the world. Majestic remnants of tall rainforest growing on sand and half the world's perched freshwater dune lakes (formed when organic matter accumulates and hardens in depressions made by the wind) are found inland from the beach.

The island's long, uninterrupted white beaches flanked by strikingly coloured sand cliffs are spectacularly beautiful, as are its 100 lakes, some of which are tea-coloured and others clear and blue – all are ringed by white sandy beaches. In spring and summer, the island's low heaths provide magnificent wild-flower displays.

This is a great destination for four-wheel-driving. **Seventy-Five Mile Beach** is an actual highway that runs up the surf side of the island, and sand tracks cross the island linking lakes and rainforests.

The island is visited by up to 40,000 migratory shorebirds every year. Rare, vulnerable or endangered species include dugongs, turtles, Illidge's ant-blue butterflies and eastern curlews.

Tour operators include **Footprints on Fraser** (tel: 07-4126 8258; www. footprintsonfraser.com.au), which offers guided walking tours; and

Fraser Experience (tel: 07-4124 4244; www.fraserexperience.com), which offers four-wheel-drive tours and hire.

Lord Howe Island

This remarkable example of an isolated oceanic island (www. lordhoweisland.info) was born of volcanic activity more than 2,000m (6,560ft) under the sea and boasts a spectacular topography. The marine park (www.environment.nsw.gov. au/NationalParks) surrounding the island contains the world's southernmost barrier coral reef and hosts over 450 species of fish, around one-tenth of which are unique to the area. Green and hawksbill turtles are common in summer, but may be observed throughout the year.

Swimming, snorkelling and scuba diving are all popular in the crystal waters of the park, and boat trips and diving tours operate from the island. Operators include **Howea Divers** (tel: 02-6563 2290; www. howeadivers.com.au), a locally owned and operated dive school

World Heritage Landscapes

Lord Howe Island boasts a spectacular topography

with extensive local knowledge of Island dive sites; **Marine Adventures** (tel: 02-6563 2243; www.marineadventures.com.au), which runs snorkelling and diving tours, fishing trips, and tours to see Green and hawksbill turtles; **Islander Cruises** (tel: 02-6563 2114; www.lordhoweisland.info), offering a half-day tour where you can snorkel, bushwalk, visit sea-bird colonies, fish and reef walk; **Lord Howe Island Tours** (tel: 02-6563 2214; www.lordhoweislandtours.com), which runs snorkelling, coral viewing and sea kayaking tours; and **Pro Dive** (tel: 02-6563 2253; www.prodivelordhowe.com), which offers introductory, PADI Openwater and PADI Advanced Openwater dives.

There are also bushwalks and more strenuous hikes to do, including the spectacular day walk to Mt Gower. **Lord Howe Nature Tours** (www.lordhowe-tours.com.au), operated by naturalist Ian Hutton, offers full- or half-day tours that are great ways to observe the island's rich flora and fauna.

Wilderness Landscapes

If you are keen to get back to nature in a true wilderness area, Australia is the place to do it.

Tasmanian Wilderness

The **Tasmanian Wilderness World Heritage Area** (www.parks.tas.gov.au) protects one of the last true wilderness regions on earth. Covering approximately 1.38 million hectares (3.46 million acres), it represents about one-fifth of the island state's area. The wilderness conserves a diverse

array of both natural and cultural features and provides secure habitats for some of the world's unique and rarest animals, including the Tasmanian devil, spotted-tail quoll, eastern quoll, pademelon and Tasmanian bettong. Endangered species found here include the orange-bellied parrot, white goshawk, swift parrot and Pedra Branca skink, a small lizard.

There are four distinct types of landscape within the wilderness area: temperate rainforest, alpine plains, moorlands and old-growth sclerophyllous forests.

The cathedral-like cool temperate rainforests of the wilderness are silent, dark and damp places where both the trunks of trees and the forest floor are covered with a luxuriant

The Tasmanian Wilderness covers around one-fifth of the island's area

carpet of mosses and lichens. They harbour the descendants of some of the most ancient of Australia's plants, including the myrtle-beech, native plum and leatherwood.

In the fragile alpine sections of the wilderness, the dominant species are cushion plants, scoparia and Tasmania's only native deciduous species, the deciduous beech. This provides superb autumnal colours. The buttongrass moorlands are covered in low vegetation dominated by sedges (grass-like plants), while the stunning sclerophyllous forests are dominated by eucalypt species including the tallest flowering plant in the world, the swamp gum, which can grow to heights in excess of 100m (328ft).

Self-guided bushwalking is the most popular activity in the

Exploring the Wilderness by zip wire

wilderness, with the **Overland Track** (see p.52) being the most famous route. With over 1,000km (620 miles) of tracks and routes, there are plenty of options to choose from, including the three-day Frenchman's Cap Walk and seven-day South Coast track. There are also popular day walks at Cradle Mountain, Lake St Clair, Hartz Mountains and the Franklin River. One of the major local companies offering guided walks is **Tasmanian Expeditions** (tel: 1300 666 856; www.tasmanianexpeditions.com.au).

The other main activity here is rafting and kayaking on the Franklin River. The full trip down the river is a magnificent 12-day wilderness rafting experience. The best time to do this is during the warmer months (Dec–Mar). Companies offering rafting tours include **Rafting Tasmania** (tel: 03-6239 1080; www.raftingtasmania.com), **Tasmanian Expeditions** (see above) and **Water by Nature – Tasmania** (tel: 0408 242 941; www.franklinrivertasmania.com).

World Heritage Landscapes

Minimal Impact Bushwalking

Australia's wilderness areas are notable for their pristine environmental state. To help keep them this way, follow these rules:

- Use a fuel stove instead of a campfire to reduce wildfire risk and campsite degradation
- Bury faecal waste 100m/yds (or as far as possible) away from watercourses
- Do not use soap and detergents in rivers or waterways as these can damage aquatic life
- Don't feed the wildlife
- Carry out all rubbish
- When camping, don't enlarge campsites, dig ditches around tents, cut saplings for tent poles or erect rock shelters

Beach and Surf Culture

A love of the beach is bred into the Australian character. Sand, surf and sun are a potent combination here, one that seduces almost every local from birth. Age, profession, income and cultural background – none of these signifies at the beach, where everyone has the same sand between their toes and waves breaking over their heads.

Aussie children start with a sand-bucket and spade, quickly progress to wetsuits and boogie boards and inevitably move on through Nippers (junior surf lifesaving programmes) to surfing and surf lifesaving. When they get older, they see this process of beachification repeated by their own children, and wouldn't have it any other way.

The Christmas holiday from late December through January is when families throughout the country flock to the coast to slather themselves in sunblock and insect repellent and claim a daily patch of paradise. There's none of that European habit of privatising the beach – everyone just lays down their beach towel or sets up a sun shelter, puts on a hat and relaxes with a book, an esky (coolbox) full of provisions and regular forays into the surf. At night, coastal resorts are redolent with the smell of barbecued meat, the queues at the local fish-and-chip joints are long and choruses of cicadas provide a distinctive soundtrack.

Visitors can easily share this enchantment if they organise themselves early enough. Most accommodation on the southern coast over the summer holiday period books up very early in the year, and the same applies to northern New South Wales and Queensland during school holiday periods. But outside these times, it's easy to find a place to stay near an idyllic beach – the country is full of them.

Swimming, boogie-boarding and surfing are the most popular beach activities on offer, with beach cricket a popular out-of-the-water activity. Many beach resorts also offer activities such as paragliding, snorkelling, diving, windsurfing, kitesurfing, sea-kayaking,

A surfer waxes his board

surf-fishing and sailing. Jet-skiing is sometimes offered but is despised by most beach-goers, as the loud machines disturb the laid-back ambience.

Sensational Surf Beaches

The East Coast of Australia is known for its magnificent surf beaches. To embark on the surfing safari of a lifetime, start in Victoria in January or February and make a leisurely trip north to Rainbow Beach in Queensland.

Bells Beach, Victoria

This is the most famous surf beach in Australia, and possibly the world. Home to the **Easter Classic Rip Curl Pro Surf & Music Festival** (http://live.ripcurl.com), which is held each Easter, it's where serious surfers come to catch Bells' famous powerful break by day and then brag about their achievements in the pubs of the nearby Surf Coast town of Torquay at night.

Bells and nearby Jan Juc are great places to take surfing lessons, and there are a number of reputable companies who will teach everyone from beginners to grommits (young surfers) wanting to improve their technique. All provide boards and wetsuits. They include **Go Ride a Wave** (tel: 1300 132 441; www.gorideawave.com.au [M]) and the **Torquay Surfing Academy** (tel: 03-5261 2022; www.torquaysurf.com.au [M]). Both also hire boards and wetsuits for independent surfers.

Newcastle, New South Wales

Surfers are spoilt for choice when they visit Newcastle. Nobby's Beach (home to the famous fast left-hander known

Bells Beach

as the Wedge), Newcastle Beach, Blacksmiths Beach, Caves Beach, Merewether Beach, Bar Beach, Shark Alley and Dixon Park Beach offer a variety of waves, including big swell and hectic right-handers. To sign up for some lessons, contact **Newcastle Surf School** (tel: 0405 500 469; www.newcastle-surfschool.com), **Redhead Mobile Surf School** (tel: 0404 839 585; www.redheadsurfschool.com.au) or **Surfest**

Recommended Read

Australian novelist Tim Winton is a fanatical surfer, and often sets his novels in coastal towns in Western Australia, where he lives. His 2008 work *Breath* is a powerful meditation on nature, surfing and masculinity that was awarded Australia's pre-eminent literary prize, the Miles Franklin Literary Award. Winton says he is most happy when he can 'blow the morning off and go for a surf'.

Surf School (tel: 0410 840 155; www.
surfestsurfschool.com). In March each
year, Merewether Beach hosts **Surfest**
(www.surfest.com), a surfing competition and festival that attracts contenders from around the world.

You can also go hang-gliding with
Air Sports (tel: 0412 607 815; www.
air-sports.com.au).

Crescent Head, New South Wales

This is the longboard capital of Australia, and is famous for its right-hand
point break, which is one of the longest in Australia. The Crescent Head
National Surfing Reserve stretches
for 3.5km (2 miles) along particularly
scenic coastline and is a great place to
learn to surf, with dolphins sometimes
observing your progress. You can even
stay in a surf camp here – **Mojo Surf
Australia** (tel: 1800 113 044; www.
mojosurf.com) operates a hostel-like
camp in the bush close to the waves
and can also provide lessons.

Seven Mile Beach at nearby Lennox
Head, another protected national surfing reserve, offers long right-hander
breaks and whale and dolphin spotting.

Byron Bay, New South Wales

This idyllic holiday spot has one of the
most beautiful beaches in the country
and offers activities galore. Surfers
head to the Pass, Wategos and Little
Wategos, while Main Beach is claimed
by swimmers and beachcombers. Surfing lessons are offered by **Black Dog
Surfing** (tel: 02-6680 9828; www.black
dogsurfing.com) and **Kool Katz** (tel:
02-6685 5169; www.koolkatzsurf.com).

Other beach activities include diving
in the Julian Rocks Marine Reserve,
skydiving, kayaking and gliding. Some
of the many operators are **Dive Byron
Bay** (tel: 02-66 858 333; www.byron
baydivecentre.com.au), **Sundive** (tel:
02-6685 7755; www.sundive.com.
au); **Skydive Byron Bay** (tel: 02-6684
1323; www.skydivebyronbay.com),
Cape Byron Kayaks (tel: 02-6680
9555; www.capebyronkayaks.com) and
Dolphin Kayaking (tel: 02-6685 8044;
www.dolphinkayaking.com.au).

Burleigh Heads, Queensland

The headland of this laid-back Gold
Coast town close to Surfers Paradise
has a legendary right-hand point break

Unique Experiences

The Gold Coast's Surfers Paradise is known for big buildings, as well as its waves

Noosa is a popular family destination

waters host pods of humpback whales. **Straddie Adventures** (tel: 07-3409 8414; www.straddieadventures.com.au) hires surfboards and runs sea-kayaking, sandboarding and snorkelling tours.

Noosa, Queensland

With a similar vibe to Byron and peaceful peeling right-hand waves for all levels, Noosa is another popular family or beginner surfing destination . The five point breaks in the Noosa National Park are world-famous, with the best waves appearing from February to June. Surf schools include **Go Ride a Wave** (tel: 1300 132 441; www.gorideawave.com.au), **Learn to Surf Noosa** (tel: 0418 787 577; www. learntosurf.com.au), **Noosa Surf Lessons** (tel: 0400 182 614; www.noosasurflessons.com.au) and luxury operator **Tropic Surf** (tel: 07-5455 4129; www.tropicsurf.net).

that is popular with surfers. Families also flock here because of the gorgeous swimming beach . Sign up with the **Godfathers of the Ocean Surf School** (tel: 07-5593-5661; www.godfathersoftheocean.com), operated by legendary surfer Michael 'Munga' Barry.

North Stradbroke Island, Queensland

This popular retreat for Brisbane's population has great breaks at Point Lookout and Main Beach, with the bonus of regular dolphin, manta ray and turtle sightings. From June to November, the

Rainbow Beach, Queensland

On the Fraser Coast, this long stretch of beach takes its name from the spectacular cliffs that back it, which feature 72 shades of sand. Surfers make the most of the right-hand point break at

Beach and Surf Culture

Surf Lifesaving Australia

At the beach, look for the red-and-yellow flags and lifeguard outfits of Surf Lifesaving Australia (www.slsa.asn.au). There are 305 local surf clubs across the country, all of which run surf awareness programmes and safety patrols. There are a few rules that everyone – however strong a swimmer – should follow:

- Always swim between the flags, as this area has been assessed as safe by

surf lifesavers, who also supervise it
- Read the safety signs posted outside the surf lifesaving club
- If possible, always swim with a friend
- If you need help, raise your arm and wave it from side to side to attract the attention of a lifeguard
- If you are caught in a rip (strong current), never swim against it. Swim parallel to the shore until you escape it.

Double Island Point, 13km (8 miles) south of the main beach, and increase the adrenaline rush by dropping 4,300m (14,000 ft) from the air with **Skydive Rainbow Beach** (tel: 0418 218 358). Other activities include sea-kayaking (**Rainbow Beach Dolphin View Sea Kayaking**; tel: 0408 738 192) and paragliding (**Rainbow Paragliding**; www.paraglidingrainbow.com).

Other Idyllic Beaches

As well as its surfeit of sensational surf beaches, Australia is spoilt for choice when it comes to magnificent stretches of sea and sand.

Shark Bay, Western Australia

World Heritage-listed **Shark Bay** (www.sharkbay.org), at the most westerly point of the Australian continent, is actually two bays formed by peninsulas lying side by side. Known as Gathaagudu ('two waters') by the Malgana Aboriginal people, it is a wonderland of wildlife, flora and amazing beaches.

The Bay's vast seagrass meadows pattern the aquamarine waters with dark dapples, ripples and swirls. Its coast is littered with rocky islands and fringed with sweeping beaches of glittering sand and shells set against a backdrop of rich red sand dunes. Giant surf smashes against the seaward coast of Edel Land and Dirk Hartog, Bernier and Dorre Islands.

Humpback whales skirt the coast on their annual migrations, and dugongs, cormorants, dolphins, green and loggerhead turtles, sharks, stingrays and rare birds are also found here.

In the inner gulf areas around Monkey Mia and Denham there is no swell, so there are plenty of safe places to take a dip. Monkey Mia is also home to a huge colony of bottlenose dolphins, which are fed every morning in a popular tourist event ℳ. Other activities include windsurfing and kiteboarding in summer, and sea-kayaking during the winter months, when the winds drop. Contact the **Shark Bay World Heritage Discovery Visitor Centre** in Denham (tel: 08-9948 1590; www.sharkbayvisit.com) for information about tours and equipment hire.

Cable Beach, Broome, Western Australia

This magnificent beach sports clear waters and a wide unblemished stretch of white sand backed by red dunes. After swimming, a camel ride along the shore at sunset is a mandatory activity. Operators include **Red Sun Camels** (tel: 08-9193 7423; www.redsuncamels).

Monkey Mia is home to a huge colony of bottlenose dolphins

Unique Experiences

com.au), **Broome Camel Safaris** (tel: 0419 916101; www.broomecamel safaris.com.au) or **Ships of the Desert Camel Tours** (tel: 0419 954 022; www. shipsofthedesert.com.au). Sea-kayaking is also popular – contact the **Broome Adventure Company** (tel: 0419 895 367; www.broomeadventure.com.au).

Ninety Mile Beach, Victoria
This stunning 144km (89-mile) stretch of sandy beach in the southeastern region of Gippsland is backed by dunes, swamplands and lagoons. The currents here are treacherous, so swim at patrolled **Seaspray**. Walking and surf fishing are the main activities.

Bay of Fires, Tasmania
A renowned 29km (18-mile) ribbon of sea, surf and sand often described as the most beautiful place in the world, the **Bay of Fires** is an unspoilt coastal wilderness area on the edge of Mount William National Park. The gorgeous beach at Binalong Bay offers excellent swimming, walking and views. If you yearn for deserted beaches where the only sounds to disturb your reverie are pounding surf and screeching seagulls, this is the perfect destination.

Jervis Bay, New South Wales
A beloved stretch of coastline south of Sydney, Jervis (pronounced Jar-vis) Bay incorporates the Jervis Bay National Park and Jervis Bay Marine Reserve. It is famed for its secluded white sandy beaches, birdlife and excellent walks, the most popular of which is the easy **White Sands Walk** from Greenfields Beach to Hyams Beach. The area is a hugely popular escape for Sydneysiders,

Cable Beach is backed by distinctive red dunes

who flock here over the Christmas holidays and in the dolphin- and whale-watching season (June–Nov). The highly regarded **Dolphin Watch Cruises** outfit (tel: 02-4441 6311; www. dolphinwatch.com.au) guarantees a free return cruise if no whales or dolphins are seen first time round.

Beach and Surf Culture

Great City Beaches

- **Bondi Beach, Sydney** Sensational surf and a famous social scene.
- **Bronte Beach, Sydney** Great for kids, with gentle waves, a grassed picnic area and a playground.
- **Northern Beaches, Sydney** Whale, Avalon and Bilgola are all great swimming beaches.
- **Glenelg beach, Adelaide** Offers high-speed jet-boat rides and catamaran cruises to watch or swim with dolphins.
- **Cottesloe Scarborough and Trigg Beaches, Perth** For surfing, head for Scarborough or Trigg; for a lively beach scene, opt for Cottesloe.

Australia's Great Journeys

Australia is a country where size really does matter. Outside the cities, the landscape is arranged on a stupendous scale: roads seem infinite, horizons endless, distances interminable. This can make exploration challenging, but the extraordinary range of natural wonders awaiting the visitor and the warm, down-to-earth hospitality that characterises rural Australia provide ample compensation.

In the 1970s and 1980s, Australian television screened a popular television show called *Ask the Leyland Brothers*, in which the intrepid duo visited different Outback destinations every week in their trusty four-wheel-drive, overcoming natural and mechanical obstacles aplenty on the way. The rest of us, alas, would find it impossible to emulate the Leylands – Australia is just too big, and parts of its terrain too inaccessible, for anyone to explore the entire interior in less than a lifetime. Instead, locals and visitors alike tend to choose one particular journey at a time,

following a scenery-laden route by foot, car or train.

The first great explorations of the Australian interior were made with the assistance of cameleers from the subcontinent and Middle East. From the mid-19th century to the 1930s, these handlers and their hardy beasts carried supplies and materials for expeditions to map the continent, locate natural resources and identify possible places for inland settlements. They also carried supplies and materials to the teams surveying and building great infrastructure projects such as

The open road through the Pilbara region of Western Australia

the Overland Telegraph and the rail link between Port Augusta and Alice Springs. Their hard work has given us today's Ghan railway line – which delivers one of the country's great journeys – and opened up many Outback roads and settlements.

These days, routes aren't as onerous as they were when the cameleers and explorers such as Eyre, Leichhardt, Burke and Wills opened up the interior, but they can vary wildly in time and degree of difficulty. Victoria's magnificent Great Ocean Road can be easily explored over one or two days in a standard two-wheel-drive, but to do any driving in the Outback, where the distance between roadhouses can be longer than the breadth of some European countries, a well-maintained four-wheel-drive is mandatory and drivers need plenty of time, supplies, navigational skill, energy and common sense. Here, dirt roads can be washed out by heavy rains or become dust bowls in dry heat, collisions with wildlife are commonplace and mobile phone signals are unknown. Travelling can be more hard work than holiday, and isn't for the faint-hearted.

But journeying need not always be by car. Dedicated walkers need go no further than the five-day Overland Route in the World Heritage-listed Tasmanian Wilderness. Train buffs will prefer to opt for the famous trip from Adelaide to Darwin on the *Ghan* or Sydney to Perth on the *Indian Pacific* – both are marvellous options for those who are keen to see Outback scenery in

Exploring the Great Ocean Road brings you up close to the stunning Twelve Apostles

comfort. Or to take a totally unique journey, consider signing up for the Great Aussie Cattle Drive, which herds cattle along the legendary Oodnadatta Track in South Australia.

And, of course, there are plenty of options for exploring via boat, most famously in a cruise around the idyllic Whitsunday Islands in Queensland's Great Barrier Reef.

Put simply, this is a land where every journey mixes a degree of challenge with charm and where every route – be it more or less travelled – is sure to provide lasting memories.

The Great Ocean Road

Magnificent views, maritime heritage and some of Australia's best beaches are on offer when you follow this route along Victoria's southwest coast-line. It's possible to drive the stretch from Melbourne to Port Campbell that we have outlined in one day, but a more leisurely progression is highly recommended – consider breaking your journey for one or two nights. From Port Campbell, it's possible to continue all the way to Adelaide, stopping at the Victorian towns of Warrnambool and Port Fairy and the South Australian towns of Mt Gambier and Robe on the way. To do this full trip justice, you'll need at least four nights/five days.

Start your journey in **Melbourne**, stopping for lunch on the city's outskirts at magnificent **Werribee Park** (K Road, Werribee; www. werribeepark.com.au; Nov–Apr daily 10am–6.30pm, May–Oct 10am–5.30pm; free ), a 19th-century pastoralist's mansion set in gracious gardens. From here, it's on to Victoria's second city, Geelong, and then to the Great Ocean Road proper, which starts in the surf-obsessed town of **Torquay**, home to popular beaches and the world's largest surfing museum, **Surfworld**

(Surf City Plaza, Beach Road; www. surfworld.com.au; daily 9am–5pm; charge ).

Next stop is **Anglesea**, famous for its beach, rockpools and the kangaroo-filled **Anglesea Golf Club** (Golf Links Road, Anglesea; tel: 03-5263 1582; www. angleseagolfclub.com.au). In relatively quick progression, the coastal hamlets of Aireys Inlet, Fairhaven and Moggs Creek – all with great beaches – are passed and you will arrive in **Lorne**, a large resort town offering gentle waves and a wide range of eating and accommodation options.

The most scenic stretch of the drive is between Lorne and Apollo Bay, gateway to the Great Otway National Park. You can visit the 1848 **Cape Otway Lightstation** (Great Ocean Road, Cape Otway; www.lightstation. com; daily 9am–5pm, Shipwreck Discovery tours at 10am and 2pm; charge ) or continue on to the magnificent **Port Campbell National**

Unique Experiences

The *Ghan* is one of the world's most famous train journeys

Stopping to take in the view along the Overland Track

The Indian Pacific

Stretching between the Indian and Pacific Oceans, the mighty *Indian Pacific* (Great Southern Rail; tel: 08 8213 4592; www.gsr.com.au) traverses 4,352km (2,698 miles) between Perth and Sydney and is one of the longest rail journeys in the world.

This three-night crossing of the continent sets off from Perth, making its way through the scenic Avon Valley, past the goldfields town of Kalgoorlie and across the Nullarbor Plain to Adelaide. It then proceeds to the outback town of Broken Hill, continues through the Blue Mountains and arrives in Sydney. You can break the trip in Kalgoorlie, Adelaide and Broken Hill, and it's also possible to take the journey from Sydney to Perth.

Park, home to the stunningly photogenic Twelve Apostles rock formations, from where you can make your way to the Wimmera, the Goldfields or on to Adelaide.

The Ghan

To travel from one edge of the continent to the other, hop aboard one of the world's most famous trains, the *Ghan* (Great Southern Rail; tel: 08 8213 4592; www.gsr.com.au). Traversing a route between Adelaide and Darwin, this rail journey through the Adelaide Hills, Flinders Ranges, Red Centre and Top End covers 2,979km (1,852 miles) and takes two nights/three days. You can break your trip in Alice Springs, close to Uluru-Kata Tjuta National Park, and at Katherine, home to Nitmuluk (Katherine Gorge) National Park. And of course you can set off from either Adelaide or Darwin. Along the way, the scenery is stark and the sunsets magnificent.

Journey Calendar

April The changing colours of the deciduous beech trees on the Overland Track are magnificent

April–October Take the *Ghan* when the temperatures are relatively mild in the Red Centre and Top End

June–September Sailing conditions in the Whitsundays are ideal during winter and early spring

July–November The best time of the year to take the *Indian Pacific* trip is during Western Australia's wild-flower season

August Great Australian Outback Cattle Drive

Early December or late February The weather on the Great Ocean Road is perfect, and the holiday crowds are relatively unobtrusive

For a taste of Outback life, join the Great Aussie Cattle Drive

The Overland Track

This internationally renowned six-day walk traverses 65km (40 miles) of the **Tasmanian Wilderness World Heritage Area** from Cradle Mountain to Lake St Clair, passing mountains, waterfalls, lakes and dense native forest on the trail.

The walk's extraordinary popularity has led to concerns about environmental degradation and overcrowding, so numbers are now limited and it is essential to book a spot with the **Tasmanian Parks and Wildlife Service** (tel: 03-6233 6047; www.parks.tas.gov.au) and pay a fee during the peak walking season (1 November – 30 April).

This is serious trekking, and it is imperative that walkers are fit, thoroughly prepared and suitably equipped. During the peak season, walkers are required to walk the track from north to south (Cradle Mountain to Lake St Clair). Aside from the main track there are also several alternative side tracks, including to the summits of Cradle Mountain and Mount Ossa, the tallest mountain in Tasmania. Taking these extends trekking time.

The Great Australian Outback Cattle Drive

City slickers who want an authentic taste of the Outback need go no further than the five-day **Great Aussie Cattle Drive** (tel: 08-84634547; www.cattledrive.com.au), in which participants lend a hand droving cattle along the dusty **Oodnadatta** or **Birdsville Tracks** in South Australia. During the drive, you are based in an Outback camp complete with bar, dining marquee and luxury tents with hot showers and flushing toilets – hardly the lot of the average Outback drover, but most welcome. Each day in the saddle sees the cattle move around 14km (9 miles) along old droving trails in the lonesome but diverse landscape.

Sailing or Kayaking the Whitsundays

The **Whitsunday Islands** form one of the world's most scenic adventure playgrounds. Hundreds of secluded bays, coves and beaches are dotted throughout these calm waters of the Coral Sea, sheltered by the Great Barrier Reef.

Most people experience the islands by staying at an island resort, but the best way to travel here is by yacht or under your own steam in a sea kayak. By doing this you will avoid the resort crowds and associated tourist hoopla, sleep to the sound of lapping waves and enjoy uncrowded snorkelling and swimming in the crystal-clear waters.

Most sailing companies and kayak-hire outfits are based at **Airlie Beach**, the departure point for the island group. Companies offering choices of sailing packages include **Whitsundays Sailing Adventures** (tel: 07-4940 2000; http://whitsundayssailingadventures.com.au) and **Whitsunday Bookings** (tel: 07-4948 2201; www.whitsundaybookings.com.au). Both offer a range of sailing holidays on catamarans, tall ships, luxury vessels and a variety of racing and cruising sloops, where you can choose to assist the crew or just lie back on deck and soak up the sun and sublime scenery.

To get even closer to the water, consider island hopping by sea kayak. **Salty Dog Sea Kayaking** (tel: 07-4946 1388; www.saltydog.com.au) offers a range of one-day or extended guided kayaking expeditions or will rent you a kayak if you want to go it alone.

Discovering the Whitsundays by sea kayak

Aboriginal Australia

Australia is home to the oldest living culture in the world – that of Indigenous Australians (Aboriginal and Torres Strait Islander peoples). These First Australians have a complex and mutually supportive relationship with the landscape and a rich social, cultural and linguistic heritage. For the visitor, gaining an understanding – however superficial – of this heritage is extraordinarily rewarding.

For too long, the culture and rights of Australia's Aboriginal and Torres Straits Islander peoples were suppressed by the white majority. That they have survived is in many ways a miracle – the First Australians have endured the appropriation of their land, innumerable massacres and the removal of their children by the Church and state, but still their cultures and spirits flourish.

Aboriginal culture is underpinned by 'the Dreamtime', a belief system that puts Aboriginal history, traditions and culture under a single mythological roof. Dreamtime stories recount how ancestral heroes created the stars, the earth and all creatures. They explain the origins of Australia's unique animals and plants, and how humans can live in harmony with nature.

The land plays a crucial part in Dreamtime lore, and responsibility for protecting significant sites is central to Aboriginal spiritual life. This is one of the reasons why land rights have always been a top political priority for the Aboriginal and Torres Strait Island peoples, and why the 1992 decision by Australia's High Court to award Eddie Mabo, a representative of the Meriam people, native title to the Murray Islands in the Torres Strait was greeted with elation and a sense of vindication by the Indigenous population. The Mabo judgement led to the Native Title Act 1993, and many subsequent claims have been awarded. Others are still to be negotiated and agreed, but a number of the country's national parks and Aboriginal sacred sites are now under Indigenous ownership and management, bringing Aboriginal and Torres Strait cultures closer than ever before to visitors.

Two generations of Aborigines in Sydney

Today, the cultures and traditions of Indigenous Australians are integral to Australian society and identity, even though citizens of Aboriginal and Torres Strait Islander descent make up less than three percent of the national population.

Understanding the Culture: Contemporary Encounters

More than half of Australia's Indigenous population lives in either New South Wales or Queensland. Although actual numbers are nowhere near as high in the Northern Territory as they are in these two larger states, the Territory's population has the largest proportion of Indigenous people (almost 30 percent). This means that visitors are far more likely to encounter Aboriginal culture in these states than they are in the south or west of the country.

Indigenous Australians are also more likely to live in rural or remote areas than the rest of the population, meaning Outback trips offer more chances to gain an understanding of Indigenous culture than do city sojourns.

National Parks and Reserves

One of the most satisfying experiences that visitors can have while in Australia is to spend time in an Indigenous-owned or -run national park or reserve. By supporting these enterprises, you will learn about and contribute materially to Indigenous culture and heritage.

Northern Territory

A number of remote Aboriginal reserves require visitors to obtain a permit before entering. **Arnhemland**, near Kakadu National Park in the

Uluru, the world's largest monolith, is sacred to the local Anangu people

Aboriginal Australia

Northern Territory, is one of these. Here, in a vast and mysterious landscape, Aboriginal people live a semi-traditional existence. To visit, you will probably need to take an organised tour; operators include **Lord's Kakadu and Arnhemland Safaris** (tel: 08-8948 2200; www.lords-safaris. com), **Nomad** (tel: 08-8987 8085; www.nomadcharters.com.au), **Magela Cultural and Heritage Tours** (tel 08-8941 9611; www.kakadutours.com. au) and **Arnhemlander** (tel: 08-8979 2411; www.arnhemlander.com.au).

Uluru-Kata Tjuta National Park (www.environment.gov.au/parks/uluru) is owned by the Anangu people, and is managed in association with Parks Australia. The park's **Uluru-Kata Tjuta Cultural Centre** (tel: 08-8956 3138; daily 7am–6pm; free) has fascinating exhibits on Aboriginal law, tradition and customs.

Nitmuluk (**Katherine Gorge**) **National Park** is jointly managed by the Jawoyn people and the Northern Territory's Parks & Wildlife Service. **Nitmiluk Tours** (08-8972 1253; www. nitmiluktours.com.au), an Indigenous-owned and operated tour company, organises camping, canoeing and walking tours, as well as helicopter flights, rock art tours and bush tucker walks.

Visiting a Cultural Centre

Many Outback towns and national parks have impressive, Indigenous-run cultural centres that welcome visitors and give an insight into Indigenous culture.

Northern Territory

The **Nyinkka Nyunyu Art and Culture Centre** in Tennant Creek (Paterson Street; tel: 08-8962 2699; www.

Nitmuluk, or Katherine Gorge

nyinkkanyunyu.com.au; May–Sept Mon–Sat 8am–6pm, Sun 10am–2pm, Oct–Apr Mon–Fri 9am–5pm, Sat–Sun 10am–2pm; charge) features multimedia and other displays that offer a great introduction to the local Warumungu culture. The centre also runs tours of its indigenous garden and of surrounding bushland, focusing on bush tucker.

Victoria

The stunning **Brambuk Cultural Centre** (Hall's Gap; tel: 03-5361 4000; www.brambuk.com.au; daily 9am–5pm; free) in Victoria's Grampians (Gariwerd) National Park is run by five local Indigenous groups in association with Parks Victoria. The displays offer an insight into local culture and history through stories, art, dance and objects. The centre also runs tours of nearby rock art and sacred sites.

Top Indigenous Festivals

March Tiwi Islands Football League Grand Final, Bathurst Island

June Barunga Festival, NT (www.barungafestival.com.au)

June Merrepen Arts Festival, NT (www.merrepenfestival.com.au)

June in odd-numbered years Laura Aboriginal Dance Festival, Laura, Queensland (www.lauradancefestival.com)

June The Dreaming Festival, Woodford, Queensland (www.thedreamingfestival.com)

August Stone Country Festival, NT (www.gunbalanya.org)

August Garma Festival, NT (www.garma.telstra.com)

A tour guide explains the cave paintings at Mossman Gorge

Cultural Tours

There are more cultural tourism opera-tors working in the Australian Outback than there are flies – and that's saying a lot. Choosing the right one can be a challenge, but there's a lot to be said for taking an Indigenous-owned and/or-run tour such as those listed below.

Northern Territory

Alice Springs–based **Anangu Tours** (tel: 08-8950 3030; www.ananguwaai. com.au) offers camel tours in the Uluru-Kata Tjuta National Park as well as dot-painting workshops and a cultural walking tour of Uluru led by an Anangu guide.

The **Jawoyn Association Aborigi-nal Corporation** (tel: 1800 644 727; www.jawoyn.org/manyallaluk-tours. htm) runs cultural heritage tours in its community of Manyallaluk, approxi-mately 100km (62 miles) from Kather-ine. These interactive, hands-on tours, which leave from Katherine, include a

bush-tucker and bush-medicine walk, traditional bark painting, fire lighting, spear throwing and basket weaving.

The Tiwi Land Council leases the rights to run tours of Bathurst Island to **Aussie Adventure Holidays** (tel: 08-8923 6523; www.aussieadventures. com.au). The tours include a smoking ceremony, morning tea with members of the local community and an exhibi-tion of traditional dancing. They can be extended to include wildlife spotting and participation in traditional food hunting and gathering.

Queensland

Tjapukai Cultural Park (Cairns Western Arterial Road, Caravonica; tel: 07-4042 9900; www.tjapukai. com.au), near Cairns, offers full- and half-day tours showcasing Indigenous culture. Guests watch theatrical per-formances and engage in interactive activities to learn the traditional cus-toms of the Tjapukai people.

Aboriginal Australia

The **Kuku-Yalanji**, traditional owners of the Mossman Gorge outside Port Douglas, operate daily 'Dreamtime Guided Rainforest Walks' (tel: 07-4098 2595; www.yalanji.com.au) demonstrating traditional plant use, identifying bush tucker sources, sharing Dreamtime legends and explaining the history of cave paintings.

South Australia

Small company **Arabunna Tours** (tel: 08-8675 8351; www.arabunnatours. com) offers one- to seven-day tours of the Flinders Ranges, Marree, Oodnadatta Track and Lake Eyre.

Bookabee Tours (tel: 08-8285 5033; www.bookabee.com.au) runs 'Dreamtime tours' focusing on storytelling, Aboriginal cultural experiences and visits to unique and culturally rich locations. These cover the Northern Flinders Ranges, Southern Flinders ranges and the Outback. It also runs a five-day 'Australia – the Movie' tour.

Indigenous Art

Artists such as Emily Kngwarreye, Rover Thomas and Cifford Possum Tjapaltjarri gave Australian Indigenous art an international profile in the 1980s and 1990s that it continues to enjoy today. Its various forms – including bark painting, dot painting, rock painting, rock engravings, body painting and weaving – are being practised in communities throughout the country, and art is a major source of Indigenous income, particularly in the Outback.

Key Aboriginal rock art sites include Nganalang in Keep River National Park, the Kimberley region of Western Australia, Carnavon Gorge in Queensland, the Burrup Peninsula in the Pilbara region of Western Australia, Sacred Canyon in South Australia's Flinders Ranges, the town of Laura in Queensland, and the Ubirr and Nourlangie Rocks in the Northern Territory's Kakadu National Park.

Northern Territory

Tiwi Art (tel: 08-8941 3593; www.tiwiart.com) operates small tours from Darwin to the three main art centres on the Tiwi islands. Participants meet local Torres Straits Islander artists while they work, and are offered the opportunity to make purchases.

The **Araluen Cultural Precinct** (corner Larapinta Drive and Memorial Avenue; www.araluenartscentre. nt.gov.au; Mon–Fri 10am–4pm, Sat–Sun 11am–4pm; charge) in Alice Springs is home to the Araluen Arts

A young Aboriginal dancer

Centre and the Central Craft studio and shop. Its guided cultural art tours (tel: 08-8951 1121; charge) focus on the connection between the Dreaming, contemporary Aboriginal art and the land of Mparntwe (Alice Springs).

Queensland

Aboriginal-owned and -operated company **Indij-n-Arts** (270 Montague Road; West End; tel: 07-3846 0455; www.theaboriginalexperience.com.au; daily 9am–5pm) runs workshops aimed at promoting the local indigenous artists of southeast Queensland and Northern New South Wales. Choose from traditional weaving, making didgeridoos and making boomerangs.

Bush Tucker Tours

Edible native foods and plants ('bush tucker') are slowly building a culinary profile in Australia. It is increasingly common to see ingredients like lemon myrtle, pepper leaf, quandong, wild honey, wild lime and Kakadu plum on restaurant menus, and bush tucker tours are becoming popular activities.

Try a bush tucker tour while in Australia

Northern Territory

Aboriginal-guided full-day tours combining a wildlife safari with bush tucker-gathering and a campfire cook-up at sunset are offered by **Kakadu Animal Tracks** (Cooinda Lodge, Kakadu Highway, Cooinda; tel: 08-8979 0145; www.animaltracks.com.au).

New South Wales

In Sydney, learn about the Aboriginal heritage of the Royal Botanic Gardens and sample indigenous bush foods in an **Aboriginal Heritage Tour** (Mrs Macquaries Road; tel: 02-9231 8111; www.rbgsyd.nsw.gov.au).

Victoria

Melbourne's **Royal Botanic Gardens** (Birdwood Drive, The Domain; tel: 03-9252 2429; www.rbg.vic.gov.au; charge) offers an Aboriginal Heritage Walk around the gardens with Indigenous Guides, in which you can experience a traditional smoking ceremony and discover traditional uses of plants for food, tools and medicine.

Aboriginal Australia

> **Further Information**
> - **Aboriginal Australia**
>   www.aboriginalaustralia.com.au
> - **Aboriginal Culture in Victoria**
>   www.aboriginaltourismvictoria.com.au
> - **Aboriginal Tourism Australia**
>   www.australiaonnet.com/tourism/aboriginal-tourism.html
> - **Indigenous Australia**
>   www.indigenousaustralia.info
> - **Western Australian Indigenous Tourism Operators Committee**
>   www.waitoc.com

PLACES

Getting Your Bearings

Australia is made up of six states – New South Wales, Victoria, Queensland, Western Australia, South Australia and Tasmania – and two territories – Australian Capital Territory (ACT) and Northern Territory. All but Tasmania are on the mainland and each has its own character and tier of government.

For easy reference when using this guide, each state and territory has a dedicated chapter and is colour-coded for quick navigation. Our coverage of the ACT only includes Canberra, as there is little to see or do elsewhere in the territory. Detailed regional maps are found at the beginning of each chapter.

WESTERN AUSTRALIA
Pages 216 – 239

Additionally, every chapter provides in-depth information on what to expect in each place. A listings index is located at the end of each chapter and it features the best hotels, restaurants, cafés and activities the region has to offer. The listings cater to all budgets, from those on a shoestring through to those who like to travel with no expense spared.

Distances across the continent are massive and much of the interior comprises inhospitable desert, meaning that most locals and visitors fly between states rather than drive. Tasmania can be visited by plane or by taking the Spirit of Tasmania passenger/car ferry across Bass Strait.

PACIFIC OCEAN

Torres Strait

Arafura Sea

Melville I.
GurigGunak Barlu N.P.
C. York
C. Grenville

win

C. Arnhem

Kakadu N.P.
Jabiru
Weipa

River
field N.P.

Katherine

Gulf of Carpentaria

Arnhem Land

Groote Eylandt

Mitchell

Cape York Peninsula

Coral Sea

Lakefield N.P.
Cooktown

Cairns

Great

ami

 sert

Victoria River Downs

Daly Waters

Larrimah

Wellesley Is

Karumba

NORTHERN TERRITORY
Pages 148 – 167

Tennant Creek

Barkly Tableland

Normanton

Tully
Hinchinbrook I.

Townsville

Barrier

Camooweal

Gregory Range

Whitsunday Islands

Mackay

Reef

o r t h e r n

Burketown

Mount Isa

Cloncurry

Sarina

r r i t o r y

Hughenden

Dajarra

Great

Dividing

Rockhampton
Gladstone

onnell Ranges

West MacDonnell N.P.

Lake Amadeus

Alice Springs

Boulia

Simpson Desert

Artesian Basin

Yaraka

QUEENSLAND
Pages 118 – 147

Q u e e n s l a n d

Emerald

Bundaberg
Fraser I.
Maryborough

ou

L. Eyre North

Birdsville

Quilpie

Charleville

Roma

Gympie

Range

Toowoomba
Warwick

Brisbane

S o
s t

SOUTH AUSTRALIA
Pages 198 – 215

Cooper Creek

Lake Eyre N.P.

South

Marree

Gammon Ranges N.P.
Leigh Creek
Flinders Ranges N.P.

Lake Torrens

Lake Frome

Sturt N.P.

Milparinka

Cunnamulla

Tibooburra

Murwillumbah
smore
Grafton

Glen Innes

Woomera

Broken Hill

Range

NEW SOUTH WALES
Pages 64 – 107

Moree

Walgett

Emidale

Port Macquarie

Ceduna

Penong

Streaky Bay

ralian Bight

Whyalla
Eyre Pen.

Augusta

Pod Pirie

Kinchega N.P.

Port

Mungo N.P.

N e w   S o u t h

Narromine

W a l e s

Dubbo

Wollemi N.P.

Taree
Myall Lakes N.P.
Newcastle

oor

Port Lincoln

York Pen.

Adelaide

Mildura

Hay

Parkes

Bathurst

Blue Mountains

Hunter Valley

Sydney

Wollongong

Kingston
Victor Harbor
Coorong N.P.
Naracoorte

Kangaroo I.

Wyperfeld N.P.

V i c t o r i a

Wagga Wagga

Albury

Kosciuszko

anberra

VICTORIA
Pages 168 – 197

Grampians N.P.

Great

CANBERRA AND THE ACT
Pages 108 – 117

C. Howe

Mount Gambier
Portland
Warrnambool
C. Otway

Melbourne
Geelong

Gippsland Lakes N.P.

Croajingolong N.P.

South East Cape

T a s m a n   S e a

King I.

Bass Strait

Furneaux Group

Marrawah

Burnie

Devonport

Queenstown

Tasmania

South West N.P.

South West Cape

Southport

Hobart

TASMANIA
Pages 240 – 257

New South Wales

To many visitors, the names 'Sydney' and 'New South Wales' are synonymous. However, there's a lot more to Australia's most populous state than its capital city. Here, visitors can unwind by hiking in a rainforest, diving on a coral reef, visiting a vineyard set amidst rolling green hills or watching a cattle muster in the dry and dusty Outback.

Sydney

Population: 4.5 million

Local dialling code: 02

Tourist offices: Palm Grove, Darling Harbour; corner of Argyle and Playfair Streets, The Rocks; both tel: 02-9240 8788; www.sydneyvisitorcentre.com

Main police station (24hr): 192 Day Street; tel: 02-9265 6499

Main post office: 1 Martin Place

Hospital (24hr emergency department): St Vincent's Hospital; 390 Victoria Street, Darlinghurst; tel: 02-8382 1111; www.stvincents.com.au

Local newspapers: *The Sydney Morning Herald*; www.smh.com.au. *The Daily Telegraph*; www.dailytelegraph.com.au

Time zone: Eastern Standard Time (GMT plus 10 hours)

When the First Fleet sailed into Sydney Harbour on 26 January 1788, the first passengers to disembark were a seasick gaggle of male convicts and their jailers – an unsavoury group of naval recruits well schooled in rum, sodomy and the lash. Understandably, the local Aborigines took one look at the new arrivals, let out furious howls and threw stones to drive them away – most of us would surely have done the same.

After a shaky start, the colony began to prosper in the early 19th century, largely due to the development of a successful wool industry serviced by Sydney, Newcastle (founded in 1797)

and Bathurst (founded 1815). By the 1820s the colony's interior was being surveyed and settled by 'squatters', free settlers who occupied large tracts of Crown land in order to graze livestock – at first illegally and then under licence. The properties and towns they established still thrive today.

Sydney

If the world had a lifestyle capital, **Sydney ❶** would be a strong contender – something that is richly ironic, considering that the city started out as a British penal colony. This is a city where leisure has been elevated to an art form, where the sun always shines and where the standard of living is one of the highest in the world.

Despite all this, Australia's largest metropolis can be off-putting. The natural beauty of the harbour and beaches often stands in stark relief to the man-made landscape: the narrow, traffic-clogged streets, the lacklustre inner-city architecture, and the endless orange-roofed expanse of suburbia. But fear not: when such elements become oppressive, one has merely to wander around spectacular Circular Quay or plunge into the surf (and scene) at Bondi Beach for all to be forgiven and for the magic of this sybaritic city to reassert itself.

Circular Quay

This is the gateway to Sydney Harbour. Ferries, RiverCats and

Sydney Harbour Bridge is one of the world's most recognisable landmarks

HarbourCats (commuter catamarans), water taxis and tour boats of every stripe plough in and out of its docks, taking passengers up and down the city's magnificent waterway.

The cluster of iconic structures surrounding the quay is postcard-perfect. Sydney's single-span **Harbour Bridge** was erected during the depths of the 1930s Depression as a symbol of hope in the future. Dubbed the Coathanger, the Toast Rack and the Iron Lung (the latter for the number of people given work on its construction, which kept Sydney breathing), this major link between the city's northern and southern suburbs can be climbed with an outfit called **Bridge Climb** (3 Cumberland Street, The Rocks; www.bridgeclimb. com; daily; charge). The southeastern pylon of the bridge is home to the **Pylon Lookout Museum** (www.pylonlookout.com.au; daily 10am–5pm; charge), which leads up to a viewing platform with superb views of the harbour and city. From here, you can walk across the bridge to the North Shore in 15–20 minutes.

Circular Quay is the gateway to Sydney Harbour

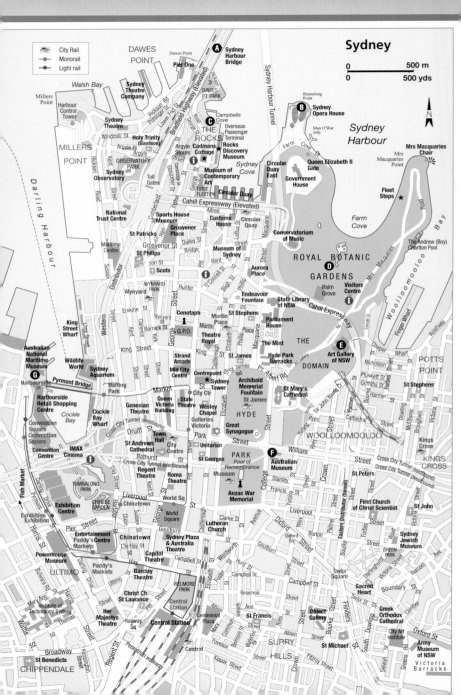

Sydney Opera House

The magnificent **Sydney Opera House** ❸ (www.sydneyoperahouse. com; guided one-hour tours daily between 9am–5pm; charge) was designed by Danish architect Jørn Utzon, and is best visited by attending a performance in the concert hall. Construction began in 1959 but Utzon's project was fraught with difficulties. Escalating costs and a slew of misunderstandings eventually led to his resignation in 1966. By the time the completed building was opened by the Queen in 1973, it had cost A$102 million – 15 times its initial budget.

The quay itself is home to a lively scene. Buskers, pedlars, tourists, ferry commuters and city office workers

Sydney Transport

 Airport: Sydney Airport (tel: 02-9667 9111; **www.sydneyairport.com. au**) is 10km (6 miles) south of the city centre. Transport to Sydney: taxi (15 minutes; A$30); Airport Link train to Central Railway Station (tel: 02-8337 8417; **www.airportlink. com.au**, every 5–30 minutes, 5am–12.40am, adult A$15 one way, A$25 return)

 Buses: Operated by Sydney Buses (**www.sydneybuses.info**). MyBus/MyTrain/MyFerry/MyMulti travelcards and tickets can be used on buses, ferries and trains. These can be purchased on transport or from TransitShops and ticket resellers displaying MyZone PrePay signage. An unlimited one-day travelcard costs A$20 and a one-trip ticket costs A$2–6 depending on the route. Buses usually run from

4.30am–midnight; NightRide buses every 30 minutes–one hour from midnight–4.30am, from Queen Victoria Building or Circular Quay. All transport information: tel: 131 500; **www.131500.com.au**

 Ferries: Operated by Sydney Ferries (tel: 131 500; **www.sydneyferries. info**) and run from 6am–midnight

 Trains: Operated by CityRail (tel: 131 500; **www.cityrail.info**) and run from 5am–midnight

 Taxis: Yellow, metered Legion Taxis (tel: 131 451; **www.legioncabs.com. au**). Taxis Combined (tel: 133 300; **www.taxiscombined.com.au**)

 Parking: Road parking is metered; there are plenty of privately operated undercover car parks

Take in Australia's early history by strolling through The Rocks

bustle about, and art-goers pass by on their way to the **Museum of Contemporary Art** (MCA; 140 George Street, The Rocks; www.mca.com.au; daily 10am–5pm; free except when special exhibitions are staged), known for its challenging exhibition programme and wonderfully sited café.

The Rocks and Observatory Hill

Sydney's most historic district is named after the sandstone bluffs from which the first convicts cut golden bricks for public buildings. Almost immediately the area became the colony's main port, and warehouses grew up along the waterfront, backed by merchants' shops, offices, hotels, banks, bars and brothels that went along with the seafaring trade of the 19th century. Today **The Rocks** ❸ is an open-air museum where

you can absorb Australia's early history during a leisurely stroll. To underpin the history lesson, visit the **Rocks Discovery Museum** (Kendall Lane, The Rocks; www.rocksdiscoverymuseum.com; daily 10am–5pm; free), an interactive display on the area's past, including the lives of its traditional residents.

Beyond the Argyle Cut, a tunnel excavated by convicts, are pretty Argyle Place and the 1840 Garrison Church; further up a steep path is the 1850s **Sydney Observatory** (Watson Road, Observatory Hill; www.sydneyobservatory.com.au), now a museum of astronomy with an imaginative **3-D Space Theatre** (daily 10am–5pm, nightly by arrangement; charge 🌀).

Botanic Gardens and Domain

East of the Opera House are the **Royal Botanic Gardens** ❹ (Mrs

Macquarie's Road; www.rbgsyd. nsw.gov.au; daily 7am–sunset; free except for Tropical Centre), a vast and voluptuous collection of Antipodean flora, including some truly majestic Moreton Bay figs. Hidden amongst the sculpted lakes and exotic fronds is an excellent café-restaurant. If you decide to picnic on the lawns, be warned – the strutting, long-beaked ibis are notorious lunch burglars.

In the gardens is the lookout known as Mrs Macquaries Chair, which overlooks the tiny island of Fort Denison. The point is also the site of the summer **Open Air Cinema** (Jan and Feb every year; www.stgeorgeopenair.com.au), where films are shown on a screen that seems to rise out of the harbour.

In the northwest corner of the gardens, overlooking the Opera House, is **Government House** (Macquarie Street; www.hht.net.au; entry by guided tour only Fri–Sun 10.30am– 3pm; free), formerly home to state governors and now open to the public. The ground-floor staterooms have some beautiful 19th- and 20th-century furniture and decoration.

Paths continue through the gardens to the **Art Gallery of New South Wales** ❺ (www.artgallery.nsw. gov.au; Thur–Tue 10am–5pm, Wed 10am–9pm; free except for special exhibitions). This imposing edifice contains one of the country's finest groupings of Australian art and hosts regular blockbuster exhibitions from Australia and overseas.

The Royal Botanical Gardens are home to a unique array of flora

Fabulous Ferry Trips

Sydney is as famous for its jaunty yellow and green ferries as London is for its red double-decker buses – and then some. These gracefully ageing vessels are as popular with local commuters as they are with visitors to the city, and a trip across or around the harbour is the quintessential Sydney experience. Great ferry, RiverCat and HarbourCat trips from Circular Quay include those to:

Balmain, a leafy enclave in Western Sydney replete with 19th-century buildings

Manly, a seaside suburb at North Head, at the entrance to Sydney Harbour

Cremorne Point on the Inner Harbour, from where it's possible to take a leafy harbourside walk to Mosman

Parramatta, home to colonial buildings including Old Government House

Watsons Bay, near South Head, home of the legendary Doyle's seafood restaurant (see p.101).

Central Business District (CBD)

Sydney's CBD is an oddly anonymous hodgepodge of glass skyscrapers and architectural styles from the past two centuries, all squeezed onto a street plan drawn up in Georgian times. It is best seen by strolling up Young Street from Circular Quay, past the 1846 classical revival **Customs House** (31 Alfred Street; www.cityofsydney. nsw.gov.au/customshouse; Mon–Fri 8am–midnight, Sat 10am–midnight, Sun 11am–5pm; free). At the end of the street is the impressive **Museum of Sydney** (www.hht.net.au; daily 9.30am–5pm; charge 🅼), built on the site of Australia's oldest building – the first Government House.

Next, cut over to Macquarie Street for a view of official Sydney: in quick succession come the **State Library of NSW** (www.sl.nsw.gov.au; Mon–Thur 9am–8pm, Fri 9am–5pm, Sat–Sun 10am–5pm; free); **Parliament House** (www.parliament.nsw. gov.au; tours on non-sitting days Mon–Fri 9am–5pm; free); and **Hyde Park Barracks Museum** (www.hht. net.au/visiting/museums/hyde_park_ barracks_museum; daily 9.30am– 5pm; charge), designed in 1817 by convict architect Francis Greenway and completed in 1819.

At the end of Macquarie Street lies **Hyde Park**, with the powerful Art Deco Anzac War Memorial. To the east of the park on College Street stands the **Australian Museum** 🅶 (http://australianmuseum.net.au; daily 9.30am–5pm; charge 🅼), the oldest museum institution in the country and the foremost showcase of Australian natural history.

Cut back across Hyde Park to visit **Sydney Tower** (corner Pitt and Market Streets; http://sydneytower.myfun.

Overlooking the Central Business District

Fresh and delicious produce at the Sydney Fish Market

Street; www.anmm.gov.au; daily 9.30am–5pm, Jan until 6pm; charge ) and **Sydney Aquarium** (http://sydneyaquarium.myfun.com.au; daily 9am–10pm; charge).

From Darling Harbour (near the Convention Centre), the Metro Light Rail takes passengers to the **Sydney Fish Market** (Bank Street, Pyrmont; tel: 02-9004 1143; www.sydneyfishmarket.com.au; daily from 7am), a mix of fish auctions, market stalls, restaurants and a seafood cooking school. Behind-the-scenes market tours run on Mondays, Thursdays and Fridays (bookings essential; charge).

From the market, the Light Rail travels back to Darling Harbour and to Paddy's Markets, close to the **Powerhouse Museum** (500 Harris Street, Ultimo; www.powerhousemuseum.com; daily 10am–5pm; charge), a huge space devoted to science and technology. From the museum, it's a short stroll east to Sydney's **Chinatown**, with its wall-to-wall Asian food.

71

New South Wales

com.au; daily 9am–10.30pm; charge), regarded as a phallic eyesore by many, but offering great views from its observation deck. On nearby George Street is the gorgeous **Queen Victoria Building** (QVB; www.qvb.com.au; Mon–Sat 9am–6pm, Thur until 9pm, Sun 11am–5pm; free). Built during the 1890s Depression as Sydney's main market, the arcade was lovingly restored in the 1980s as an upmarket shopping centre.

Darling Harbour and Chinatown

Slithering its way past the QVB is the city's Disney-esque Monorail. This is the easiest way to get to Darling Harbour, once a seedy area where trading ships docked but now a touristy collection of shops, restaurants and attractions, including the **Australian National Maritime Museum** (2 Murray

Inner East

In Victorian times, **Kings Cross** ('The Cross') was an elegant, tree-lined residential suburb. The 1920s and 1930s saw it take the mantle of Sydney's bohemian mecca, something it retained until the 1960s, when it turned into the city's sleazy red-light strip, a dubious honour it retains to this day. Despite this, The Cross and its neighbouring enclave of **Potts Point** house some of the city's most popular nightspots, bars, restaurants and boutique hotels.

⬛ PADDINGTON AND WOOLLAHRA WALK

This walk through two up-market inner-city neighbourhoods showcases some of Sydney's best shopping, eating and heritage architecture.

Kick off your walk in Paddington, once a notorious slum and now one of the city's most desirable residential addresses. In the early years of the colony, this part of town was dominated by British troops, who built the magnificent Georgian-era **Victoria Barracks** *(see p.74)*. Following Federation in 1901, the site remained the focal point of military activity in New South Wales and it is still in active use today. Many of the cottages built to house the convict workforce who laboured during its construction can still be seen in the streets that run off Oxford Street opposite the barracks, such as Bourke Lane and Shadforth Street.

Heading east up Oxford Street, the second street on your left after Greens Road is **Glenmore Road**. This was Paddington's first major road, created by the bullock carts hauling gin to Oxford Street from the Glenmore Distillery near Rushcutters Bay. Today the stretch of Glenmore Road adjoining Oxford Street is home to boutiques and art galleries.

Walk down Glenmore Road, passing the popular **Jackies Café** at No 1c and **Barry Stern Gallery** at No 19, and you will eventually arrive at one of the suburb's loveliest enclaves, **Five Ways** (its epicentre is at the junction of five streets). From here, veer southeast up Heeley Street and turn left almost immediately into Broughton Street. At the sixth street on your right (Hopetoun Street) veer right to reach one of Paddington's best shopping strips, **William Street**. Fashion designers such as Collette Dinnigan and Leona Edmiston ply their wares from converted terrace houses.

Run the shopping gauntlet back to Oxford Street. From here head west

Elegant houses in Paddington

Tips

- Distance: 8km (5 miles)
- Time: Half a day
- From the city, catch a bus going to Oxford Street and ask to be let off at the Victoria Barracks stop.
- The tour is best done on a Saturday in order to visit Paddington Markets; allow a couple of hours to see the markets in full, if possible.

(towards the city) to visit the cutting-edge **Australian Centre for Photography** (www.acp.org.au; Tue–Fri noon–7pm, Sat–Sun 10am–6pm; free) at No 257. Slightly further, on the corner of Ormond Street, is Paddington's finest historic building, **Juniper Hall**, built for Robert Cooper, ex-convict and gin distiller, and completed in 1824. This elegant villa – named after the key ingredient in gin – now belongs to the National Trust and is occupied by tenants.

Backtracking east up Oxford Street, you'll pass the Paddington Uniting Church on the southern side of the street. On Saturdays, the grounds here host the popular **Paddington Markets** *(see p.74).* A bit further east, go left at the Light Brigade Hotel and wander down Jersey Road to get a taste of the up-market suburb of Woollahra, home

Paddington Markets is the place to come for fashions and foodstuffs

to huge mansions. If you walk to the end of Jersey Road, head into Rush Street and then turn right (south) into Moncur Street you will encounter a tempting array of cafés and restaurants – **Bill's** and **Bistro Moncur** *(see p.101)* being two of the most popular.

From Moncur Street, turn right (west) into Queen Street, another fashionable shopping strip. At its junction with Oxford Street, set off to Centennial Park or get a bus to the Eastern Beaches or CBD.

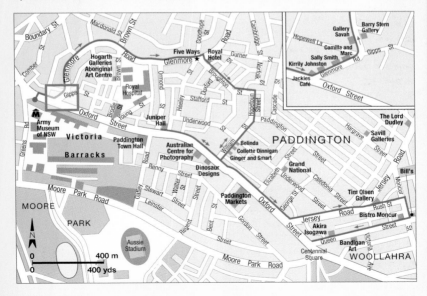

From The Cross, Darlinghurst Road wends its way south to **Oxford Street**, where Sydney's gay community reigns supreme. Gay-friendly clubs, bars and shops snuggle happily together around Taylor Square, and every February the area hosts the world-famous Sydney Gay and Lesbian Mardi Gras parade. South of Taylor Square, in the boho-chic suburb of **Paddington** ❶ ('Paddo'), is the magnificent **Victoria Barracks** (corner Oxford Street and Greens Road; guided tours Thur 10am; charge), built in 1841–48. The barracks complex is home to the **Army Museum** (visit Sun 10am–2.30pm or on the Thur tour).

Paddo is home to a number of Sydney's best shops, restaurants and commercial art galleries, as is the ritzy adjoining suburb of **Woollahra**. As you reach the summit of Oxford Street, before it heads along the dual carriageway to Bondi, you hit huge, leafy and much-loved **Centennial Park**. Sydneysiders run, rollerblade, picnic, cycle and horse ride here year-round. In summer, a huge screen is erected in the park's Belvedere Amphitheatre for the **Moonlight Cinema** (www.moonlight. com.au) – picnicking while watching a new-release film (and the passing parade that is the audience) is one of Sydney's finest outdoor experiences.

Eastern Beaches

From Paddington, it's a short bus or taxi ride to any of the eastern beaches – of which the most famous is certainly **Bondi** ❶ (pronounced 'Bond-eye'). In summer, activity here kicks off at dawn, with the joggers on

---

To Market, to Market

Sydneysiders far prefer the outdoor market to the indoor shopping mall. Three of the city's most popular are: **Balmain Market** (St Andrew's Congregational Church, corner Darling Street and Curtis Road; www.balmain market.com.au; Sat 8.30am–4pm) for food, arts and crafts, and vintage clothing; **Bondi Markets** (Bondi Beach Public School, corner Campbell Parade and Warners Avenue; www.bondimarkets. com.au; Sun 10am–4pm) for up-and-coming fashion and jewellery as well as retro clothing and bric-a-brac; **Paddington Markets** (St John's Church, 395 Oxford Street; www. paddingtonmarkets.com.au; Sat 10am–4pm), known for its avant-garde fashion and wide variety of food stalls.

Bondi Beach

The isthmus of Manly boasts a glorious beach

the promenade, bodybuilders by the shore and surfies catching a few waves before work. Sun-worshippers arrive early, closely followed by busloads of Japanese tourists. The Bondi Pavilion opens up, selling ice creams and souvenirs; picnickers arrive with their fish and chips; and the activity continues until well after dark, when lovers take over the sands.

Campbell Parade, the main beach-front thoroughfare, is a motley string of 1930s-era storefronts that seems to resist all improvement ('one of the great disappointments of Sydney', according to the travel writer Jan Morris). Despite the occasional attempt to open a sleek shop or café, the parade hangs on to its raffish, sand-gritted per-sonality – and most Sydneysiders really would have it no other way.

The other eastern beaches are smaller than Bondi, but don't attract its often-overwhelming crowds. The easiest way to see them all in a day is to take the Eastern Beaches Walk *(see p.76)*.

North Shore

A five-minute ferry ride from Circular Quay is the North Shore suburb of **Kirribilli**, where the prime minister and governor-general have official residences.

To its west, on either side of Lavender Bay, are the suburbs of **McMahons Point**, held to have the best view in Sydney, and **Milson's Point**, location of **Luna Park** (1 Olympic Drive; www.lunaparksydney. com; opening hours vary; free entrance and paid rides 🅜), which has retained many original 1935 fixtures including its distinctive harbour-facing laughing face and towers.

Spectacularly sited **Taronga Zoo** ➋ (www.taronga.org.au; daily 9am–5pm; charge 🅜) is also easily accessible by ferry from Circular Quay. Surrounded by virgin bush, the zoo commands a heart-stopping panorama of the city (taronga is an Aboriginal word for 'view across the water') and is home to more than

This is the most famous walk in Sydney for good reason – the stretch from Bondi to Bronte takes less than one hour, the coastal views are magnificent and the walk is relatively easy.

A showcase of sun, surf and Sydney itself, Bondi is probably the most famous beach in the world. Home to the world's first lifesaving club (established in 1906), its wide golden sands, ragged sandstone headlands and white-crested waves lend it a potent charm that is as irresistible to sightseers as it is to sun worshippers.

This walk starts at the Bondi Icebergs Club, with its spectacularly sited **outdoor pool** (Mon–Fri 6am–6.30pm, Sat–Sun 6.30am–6.30pm; charge),

glamorous restaurant *(see p.102)* and down-to-earth bistro. Follow the signposts south around the cliff path towards the small reserve known as **Mark's Park** – there are plenty of scenic vantage points (and a number of benches) along the way. On your way, look out for plaques recounting local Aboriginal myths and stories associated with this part of Sydney.

From Mark's Park it's a short distance to diminutive **Tamarama Beach**. The surf lifesaving club here has been fundraising for years to replace its ugly concrete clubhouse with a structure more visually attuned to its surrounds – at present walkers have no choice but to ignore this ugly intervention on an otherwise picture-perfect route. As at Bondi, Bronte and Coogee, the beach here is patrolled

Soaking up a few rays on Bondi Beach

Tips

- Distance: 5.5km/3½ miles (the first section, to Bronte Beach, is just 1.5km/1 mile)
- Time: A half-/full day
- Bring your togs and a towel – there are plenty of swimming opportunities.
- Wear a hat and sunscreen.
- To access Bondi Beach, Tamarama, Bronte and Coogee by public transport, catch the Bondi Explorer bus service *(see p.67)*.
- The best time of the year to do this walk is between late October and mid-November, when the wildly popular Sculpture by the Sea exhibition (http://sculpturebythesea.com) transforms the route between Bondi and Bronte.

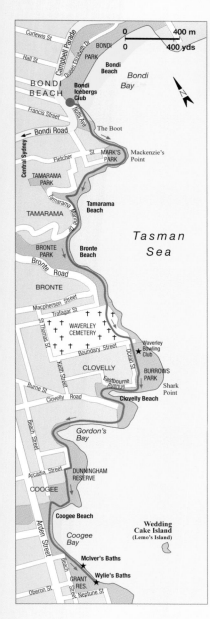

Lovely Bronte Beach is fringed
by Norfolk Island pines

– be sure to swim only between the
yellow-and-red flags.

Follow the path around the perimeter
of the small grassed reserve and continue on to charming **Bronte Beach** with
its Norfolk Island Pines, picnic ground
and popular children's playground.
Named after Admiral Lord Nelson, who
was also the Duke of Bronte (Sicily), this
has been a popular spot for Sydneysiders to frolic ever since its ocean pool
was opened in 1887.

Those only interested in a short walk
can stop here to swim, picnic or claim
a table at one of the cafés on Bronte
Road above the beach. For those who
are keen to continue walking, the route
follows the cliff top and continues along
a newly constructed boardwalk edging
the picturesque **Waverley Cemetery**
and on to **Clovelly** (a popular snorkelling spot), **Gordon's Bay** and **Coogee
Beach**. At Coogee, the historic **Wylie's
Baths** (www.wylies.com.au; daily during
daylight saving hours 7am–7pm, rest
of year 7am–5pm; charge), a tidal pool
built in 1907 and magnificently restored
in 1994, commands sweeping ocean
views. If you've worked up an appetite,
it's hard to beat the fish and chips at **A
Fish Called Coogee** (229 Coogee Bay
Road; daily 11.30am–10pm).

5,000 animals, including the full panoply of local critters.

The suburb of **Manly**  was given its name by Captain Phillip in 1788 when he was struck by the 'manly' bearing of the Aborigines he met there. In the 1930s, the isthmus became Australia's favourite holiday resort and the vacation atmosphere has lingered, with a bustling pedestrian mall and loads of eateries. On West Esplanade are the **Manly Art Gallery and Museum** (www.manlyaustralia. com.au/manlyartgallery; Tue–Sun 10am–5pm; charge, free Wed), with a good selection of Australian paintings; and **Oceanworld** (http://oceanworld. myfun.com.au; daily 10am–5.30pm; charge 🖼), where visitors can walk through a shark tunnel, see a Great Barrier Reef exhibit, feed fish or take diving and snorkelling classes. On weekends, guided tours of the historic **Manly Quarantine Station** (North Head; tel: 02-9977 5145; www.qstation. com.au; Sat–Sun 3pm, bookings essential; charge) are popular; spooky ghost tours (charge) are also conducted here at least four nights per week.

Sydney Excursions

After spending a few high-velocity days in Sydney, many visitors choose to retreat to the surrounding countryside for a day or two of R&R amidst spectacular bushland scenery. In doing so, they follow a tradition that was established by Sydneysiders in the early 20th century and is still enthusiastically embraced by locals on weekends.

The Blue Mountains

Sixty-five kilometres (40 miles) west of Sydney lie the World Heritage-listed

---

A Cattle-Rustler's Hideout

In 1838, pastoralist James Whalen was tracking an escaped convict and cattle rustler called James McKeown when he came across an entrance to the prehistoric **Jenolan Caves** (www.jenolancaves.org.au; guided tours daily 9.30am–5.30pm; charge), a spectacular series of 350 underground limestone halls encrusted with stalactites and stalagmites, just over an hour's drive west of Katoomba. McKeown's hideout emerged as a popular tourist destination in the 1880s, and subsequent explorations by guides and members of spelaeological societies led to the discovery of many new caves, the most recent being Spider Cave in 1975.

The dramatic landscape of the Blue Mountains, a stone's throw from Sydney

Blue Mountains, a dramatic region of forested ravines and pristine bushland. The name derives from the mountains' distinctive blue haze, produced by eucalyptus oil evaporating from millions of gum trees. Well-marked walking trails of all grades crisscross **Blue Mountains National Park** ❶ (charge for vehicle entry), passing streams and waterfalls, descending into cool, impressive gorges, and snaking around sheer cliffs.

The region's 26 small towns are riddled with fine restaurants, old-style cafés and antique stores catering to weekenders. Its best-known natural feature is The Three Sisters, a trio of pinnacles best viewed from Echo Point at the town of Katoomba. The

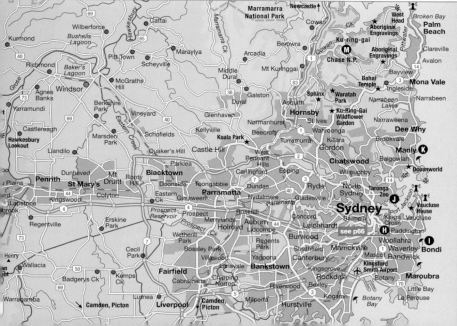

Scenic Railway (corner Violet Street and Cliff Drive; daily 9am–5pm; charge ), the world's steepest railway, descends from the clifftop at Katoomba into the Jamison Valley.

Ku-ring-gai Chase

Twenty-five kilometres (15½ miles) north of Sydney is **Ku-ring-gai Chase National Park**  (daily 6am–8pm daylight saving hours, 6am–5.30pm rest of year; charge for vehicle entry), an area of unspoilt forests, cliffs and heathland fringing the Hawkesbury River. There are many good walking trails through bushland here, including a signposted Aboriginal Heritage Walk that passes rock carvings left by the Guringai people who lived in this area long before the foundation of New South Wales. The park's **information centre** (Bobbin Head Road, Mount Colah; daily 10am–noon and 12.30–4pm) can supply information on the park's cultural heritage as well as maps of walking tours. Guided tours are run by the park's **Kalkari Discovery Centre** (tel: 02-9472 9300).

Royal National Park

Only 32km (20 miles) south from Sydney, the **Royal National Park** (daily sunrise–8.30pm; charge for vehicle entry) was established in 1879 and is the world's second-oldest national park – after Yellowstone in the USA. It offers riverside picnics, great surf beaches, cliff-top heathland walks, rainforest cycle tracks, and guided cultural and wildlife walks.

North From Sydney

For generations, the Pacific Highway has been Sydney's escape route to the sun. With the pedal to the metal, you can make the drive to Queensland in 12 hours, but it's much better to give yourself between three and five days to explore the wealth of national parks, wineries, laid-back holiday towns and fabled surf beaches en route.

Hunter Valley is one of Australia's foremost wine-growing regions

Among Newcastle's attractions are its fine surf beaches

the river in 1827. A free car ferry takes you to the rugged bush-clad sandstone cliffs of **Dharug National Park**. Here, walkers, cyclists and horse riders can travel a stretch of the Great North Road literally carved out of the rock by convicts in the 1830s.

The commercial hub of this central coast region (a mixed bag of retirees, new industries and Sydney commuters) is a detour away at the not-terribly-alluring Gosford. But beyond the urban sprawl are the orchards and forests of the Mangrove Mountain area, plus a string of beautiful beaches. At Doyalson, the highway heads along a ridge between the ocean and Lake Macquarie before eventually arriving at **Newcastle ❷**, the second-largest city in New South Wales. Long lumbered with a reputation as an unsophisticated industrial hub, Newcastle has reinvented itself in recent years, and now boasts a thriving university, the excellent **Newcastle Region Art Gallery** (1 Lamen Street; www.newcastle.nsw. gov.au/nag; Tue–Sun 10am–5pm; free), a lively waterfront development, beautifully preserved heritage buildings and impressive surf beaches.

The Central Coast

The trip north starts at Sydney Harbour Bridge and proceeds through the well-heeled upper North Shore to the beginning of the Newcastle Freeway at Wahroonga. Where the highway crosses the Hawkesbury River at Brooklyn, a vista of ridges, valleys and arms of open water spreads east and west. Among the many outfits offering cruises is the **River Boat Mail Run** (www. hawkesburyriverferries.com.au; charge **M**), the local post service that departs from Brooklyn Wharf every weekday at 9.30am and allows passengers to come along for the three- to four-hour trip.

Upstream lies Wiseman's Ferry, where former convict Solomon Wiseman opened the first ferry across

Hunter Valley

Nearby, accessed via the New England Highway (A15), is the **Lower Hunter Valley ❸**, one of Australia's premier wine-growing districts (*see p.29*). From Maitland, a city rich in historic buildings, roads lead west through one winery after another, with most centred around the town of Pokolbin, home to **The Hunter Valley Tourism and Visitors Information Centre** (455 Wine Country Drive; www.

winecountry.com.au; daily 9am–4pm), a veritable vat of information about the local wine industry.

Mid-North Coast

Back on the Pacific Highway, the road crosses the Hunter River at Hexham and skirts the western shore of the **Port Stephens area**, home to a number of popular resorts such as the sophisticated Nelson Bay, and quieter settlements such as Tea Gardens and Hawks Nest. The bay's most famous attraction is its large population of bottlenose dolphins. Between May and November it also offers whale-watching opportunities.

About 40km (25 miles) north of Port Stephens you reach Bulahdelah, the gateway to the beautiful **Myall Lakes**. Here, paperbarks, palms and other wetland vegetation crowd the shores, while the waterways are filled with birdlife. Surrounding the chain of lakes is **Myall Lakes National Park** (charge for vehicle entry), where nature-lovers can camp in the wild.

A string of beaches at the northern end of the lakes leads to the holiday resort of **Forster**, the southernmost of the North Coast beach towns. Travelling north, it's worth detouring off the highway to the coastal town of **Port Macquarie ❹**, a former penal settlement that was founded in 1821 and is still full of historic sandstone buildings.

It's also worth taking the 24km (15-mile) detour to the resort of **Crescent Head** – a pretty, peaceful town with fine surf and good golf. Nearby is the town of South West Rocks and the picturesque ruins of the 1886 **Trial Bay Gaol** (www.trialbaygaol. com; daily 9am–4.30pm; charge).

The timber port of **Coffs Harbour ❺** is reputed to have Australia's best

The charming resort of Crescent Head is worth a visit

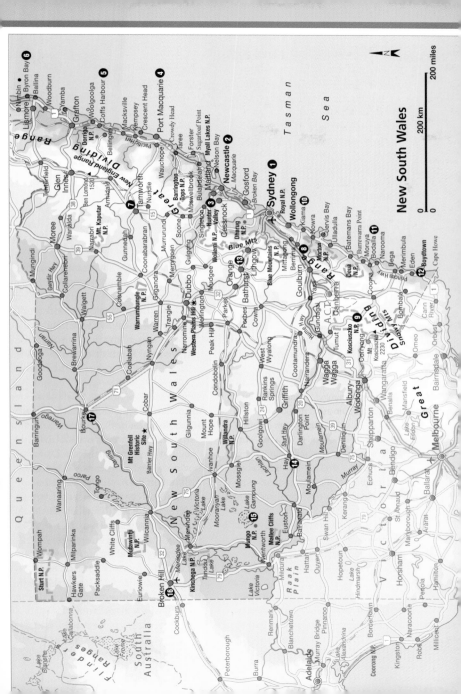

New South Wales

Sydney ❶
Newcastle ❷
❸
Port Macquarie ❹
❺
Byron Bay ❻
❼
Wollongong ❿
❽
⓫
⓬
Kosciuszko N.P. ❾
⓭
⓮
⓯
⓰
⓱

0   200 km
0   200 miles

Lord Howe Island

This coral isle 483km (300 miles) east of Port Macquarie offers splendid snorkelling and scuba diving as well as numerous walking trails, many birds and some unique vegetation.

Its World Heritage-listed forests, beaches and mountains are jammed into what amounts to a lush green speck in the vastness of the ocean and its permanent population is a mere 350 or so; tourist numbers are capped at 400 at any one time. Flights from Sydney or Brisbane take two hours.

climate, and has developed into a major centre of North Coast tourism. Unfortunately, most motorists know Coffs only as the city of the Big Banana, erected in 1964 to attract custom to a plantation and a manifestation of rural Australia's love of bizarre 'Big Things'. Coffs is more or less the midway point between Sydney and Brisbane – around seven and six hours' driving distance, respectively. Parasailing, four-wheel-drive tours into the surrounding forests, the beach, golf and galleries fill the days here.

The beautiful inland village of **Bellingen** was, along with Byron Bay and Nimbin to the north, once the heart of hippy culture in NSW. These days, the cultures here and in Byron are no longer drug-dazed – organics remain in vogue, but only in the form of the foodstuffs used by local chefs at the towns' gourmet restaurants and cafés. Time-warped Nimbin is another matter (*see p.86*).

In Bellingen, local arts and crafts are on offer at the Old Butter Factory and designer goods can be browsed at the beautifully restored Hammond and Wheatley Emporium department store. From Bellingen, take the Dorrigo Road to the small town of Dorrigo, a great base for exploring the **Dorrigo National Park**. The park is a fragment of the massive rainforest that covered the area until the 1920s, when loggers cleared the area in their search for Australian cedar, a timber so valuable it was known as 'red gold'. From the **Dorrigo Rainforest Centre** (Dome Road; Mon–Fri 8.30am–4.30pm, Sat-Sun 9am–4.30pm), you can take a number of walks including the Skywalk, a wooden walkway stretched high over the forest canopy.

Lush, green Lord Howe Island

A lighthouse presides over magnificent Byron Bay

Far North Coast

The Pacific Highway swings inland yet again through the forests, this time emerging at **Grafton**, a lovely old town situated on a bend of the Clarence River. After a stretch of alternating river and cane scenery, the Pacific Highway clips the coast again at **Ballina**, the southernmost beach town in a string reaching to the Queensland border. It then heads due north through magnificent rolling hills, but the alternative coastal route takes in some equally breathtaking coastal scenery, including the village of Lennox Head, often described as one of the top 10 surfing spots in the world (the big waves come from May to July).

Byron Bay ❻ ('Byron') is surrounded by almost 30km (19 miles) of sandy beaches fringed by a fertile hinterland. This magnificent setting combined with the town's vibrant festival programme, spas and excellent cafés has made it a favoured destination for wealthy holiday-makers from Sydney, Melbourne and Brisbane

– meaning that staying here has become a pricey proposition.

Fortunately, the growth of tourism has not marred Byron's natural beauty. While the beaches are a major attraction, the hinterland features a number of national parks and nature reserves, including **Tyagarah Nature Reserve** (charge for vehicle entry), **Broken Head Nature Reserve**, **Arakwal National Park** and **Cape Byron State Conservation Area** (lighthouse precinct daily 8am–sunset; charge for vehicle entry to lighthouse precinct). Then of course there's the underwater world. Byron's most famous dive spot, **Julian Rocks** (www.julianrocks.net), is located where temperate waters and tropical waters meet, giving divers the opportunity to view an astonishing array of marine wildlife.

New England

In the Northern Tablelands of the Great Dividing Range is the New England Plateau and the city of **Tamworth** ❼. This pretty centre, surrounded by hills, has a thriving

★ NEW AGE NORTH COAST

In May 1973, a counter-cultural arts and music event called the Aquarius Festival was staged in the farming hamlet of Nimbin, in the far north coast hinterland of NSW. This celebration of alternative thinking and sustainable lifestyles prompted many people to stay in the area and pursue the hippy dream of sustainable communal living, leading to the region being branded as the epicentre of Australian New Age culture – a tag it retains to this day.

Nimbin hasn't changed much since the festival dubbed 'Australia's Woodstock' brought it to national prominence. It retains a number of the communes established in the wake of the festival, and many of its residents remain firm believers in the positive power of the marijuana plant – they even stage an annual 'Mardigrass' Festival (www.nimbinmardigrass.com) to celebrate its medicinal and other values. It's not a place that is to everyone's taste – some accuse it of being stuck in a drug-hazed hippy-era time warp.

The small town of **Bellingen**, set in lush tropical hinterland behind Coffs Harbour, also attracted urban escapees in search of a new lifestyle in the 1970s. These days a significant number of performance artists, painters, sculptors and craftworkers call it home, and its New Age tendency is obvious in the whimsical architecture and street signage of the town centre.

Marijuana still reigns supreme on Nimbin High Street

The Bellingen Global Carnival (www.globalcarnival.com) in October is a popular World Music festival.

Poised on the easternmost edge of Australia, beautiful **Byron Bay** deserves its reputation as Australia's alternative therapy heartland. Practitioners offer acupuncture, aromatherapy, homeopathy and reflexology, among many other treatments. For a full list, check www.byronbodyandsoul.com.

For those who wouldn't have the faintest idea what most of these therapies are, the Byron area offers an alluring array of luxury spas where massages, detox treatments and facials can be enjoyed. Some even have luxe accommodation and gourmet restaurants with organic menus. One of the best known of these is Gaia Retreat and Spa (www.gaiaretreat.com.au), owned by singer and actress Olivia Newton-John. Other day-spa options include Buddha Gardens Day Spa (www.buddhagardensdayspa.com.au), Botanica Rainforest Day Spa (www.brdayspa.com.au), Azabu Day Spa Retreat (www.azabu.com.au) and The Byron Spa and Wellness Centre (www.thebyronatbyron.com.au) at the Byron at Byron resort.

Yoga vies with surfing as the most popular physical activity in Byron, and there are plenty of styles to choose from. Bikram Hot Yoga (www.bikramyogabyronbay.com.au), The Yoga Room and Life Centre (www.theyogaroom.com.au), Byron Bay Yoga (www.byronbayyoga.com) and the Byron Yoga Centre (www.byronyoga.com) are all well-known centres; Byron Yoga Centre and Byron Bay Yoga also offer yoga retreats.

Since the 1973 Aquarius Festival, Nimbin has been at the forefront of New Age culture

New Age North Coast

A Byron Bay resident enjoying a spot of yoga on the beach

Norfolk Island

A rich and fascinating cultural heritage, relaxed lifestyle and rolling green pastures characterise Norfolk Island, 1,700km (1,050 miles) northeast of Sydney. A British penal settlement was established here in 1788 and operated until 1852, when the British government decided it was too expensive to run. Today fewer than 1,800 people live on the 3,500-hectare (8,750-acre) island. The island's museum complex (www.museums.gov.nf; daily 11am–3pm; charge) brings its history to life, and there are plenty of outdoor activities to indulge in, including diving and cycling. Flights from Sydney and Brisbane take two and a half hours.

local economy based on sheep and cattle. It's also known as 'the country music capital of Australia' and the annual music festival (www.tamworthcountrymusic.com.au) in January is a major tourist drawcard. During the rest of the year, visitors

can mosey along down to the **Australian Country Music Hall of Fame** (93 Brisbane Street; www.countrymusichalloffame.com.au; Mon–Fri 10am–4pm, Sat 10am–2pm).

As its name suggests, New England bears striking similarities, in both topography and climate, to 'the mother country'. Its altitude gives it frosty mornings nine months of the year, occasional snow and a year-round freshness. Nowhere is this more evident than in the city of **Armidale**, a university town greened by parks and gardens, with two cathedrals and tree-lined streets.

Southern Highlands, Snowy Mountains and South Coast

The Hume Highway (Highway 31) is the main road running south from Sydney to Melbourne, passing the area known as the Southern Highlands and crossing the Great Dividing Range near the Snowy Mountains. The alternative route to Victoria is via the

Norfolk Island

scenic Princes Highway (A1), which hugs the South Coast.

Southern Highlands

Mount Gibraltar, a denuded volcanic plug known locally as 'The Gib', rises above Mittagong and the surrounding terrain, marking the gateway to the Southern Highlands. Few people take the time to stop in Mittagong; they're heading either for the limestone **Wombeyan Caves** (Wombeyan Caves Road, Wombeyna; daily 9am–4.30pm; charge ) in the nearby **Wombeyan Karst Conservation Reserve**, or the collection of picturesque country towns that have made the Southern Highlands a favourite weekend getaway for Sydneysiders.

The first of these towns is **Bowral**, 5km (3 miles) from Mittagong, which combines wide small-town streets with elegant big-city-style boutiques and one of the most sophisticated dining scenes outside Sydney. Its attractions include the **Bradman Museum** (www.bradman.org.au; daily 10am–5pm; charge) on Jude Street, which details the career of Australia's most revered sportsman, cricketer Don Bradman, who died in 2001.

The gem of the Southern Highlands is **Berrima** ❶, a small village off the Hume Highway, about 8km (5 miles) west of Bowral. Established in 1831, many of its impressive old sandstone buildings have been converted to antique and craft galleries; most of those with historical artefacts are open from 10am to 5pm daily. These include the Surveyor General Inn (1834), said to be the oldest continuously licensed pub in Australia; the

One of two classical cathedrals in the country town of Goulborn

Court House (1839), now the information centre and museum (www.berrimacourthouse.org.au; daily 10am–4pm; free); the Gaol (1839), now a prison rehabilitation training centre; the Church of Holy Trinity (1849); and St Francis Xavier's Roman Catholic Church (1851).

The big country town of **Goulburn** is located 200km (120 miles) southwest of Sydney, about midway between the Southern Highlands and Canberra. Goulburn's peaceful Georgian homes and two classical cathedrals belie its 19th-century history as a centre of police action against the bushrangers who plagued the surrounding roads for decades. The historic buildings at the **Goulburn Brewery** (23 Bungonia Road; Fri–Sun from 10am) were designed by noted colonial architect Francis Greenway in the 1830s.

Mount Kosciuszko is the highest peak in Australia

Iron hitching posts still stand outside some of the graceful commercial buildings on the main street of **Yass**, once home to Hamilton Hume, the explorer after whom the Hume Highway is named. Hume spent the last 40 years of his life living in **Cooma Cottage** (/www.national trust.com.au/cooma.html; early Aug–mid-June Thur–Mon 10am–4pm; charge), now maintained by the National Trust.

Snowy Mountains

Some might argue that the Snowy Mountains don't really live up to their name, as the ski resorts at Perisher Blue, Thredbo, Mt Selwyn and Charlotte Pass often rely on snow-making machines for backup during the short ski season. Nor are the peaks particularly impressive – Australia's highest mountain, Mount Kosciuszko (pronounced koz-ee-oss-ko), is only 2,230m (7,315ft) high. However, **Kosciuszko**

National Park ❾ (charge for vehicle entry), the largest protected area in the state, is well worth a visit, with a number of beautiful walks, some of which can be accessed by the Thredbo ski lifts.

The creation of Lake Jindabyne was part of the Snowy River Hydroelectric Project, a 25-year, A$820-million scheme to provide energy for Sydney, Melbourne and the rest of southeastern Australia while diverting water to irrigate vast stretches of the Riverina district west of the mountains. Regarded as one of the great achievements of modern civil engineering, 100,000 people worked on the scheme, mainly immigrants from 30 different countries – their stories form part of the exhibit at the **Snowy Mountains Hydro-Electric Scheme Information Centre** (Monaro Highway, Cooma; www.snowyhydro.com. au; Mon–Fri 8am–5pm, Sat–Sun 9am–2pm; free).

South Coast

From Sydney, the Pacific Highway spectacularly skirts the rim of the Illawarra Plateau until descending suddenly to **Wollongong**, a major industrial city in an impressive natural setting. South of Wollongong, past Lake Illawarra, is the fishing and market town of **Kiama ⑩**, known for its blowhole. When seas are sufficiently high to force water geyser-like through a rock fissure, the spout can reach an amazing 60m (200ft) in height. Beware – visitors have been swept to their death off these rocks.

Further south is **Kangaroo Valley**, a lovely historic township set in an isolated vale among heavily forested slopes. Established in 1829, today it is a favourite haunt of picnickers, bushwalkers and spring wild-flower lovers. Nearby is the magnificent **Morton National Park** (charge for vehicle entry), which encompasses sandstone escarpments, the Shoalhaven Gorge, waterfalls and rainforest gullies.

Surrounded on all sides but the southeast by 50km (30 miles) of headland and beaches, **Jervis Bay** (pronounced Jarvis) is one of the South Coast's most idyllic holiday spots. Once a busy working port, these days it's technically part of Australian Capital Territory – co-opted under an act that stipulated the capital must have access to the sea – and is home to the Royal Australian Naval College, HMAS *Creswell*.

Ulladulla is a beach resort and fishing port that supplies much of Sydney's fresh fish daily. The importance of its fleet can be credited to Italian immigrants of the 1930s, who created the town's artificial harbour. **Batemans Bay**, another 85km (53 miles) south, is a tourist, crayfishing and oystering centre at the mouth of the Clyde River.

Boats at the fishing port of Ulladulla

As the highway winds through the hills into **Bodalla** , 38km (23 miles) south of Moruya, it's hard to miss the little town's Big Cheese. Some 4½m (15ft) high and equally wide, it was sculpted from metal in early 1984 to bolster the community's image as a cheesemaking centre. Other dairy centres include the beautifully preserved 19th-century hamlet of **Central Tilba**, 29km (18 miles) southwest of Narooma; and **Bega**, the biggest town on the far South Coast. The locals here are inordinately proud of their eponymous cheese, so much so that there's probably a bylaw that forbids visitors to leave without sampling the local product: play it safe and take

in a factory tour and cheese tasting at the **Bega Cheese Heritage Centre** (23–45 Ridge Street, North Bega; www.begacheese.com.au; daily 9am–5pm; free).

Merimbula and its sister town of **Pambula**, on the so-called 'Sapphire Coast', offer fine surfing, boating, fishing and oystering. **Eden**, the last sizeable town before you cross the Victoria state border, is located on Twofold Bay, once a thriving whaling port and now host to whale-watching tours. The **Eden Killer Whale Museum** (www.killerwhalemuseum.com.au; Mon–Sat 9.15am–3.45pm, Sun 11.15am–3.45pm; charge) on Imlay Street recalls those 19th-century days.

During its whaling era, Eden had stiff competition as a port from **Boydtown**, established in 1842 by the banker-adventurer Benjamin Boyd on the south side of Twofold Bay. Boyd started a steamship service to Sydney and erected many buildings, but in 1850 his empire collapsed and all that remains of his grand scheme today are the Seahorse Inn – a magnificent building with stone walls, Gothic arches and hand-carved doors and windows – and Boyd's Tower, a 31m (102ft) sandstone lighthouse built in 1846 but never lit. The stunning 8,950-hectare (22,110-acre) **Ben Boyd National Park** (charge for vehicle entry) encompasses the coastal headlands north and south of Twofold Bay.

Western Slopes and Plains

West of Sydney, the rich countryside behind the Great Dividing Range has

Pelicans taking a break in Merimbula

A Western Plains Zoo resident

NSW National Parks

The NSW National Parks and Wildlife Service manages more than 600 national parks, nature reserves and historic sites in the state. To visit some of these, you will have to pay a daily entry fee for your vehicle – everywhere else you're free to come and go as you please. Where there is a fee it's sometimes a matter of purchasing a 'pay and display' ticket, so always travel with plenty of coins. For information about both the service and individual parks, go to www.nationalparks.nsw.gov.au.

always been the state's agricultural heartland. The colonists of NSW made their fortunes on these gentle slopes and wide plains, but they rarely penetrated the dry red landscape of the rugged Outback region further west, leaving this for miners to exploit.

Highway 32

The route due west from Sydney, along the Great Western Highway, passes through the Blue Mountains and the vast grazing land that begins where the mountains end. The major pastoral centre of **Bathurst** ⓭, Australia's oldest inland town, was where the heady gold rush of the 1850s kicked off, and its streets are full of grand civic buildings and mansions built with gold-era profits.

From Bathurst, the Great Western becomes the Mitchell Highway, and its first main town is **Orange**. This quaint place is, predictably, a fruit-growing centre – but, not so predictably, the crops are apples and cherries rather than citrus fruits (it was named after the Duke of Orange). An extinct volcano 14km (9 miles) southwest of the town is at the centre of the 1,500-hectare (600-acre) **Mount Canobolas State Conservation Area**, with walking trails, picnic areas and waterfalls.

From Orange, the Mitchell Highway runs 151km (94 miles) to the thriving city of Dubbo, in the middle of the state's wheat belt. The main tourist attraction here is the **Western Plains Zoo** (http://taronga.org.au/western-plains-zoo; daily 9am–4pm; charge 🅼), an excellent wildlife park associated with Sydney's Taronga Park Zoo.

Highway 24

The Mid-Western Highway runs through sheep and wheat country to **Cowra**, a prosperous agricultural centre on the Lachlan River that has strong links with Japan. During World War II, Japanese prisoners of war were interned in a camp here, and in 1944 it was the scene of a suicidal mass breakout attempt in which nearly 231 prisoners were killed. The care local people gave to the graves of the dead prisoners impressed the Japanese, who later repaid them with the gift of a classically laid-out garden – the **Japanese Garden and Cultural Centre** (Binni Creek Road; www.cowraregion.com.au/japanesegarden; daily 8.30am–5pm; charge).

It's a desolate drive on to **Hay ⑭**, through empty horizons broken only by the sight of an occasional emu, goanna or flock of budgerigars. The town, about halfway between Sydney and Adelaide, is a well-watered oasis on the banks of the Murrumbidgee River. For many years it was an important river crossing on the stock route to Victoria and it's now the centre of an extensive horticultural and wool-producing area. You can watch demonstrations of sheep losing their woollen coats at **Shear Outback** (corner Sturt and Cobb Highways; www.shearoutback.com.au; daily 9am–5pm; charge), an interpretive centre devoted to the culture and stories of Australian shearing.

Highway 20

Head west on the Sturt Highway (20) to visit the **Willandra Lakes World Heritage Site**, a 370,000-hectare (950,000-acre) system of Pleistocene lakes that contains the longest continuous record on Aboriginal habitation in Australia, stretching back 40,000 years. The most accessible part of Willandra is

Mungo National Park

Broken Hill, the remotest part of New South Wales, is still an important mining centre

Mungo National Park ⑮ (charge for vehicle entry), about 150km (93 miles) north of Balranald. Its star attraction is the Walls of China, a geological phenomenon with 30m (100ft) -high walls of white sand running for 30km (19 miles). A good base for visiting the park is the sleepy town of **Wentworth**, positioned at the confluence of the Murray and Darling rivers.

Highway 79

Head north on the Silver City Highway from Wentworth for 265km (165 miles) and you'll reach New South Wales' most remote outpost: **Broken Hill** ⑯. In this far corner, locals set their watches to South Australian time, half an hour behind, as most business is done through Adelaide, which lies much nearer than faraway Sydney.

Broken Hill's mineral wealth played a large part in changing the nation from a strictly pastoral outpost to a more industrial base. It all began in 1883 when a boundary rider and amateur geologist, Charles Rasp, stumbled across a lump of silver ore on a rocky outcrop he described as a 'broken hill'. From the claim that he and his syndicate pegged grew the nation's largest

A Rich Artistic Lode

Not every treasure in Broken Hill is found underground. It has become an unlikely centre of the arts, and is associated with several locally famous painters known as the 'Brushmen of the Bush' including Jack Absalom and the late Pro Hart. Among the city's arty attractions are the **Broken Hill Regional Art Gallery** (404 Argent Street; www.brokenhill.net.au/bhart/main.html; daily 10am–5pm; donation requested) and the **Sculpture Symposium**, a group of 12 sandstone sculptures set in the **Living Desert Flora and Fauna Sanctuary** (www.stateparks.nsw.gov.au; daily Mar–Nov 9am–5pm, Dec–Feb 6am–2pm; free), 12km (7 miles) from the city centre.

company, the Broken Hill Proprietary Co. Ltd (BHP). 'The Hill' turned out to be the world's largest silver, lead and zinc lode and these metals are all still being mined here. To get an idea of what underground working life is like, consider taking a tour of the now-abandoned **Daydream Mine** (tel: 08-8088 5682; www.daydream mine.com.au; tours daily 10am–3pm; charge), 20km (12 miles) outside town. It operated between 1882 and 1983.

The historic buildings and wharf remnants at **Wilcannia**, 196km (122 miles) northeast of Broken Hill on the Barrier Highway, are reminders of the days when its position on the Darling River made it a major inland port and earned it the title of 'Queen City of the West'. Stay on the Barrier Highway to Cobar, and about 40km (25 miles) before town, you'll find the turn-off to the **Mount Grenfell Historic Site** (tel: 02-6836 2692) with its hundreds of Aboriginal cave paintings.

Cobar typifies the resilience of the area's people as well as its hardy flora and fauna. From being a rip-roaring town of 10,000 people and 14 hotels not long after copper mining began there in the 1870s, its fortunes have fluctuated: 100 years later its population was less than 4,000 and only one mine was operating; today the figures are 6,000 people and four mines. North of Cobar, the Mitchell Highway meets the Darling River at the small township of **Bourke** ⓱. Once an important port, Bourke has become immortalised in the colloquial expression, 'out the back o'Bourke', signifying a place so remote that it is exceeded only by going 'beyond the black stump'. Take in the emptiness that surrounds Bourke, and you'll get a true sense of the Aussie Outback.

On the road to Wilcannia

ACCOMMODATION

Visitors won't have any problems finding boutique, backpacker or luxury accommodation to suit their fancy in Sydney and its immediate surrounds. Outside this cordon there are fewer boutique options, but budget hostels and luxury resorts abound.

Sydney

Hotel 59
59 Bayswater Road, Kings Cross
Tel: 02-9360 5900
www.hotel59.com.au
Located in a quiet section of Bayswater Road, this small and very friendly hotel offers fairly basic but very clean rooms with daggy (Aussie slang for unfashionable) decor. **$$–$$$**

Base Sydney
477 Kent Street
Tel: 02-9267 7718
www.stayatbase.com
Accommodation at this slick hostel ranges from twin rooms to multi-bed dormitories, all of which feature surprisingly stylish furnishings. There's also a female-only floor. **$–$$**

Bed and Breakfast Sydney Harbour
140–142 Cumberland Street, The Rocks
Tel: 02-9247 1130
www.bedandbreakfastsydney.com

A cocktail at the BLUE Sydney bar

This restored late 19th-century guesthouse has rooms fitted out with period furniture. Some have harbour views and most have their own bathroom. **$$$**

BLUE Sydney
6 Cowper Wharf Road, Woolloomooloo
Tel: 02-9331 9000
www.tajhotels.com
A renovated warehouse on Woolloomooloo wharf may seem a strange location for a boutique hotel, but super-sleek Blue works wonderfully well. **$$$–$$$$**

Bondi Beachhouse
28 Sir Thomas Mitchell Road, Bondi Beach
Tel: 0417 336 444
www.bondibeachhouse.com.au
Nine pretty rooms, a sun-drenched deck and a location only 100m/yds from the beach make this an alluring Bondi option. **$$$–$$$$**

Bondi Beachhouse YHA
Corner Fletcher and Dellview streets, Bondi Beach
Tel: 02-9365 2088
www.yha.com.au
Friendly staff, single-sex dorms and a rooftop terrace with fabulous beach view give this hostel a winning edge. **$–$$**

Establishment Hotel
5 Bridge Lane
Tel: 02-9240 3100
www.merivale.com.au
The public areas are glam and the rooms are luxurious at the Establishment. Guests

adore the scenes in the bar and the excellent Est restaurant. **$$$$**

Eva's Backpackers
6–8 Orwell Street, Kings Cross
Tel: 02-9358 2185
www.evasbackpackers.com.au
Features such as a cosy common room/ kitchen, free Wi-fi and rooftop garden with great views make this family-run backpacker joint a popular choice. **$–$$**

Fraser Suites
488 Kent Street
Tel: 02-8823 8888
www.fraserhospitality.com
This studio and suite complex is both sexy and luxurious. There's daily room servicing, a gym and rooftop lap pool. **$$$–$$$$$**

The Hughenden
14 Queen Street, Woollahra
Tel: 02-9363 4863
www.hughendenhotel.com.au
Housed in an Italianate mansion dating back to 1876, this boutique hotel is in a great location close to shops, restaurants and leafy Centennial Park. **$$$–$$$$**

Medusa
267 Darlinghurst Road, Darlinghurst
Tel: 02-9331 1000
www.medusa.com.au
If your plans include late-night clubbing and lots of shopping, Medusa is the perfect choice. It offers 18 theatrically decorated rooms with kitchenettes. **$$$$–$$$$$**

Oaks Goldsborough Apartments
243 Pyrmont Street, Darling Harbour
Tel: 02-8586 2500
www.theoaksgroup.com.au
Modern self-contained studios and apartments in a handsome 1883 building are on offer at this well-priced apartment hotel. **$$$**

Ravesi's
Corner of Campbell Parade and Hall Street, Bondi Beach

The Russell

Tel: 02-9365 4422
www.ravesis.com.au
Now this is the way to do Bondi: a prime beachside location; an intimate and stylish atmosphere; even a balcony overlooking the surf. Perfect. **$$$$–$$$$$**

The Russell
143a George Street, The Rocks
Tel: 02-9241 3543
www.therussell.com.au
An atmosphere-laden boutique hotel in The Rocks district, the recently renovated Russell has friendly, intimate surrounds and a choice of room styles. **$$$–$$$$**

Sydney Harbour YHA
110 Cumberland Street, The Rocks
Tel: 02-8272 0900
www.yha.com.au/hostels/nsw/sydney-surrounds/sydney-harbour
The only hostel in The Rocks, this recently opened place has dorms and rooms with air conditioning and en suite. There's a roof terrace with great harbour views. **$$–$$$**

Vulcan Hotel
500 Wattle Street, Ultimo
Tel: 02-9211 3283
www.vulcanhotel.com.au
The stylish Vulcan Hotel is one of Sydney's hidden gems – its 46 rooms ooze urban

chic, and the service is both intimate and friendly. **$$$**

Blue Mountains
Echoes
3 Lilianfels Avenue, Katoomba
Tel: 02-4782 1966
www.echoeshotel.com.au
With just 12 rooms and two suites, this boutique hotel is almost like a private holiday home – albeit with a day spa and jaw-dropping views of the Jamison Valley. **$$$$–$$$$$**

Lilianfels
Lilianfels Avenue, Katoomba
Tel: 02-4780 1200
www.lilianfels.com.au
The ultimate Blue Mountains retreat, set in a historic country house amid 1 hectare (2½ acres) of manicured gardens. Features include the award-winning Darley's Restaurant, an indulgent spa and a location close to the Three Sisters. **$$$$–$$$$$**

The Central Coast and Hunter Valley
Peppers Convent
Halls Road, Pokolbin, Hunter Valley
Tel: 02-4998 4999
www.peppers.com.au
The nuns would be surprised to see this luxurious transformation of their early 20th-century convent. The same company runs the slightly cheaper but equally

Ravesi's occupies a great Bondi location

impressive **Peppers Guesthouse** (Ekerts Road, Pokolbin; tel: 02-4993 8999). **$$$$–$$$$$**

Mid-North Coast
Coffs Harbour YHA Backpacker Resort
51 Collingwood Street, Coffs Harbour
Tel: 02-6652 6462
www.yha.com.au
A location close to the beach and jetty and a choice of dorms or private en-suite rooms means that this excellent hostel is almost always full – book ahead. **$–$$**

The Observatory
40 William Street, Port Macquarie
Tel: 02-6586 8000
www.observatory.net.au
An unrivalled location opposite the town beach and a choice of clean and bright rooms, apartments and penthouses makes this resort an excellent family option. 🏨
$$–$$$

Far North Coast
Bamboo Cottage
76 Butler Street, Byron Bay
Tel: 0414 187 088
www.byron-bay.com/bamboocottage
The Balinese-style garden is but one of many attractive features at this unpretentious guesthouse. **$$**

Rae's on Watego's
8 Marine Parade, Watego's Beach, Byron Bay
Tel: 02-6685 5366
www.raes.com.au
A luxurious beachside retreat where guests can swim, chill out in the spa or linger over meals in the terraced restaurant. **$$$$$**

New England
Lindsay House
128 Faulkner Street, Armidale
Tel: 02-6771 4554
www.lindsayhouse.com.au
This gorgeous B&B in the heart of Armidale offers elegant and extremely comfortable rooms with plenty of amenities. **$$$**

Listings

Southern Highlands

Milton Park
Horderns Road, Bowral
Tel: 02-4861 1522
www.milton-park.com.au
Enjoy a country house experience at this elegant estate, which boasts a spa, tennis courts, historic landscaped gardens and luxe rooms. **$$$$–$$$$$**

South Coast

Paperbark Camp
Woollamia, Jervis Bay
Tel: 02-4441 6066
www.paperbarkcamp.com.au
An Aussie version of a safari camp, complete with luxury tented accommodation, set in 40 hectares (100 acres) of pristine bushland. Dine on your private verandah or in the tree-top restaurant. **$$$$–$$$$$**

Royal Exchange Hotel

Western Slopes and Plains

Royal Exchange Hotel
Argent Street, Broken Hill
Tel: 02-8087 2308
www.royalexchangehotel.com
This Art Deco gem in Broken Hill's centre boasts 24 refurbished rooms with private bathrooms and air conditioning. **$$$**

RESTAURANTS

Sydney's chefs have a sensibility that is slightly more Asian-oriented than that of their Mediterranean-obsessed Melburnian peers. In Sydney the major eating strip is Crown Street in Surry Hills, although many of the city's fine dining establishments are clustered around Circular Quay. In coastal and rural NSW, menus tend to be inspired by top-notch local produce.

Restaurants Price Categories
Prices are for a two-course meal
$ = below A$20
$$ = A$20–45
$$$ = A$45–75
$$$$ = over A$75

Sydney

Aria
1 Macquarie Street, East Circular Quay
Tel: 02-9252 2555
www.ariarestaurant.com
Come here for a dress-circle setting near the Opera House, sleek decor, a knock-out wine list and a seasonal menu by Matt Moran that never fails to impress. **$$$$**

Bathers Pavilion
4 The Esplanade, Balmoral Beach
Tel: 02-9969 5050
www.batherspavilion.com.au
Chef Serge Dansereau offers a sophisticated and seductive menu in an Art Deco pavilion on the North Shore's prettiest beach. There's also a less expensive café. **$$$$**

BBQ King
18–20 Goulburn Street, Haymarket
Tel: 02-9267 2586
The decor is basic, but the Peking duck and Chinese barbecue pork are authentic, the servings are big, and it's open until 2am. No wonder it's a Sydney institution. **$$**

Bécasse
204 Clarence Street
Tel: 02-9283 3440

www.becasse.com.au
Exquisite French cuisine from Justin North's kitchen makes this one of Sydney's most satisfying dining experiences. **$$$$**

Bill's
433 Liverpool Street, Darlinghurst
Tel: 02-9360 9631
www.bills.com.au
Bill Granger's sunny corner café-restaurant serves perfect breakfasts. There are other branches at 118 Queen Street, Woollahra, and 359 Crown Street, Surry Hills. **$$**

Billy Kwong
355 Crown Street, Surry Hills
Tel: 02-9332 3300
www.kyliekwong.org
Chef Kylie Kwong's highly flavoured modern take on Chinese favourites has made her a local and international culinary star. **$$–$$$**

Bistro Moncur
Woollahra Hotel, 116 Queen Street, Woollahra
Tel: 02-9327 9713
www.woollahrahotel.com.au
Come here for classic French bistro cuisine served in stylish surrounds. It doesn't accept reservations, so arrive early and have an aperitif in the bar. **$$$**

Bodega
216 Commonwealth Street, Surry Hills
Tel: 02-9212 7766
www.bodegatapas.com
Bodega offers the complete package: funky surroundings, gorgeous waiters and an inviting tapas menu that makes it hard to say 'bastar' ('enough'). **$$–$$$**

Bourke Street Bakery
633 Bourke Street, Surry Hills
Tel: 02-9699 1011
This artisan bakery has a few bench seats and a huge following. Everything is delicious. **$**

Café Sopra
81 Macleay Street, Potts Point

Tel: 02-9368 6666
www.fratellifresh.com.au
Delizioso Italian dishes are served up daily at the bustling trattoria located within the Fratelli Fresh providore. There are other branches at 7 Danks Street, Waterloo and 16 Hickson Road, Walsh Bay. **$$**

Doyles on the Beach
11 Marine Parade, Watsons Bay
Tel: 02-9337 2007
www.doyles.com.au
Australia's first seafood restaurant (opened 1885) remains one of Sydney's favourite places for a Sunday lunch on a sunny day. The seafood is simple, but fresh, and the beachfront views are dazzling. There's also a takeaway outfit on the wharf. **$$$$**

Flying Fish
Jones Bay Wharf, 19–21 Pirrama Road, Pyrmont
Tel: 02-9518 6677
www.flyingfish.com.au
A converted timber wharf offering divine seafood, not to mention some of the best hand-cut chips in town. **$$$$**

Fratelli Paradiso
16 Challis Avenue, Potts Point
Tel: 02-9357 1744
Challis Avenue is the heart of Potts Point's café society, lined with intimate eateries of every description. This Italian delight is the best of them. **$$**

Doyles, a Sydney favourite since 1885

Golden Century Seafood Restaurant

393–399 Sussex Street, Haymarket
Tel: 02-9212 3901
www.goldencentury.com.au
Chinese-style seafood at its best, with all the hustle and bustle of Hong Kong. **$$$**

Guillaume at Bennelong

Sydney Opera House, Bennelong Point
Tel: 02-9241 1999
www.guillaumeatbennelong.com.au
Superb food and stunning dining space in the southern shell of Sydney's most famous building make this a dining experience to remember. **$$$$**

Icebergs Dining Room and Bar

1 Notts Avenue, Bondi Beach
Tel: 02-9365 9000
www.idrb.com
The quintessential Sydney dining experience, featuring a sun-drenched and sophisticated dining room, panoramic views over Bondi Beach, an impressive wine list and delectable Italian food. **$$$$**

Longrain

85 Commonwealth Street, Surry Hills
Tel: 02-9280 2888
www.longrain.com.au
Executive Chef Martin Boetz turns Thai food into high art. Don't let the communal tables fool you: prices are far from cheap, but the food is worth it. **$$$**

Manly Pavilion

West Esplanade, Manly Cove
Tel: 02-9949 9011
www.manlypavilion.com.au
Enjoy Mod Med dishes in the sleek dining room or on the spacious terrace of this restored 1930s bathing pavilion near the wharf. **$$$**

Marque

355 Crown Street, Surry Hills
Tel: 02-9332 2225
www.marquerestaurant.com.au
The subtle decor at this culinary temple is a reminder that you are here for the food

A glass of wine with your meal at Longrain

rather than to be seen. And what food it is! **$$$$**

Mohr Fish

202 Devonshire Street, Surry Hills
Tel: 02-9318 1326
As this tiny, unpretentious fish and chippie doesn't take bookings, most patrons end up nursing a beer in the pub next door while waiting for a table to clear. The wait is worth it. **$$**

North Bondi Italian Food

North Bondi RSL, 118 Ramsgate Avenue, Bondi Beach
Tel: 02-9300 4400
www.idrb.com
At the other end of the beach from Icebergs, which is operated by the same crew, this venue is less expensive, but the seafront ambience and food are nearly as sensational. **$$$**

Otto Ristorante

6 Cowper Wharf Road, Woolloomooloo
Tel: 02-9368 7488
www.otto.net.au
Otto is known for elevating Italian comfort

food to a fine art. All nonna's favourites are here – only better. **$$$$**

Quay
Overseas Passenger Terminal, Circular Quay West
Tel: 02-9251 5600
www.quay.com.au
It's one thing to have the best location in town; another to create food that almost exceeds the setting – Quay chef Peter Gilmore achieves both. **$$$$**

Rockpool
107 George Street. The Rocks
Tel: 02-9252 1888
www.rockpool.com.au
Other restaurants have come and gone. but after more than 20 years, Neil Perry's flagship restaurant continues to collect accolades. Perry also owns the slightly less expensive **Rockpool Bar & Grill** (60 Hunter Street; tel: 02-8078 1900) and Chinese-themed **Spice Temple** (10 Bligh Street; tel: 02-8078 1888). **$$$$**

Sean's Panarama
270 Campbell Parade, Bondi Beach
Tel: 02-9365 4924
www.seanspanaroma.com.au
A place of pilgrimage for those who love a serious weekend breakfast, but just as popular for its dinners. **$$$**

Tetsuya's
529 Kent Street
Tel: 02-9267 2900
www.tetsuyas.com
Tetsuya Wakada is one of the most acclaimed chefs in the world. His degustation menu is an essential Sydney experience for gourmets. **$$$$**

Blue Mountains
Vulcan's
33 Govett's Leap Road, Blackheath
Tel: 02-4787 6899
Have anything from the wood-fired oven, plus one of Philip Searle's classic desserts, and you will be in heaven. **$$$**

The Central Coast and Hunter Valley
Firestick Café
Poole's Rock Winery, 576 Debeyers Rd, Pokolbin
Tel: 02-4998 6968
www.rockrestaurant.com.au
Vineyard views, wood-fired pizzas and delicious food are a winning combination here. The **Rock Restaurant** ($$$$) in the same complex offers a fine-dining experience in the evening. **$$–$$$**

Muse Restaurant and Cafe
1 Broke Rd, Pokolbin
Tel: 02-4998 6777
www.musedining.com.au
The bustling dining hall at the Hungerford Hill Winery functions as a café during the day and restaurant in the evening. The food is impressive at any time. **$$–$$$**

Mid-North Coast
No 2 Oak Street
2 Oak St, Bellingen
Tel: 02-6655 9000
www.no2oakst.com.au
No 2 may have a slightly unfortunate name, but it's as well known for its friendly service as it is for its delectable food and affordable wine list. **$$$**

Zest
16 Stockton St, Nelson Bay
Tel: 02-4984 2211
A locavore's delight, Zest is testament to chef Glenn Thompson's devotion to regional produce and European cuisines. **$$$**

Listings

Chefs work their magic at Rockpool

Far North Coast
Pacific Dining Room
Beach Hotel, Bay Street, Byron Bay
Tel: 02-6680 7055
www.pacificdiningroom.com.au
The aqua decor is as soothing as the breezes
that waft in from the beach. The menu offers
something for every palate. **$$$**

Southern Highlands
Racine Restaurant
La Colline Winery, 42 Lake Canobolas Rd,
Orange
Tel: 02-6365 3275
Gorgeous vistas, gourmet Italian food and
an excellent house Riesling make La Colline
an essential stop when in these parts. **$$$**

NIGHTLIFE AND ENTERTAINMENT

Sydney has a down-to-earth pub scene, an uppity bar scene, a flamboyant gay
scene and a seriously good theatre scene.

Sydney
Ash Street Cellar
1 Ash Street
Tel: 02-9240 3000
www.merivale.com
Chic surrounds, chic people, chic menu. All
that needs to be said about this French-style
bistro and wine bar is 'ooh la la'.

The Basement
29 Reiby Place, Circular Quay
Tel: 02-9251 2797
www.thebasement.com.au
Sydney's premier jazz and blues venue, but
world music, pop and alternative acts also
make appearances.

Establishment
252 George Street
Tel: 02-9240 3000
www.merivale.com
Walk past during the day, and you would
doubt this vast space, with its 42m/138ft
marble bar and airy ceilings, could ever get
full; however, by 6.30 on a Friday evening, it
will be packed. City girls refer to this place
as The Drycleaners: it's where they go to
pick up a suit.

Hotel Bondi
178 Campbell Parade, Bondi Beach
Tel: 02-9130 3271
www.hotelbondi.com.au
Scrubbed up but still smelling of saltwater,

Enjoy the view from the Opera Bar

local youngsters and Brit backpackers head
to the Bondi's six bars to shoot some pool,
watch some sports, sink a few beers and
chat each other up.

Lord Dudley
236 Jersey Road, Woollahra
Tel: 02-9327 5399
www.lorddudley.com.au
With steaming pork pies and British beers
served in pints, this is a little bit of Old
Blighty stranded in Woollahra.

Opera Bar
Sydney Opera House, Bennelong Point
Tel: 02-9247 1666
www.operabar.com.au
It offers a choice of 30 Australian wines by
the glass and has one of the best views in
Sydney. Need we say more?

Oxford Hotel
134 Oxford Street, Darlinghurst
Tel: 02-9331 3467
www.theoxfordhotel.com.au
This 24-hour venue on Taylor Square is party central for Sydney's gay community.

Palisade Hotel
35 Bettington Street, Millers Point
Tel: 02-9247 2272
www.palisadehotel.com
Some people come here for the interiors; some come here for the excellent food; and some just come here because it is a damn good pub.

The Wharf
Pier 4 and 5 Hickson Road, Walsh Bay
Tel: 02-9250 1777
www.sydneytheatre.com.au
The acclaimed Sydney Theatre Company (STC) has a high-wattage power couple at the helm (Cate Blanchett and her playwright husband, Andrew Upton) and a stunning home in this converted wharf.

North from Sydney
Far North Coast
The Balcony Restaurant and Bar
Corner Lawson and Johnson streets, Byron Bay
Tel: 02-6680 9666
The Balcony claims to be a place 'where world flavours merge with art and seductive grooves'. Gosh. All we know is that it's a fine option for a sunset drink accompanied by tasty tapas.

Beach Hotel
Bay Street, Byron Bay
Tel: 02-6685 6402
www.beachhotel.com.au
This open-air bar opposite the beach throngs with crowds enjoying live rock and DJs in the evenings, and has a relaxed atmosphere during the day.

SPORTS AND ACTIVITIES
The gorgeous climate prompts locals to spend a lot of time outdoors, particularly in the water.

Andrew 'Boy' Charlton Pool
1c Mrs Macquaries Road, the Domain
Tel: 02-9358 6686
www.abcpool.org
This heated outdoor saltwater swimming pool near the Botanic Gardens is hugely popular.

Australian School of Mountaineering
166 Katoomba Street, Katoomba
Tel: 02-4782 2014
www.asmguides.com
Abseiling, rock climbing, canyoning and mountaineering courses in the Blue Mountains.

Dive Byron Bay
9 Marvell Street, Byron Bay
Tel: 02-6685 8333
www.byronbaydivecentre.com.au
Diving and snorkelling trips in the Cape Byron Marine Park.

North Sydney Olympic Pool
4 Alfred Street South, Milsons Point
Tel: 02-9955 2309
It's got harbour views, a fabulous restaurant and a buzzy vibe – pure Sydney.

Andrew 'Boy' Charlton Pool

TOURS

There's loads to see and do in NSW, and plenty of organised tours are on offer. For details of tours about Indigenous culture, *see p.54*. For details of guided tours and activities in the state's many national parks, check the NSW National Parks and Wildlife Service's website (www.environment.nsw.gov.au).

Australian Eco Adventures
3/158 South Creek Rd, Cromer
Tel: 02-9971 2402
www.ozeco.com.au
Luxury small-group day tours of the Blue Mountains or Hunter Valley leaving from Sydney.

Balloon Aloft
Wine Country Drive, North Rothbury
Tel: 1800 028 568
www.balloonaloft.com
See the Hunter Valley vineyards or Camden Valley from the air.

Bondi Explorer
Tel: 131 500
www.sydneybuses.info/tourist-services/bondi-explorer.htm
This hop-on, hop-off bus service covers Central Sydney, The Cross, Centennial Park and the Eastern Beaches.

Boutique Wine Tours
Tel: 02-9499 5444
www.boutiquewinetours.com.au
Visit the Hunter Valley wineries with this outfit, which offers small-group tours and customised itineraries. Aussie Wine Tours (www.aussiewinetours.com.au) offers more of the same.

Byron Bay Eco Tours
Tel: 02-6685 4030
www.byron-bay.com/ecotours
Small tours (maximum six people) of rainforests and national parks around Byron.

Dolphin Watch Cruises
50 Owen Street, Huskisson
Tel: 02-4441 6311
www.dolphinwatch.com.au
Eco-certified dolphin- and whale-watching tours in Jervis Bay between May and November.

John Arnolds Outback Safari Tours
11 Morgan Street, Broken Hill
Tel: 08-8087 7701
Four-wheel-drive tours of the Outback and Broken Hill and surrounds.

Natural Wanders
Tel: 0427 225 072
www.kayaksydney.com
Offers kayaking tours around Sydney Harbour.

The chance to spot dolphins is a New South Wales highlight

Sydney by Sail
Tel: 02-9280 1110
www.sydneybysail.com.au
This outfit offers three-hour harbour sailing tours on luxury yachts, and introductory sailing courses, from its base at Darling Harbour.

Moonshadow Cruises
Shop 3, 35 Stockton Street, Nelson Bay
Tel: 02-4984 9388
www.moonshadow.com.au
Eco-certified dolphin- and whale-watching tours on big catamarans leave from Nelson Bay between May and November.

FESTIVALS AND EVENTS

NSW has a hefty swag of arts and cultural festivals.

Tamworth Country Music Festival

January

Concerts in The Domain
Free outdoor performances by Opera Australia and the Sydney Symphony Orchestra on two January evenings. Crowds of up to 80,000 bring picnics and enjoy a great night.

Sydney Festival
www.sydneyfestival.org.au
A three-week festival of local and imported music and theatre in January.

Tamworth Country Music Festival
www.tamworthcountrymusic.com.au
Australia's most famous C&W festival is held here every January.

February

Tropfest
www.tropfest.com
The world's largest short-film festival is held in the Domain every February, often with major Hollywood actors and directors on its judging panel.

March/April

Gay and Lesbian Mardi Gras
www.mardigras.org.au
A hugely popular parade and street party in Sydney held in March.

Bluesfest
www.bluesfest.com.au
Byron Bay's annual international blues and roots festival is held over Easter.

May–August

Biennale of Sydney
www.biennaleofsydney.com.au
Internationally renowned visual arts festival held between May and August every even-numbered year.

City 2 Surf
http://city2surf.sunherald.com.au
Tens of thousands of runners join the race from the Sydney's CBD to Bondi on the second Sunday in August.

December

Sydney to Hobart Yacht Race
http://rolexsydneyhobart.com
On Boxing Day, thousands watch the start of this yacht race from vantage points around Sydney Harbour.

New Year's Eve Fireworks
www.nsw.gov.au/new-years-eve-celebrations
A spectacular display over Sydney Harbour plus a swathe of parties around town.

Australian Capital Territory

When Australia's new nationhood was proclaimed in 1901, the perennial power struggle between Sydney and Melbourne reached a deadlock. Rather than choosing either city as national capital, a new site was selected in the bush 300km (185 miles) southwest of Sydney. Where sheep had grazed, the young Commonwealth raised its flag.

Canberra

Population: 350,000

Local dialling code: 02

Tourist office: Canberra and Region Visitors Centre; 330 Northbourne Avenue, Dickson; tel: 1300 554 114, 02-6205 0044; www.visitcanberra.com.au

Main police station: Canberra City Police Station, 18 London Circuit, Civic; tel: 02-6256 7777

Main post office: General Post Office; 53–73 Alinga Street, Civic

Hospital: Canberra Hospital; Yamba Drive, Garran; tel: 02-6244 2222; www.health.act.gov.au

Local newspaper: Canberra Times; www.canberratimes.com.au

Time zone: Eastern Standard Time (GMT plus 10 hours)

Sprawling across former bush and grazing land, the Australian Capital Territory (ACT) is dominated by Canberra, Australia's national capital. The territory is made up of national parklands, rolling mountains and pastures dotted with century-old homesteads.

Canberra is essentially a company town – though the local industry here is government. The city is also an educational, research and cultural centre, but its real focus is parliament with its attendant politicians, lobbyists and hangers-on, government ministries and foreign embassies. In spite of this considerable enterprise, Australia's only sizeable inland city is both uncrowded and relaxed.

Chicago-based architect and landscape designer Walter Burley Griffin, a former employee of Frank Lloyd Wright, won an international architectural competition to create the new capital from scratch in 1912. His design, which was created in association with his wife Marion Mahony, placed great emphasis on coherent connections between the landscape of the Australian Capital Territory (ACT) and the cityscape of Canberra. This enlightened vision has led to Burley Griffin's city being one of Australia's most congenial environments, full of native flora, attractive landscaping and showcase architecture.

Canberra

Many of the capital's main attractions are clustered near Lake Burley Griffin, but you'll need three or four hours to get around the main sights on foot. Bus tours are recommended, with a choice of half-day and all-day itineraries. City Sightseeing buses run a 25km (15-mile) route stopping at all the main sights. You buy a 24-hour ticket, then hop on and off at will. Alternatively, you can drive yourself around the town or hire a bike, following itineraries that are mapped out in a free sightseeing pamphlet available from the Canberra and Region Visitors Centre.

Walking around Lake Burley Griffin is a great way to see Canberra

Parliament House courted controversy when it was completed in 1988

Capital Hill

A walk around **Lake Burley Griffin** provides great views of the city and parliament buildings. Dominating Capital Hill, **Parliament House** Ⓐ (www.aph.gov.au; Mon–Fri 8am–6pm on non-sitting days, 8am to 30 minutes after sitting on sitting weeks; free) is adorned with many fine artworks representing the best in Australian art and design, including a massive tapestry in the Great Hall designed by Australian artist Arthur Boyd. Construction of Parliament House was completed in 1988, in time for the bicentennial celebrations commemorating the arrival of the First Fleet in 1788. The combination of an unusual design as well as exploding building costs of more than A\$1 billion made the new complex a sure-fire cause célèbre during its construction, taxpayers noting the lavish offices, bars, swimming pool and sauna.

Free tours explore the public areas, and when parliament is sitting you can watch Australian parliamentary democracy in action from the Public Galleries. The livelier of the two

Australian Capital Territory

chambers is the House of Representatives, and the best time to be there is Question Time. This is generally held at 2pm and you'll need to book by calling 02-6277 4889 before 12.45pm on the day you want to visit.

A little closer to the lake is its predecessor, **Old Parliament House** Ⓑ (18 King George Terrace; http://moadoph.gov.au; daily 9am–5pm; charge 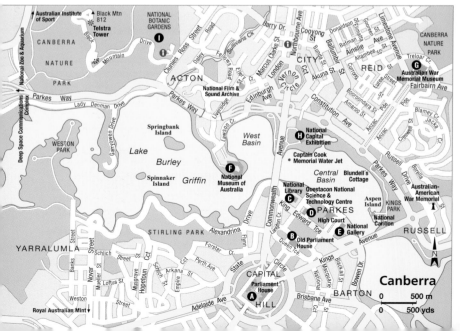), an impressive Art Deco building that's been wonderfully preserved as the Museum of Australian Democracy. Creative and entertaining interactive installations make the building a living museum of Australia's social and political history, complete with clattering typewriters, ringing phones and the gabbling voices of politicians taking the floor. Labyrinthine corridors lead to chambers and offices, the heady atmosphere of the Press Gallery, the politicians' dining room, secretarial offices and the inner sanctum, the Prime Minister's rooms.

On either side of the glass-like pond at the front of the building is the **Aboriginal Tent Embassy**, first set up here in the 1970s to focus attention on the Aboriginal land-rights campaign and a permanent fixture since 1992.

South of the Lake

Also on the lakefront is the **National Library** Ⓒ (Parkes Place; www.nla.gov.au; Mon–Thur 9am–9pm, Fri–Sat 9am–5pm, Sun 1.30am–5pm; free), which is home to more than five million books, along with journals, music and oral histories. Exhibitions of rare books are held regularly, and the reading room houses

The Aboriginal Tent Embassy draws attention to Indigenous land rights

an extensive selection of overseas newspapers and magazine publications. Nearby, hands-on science entertains children and adults alike at **Questacon** (King Edward Terrace; www.questacon.edu.au; daily 10am–5pm; charge). Architecturally, the building is an interesting study in curves – some say it looks like a flying saucer at rest.

National and international art is the focus at the **National Gallery of Australia** (Parkes Place; www.nga.gov.au; daily 10am–5pm; free), showcasing artists as varied as Monet and Matisse, Pollock and de Kooning, along with an honour roll of Australian masters including Tom Roberts, Arthur Streeton, Sidney Nolan, Arthur Boyd and Albert Tucker. Displays of art from the Pacific Islands, Africa, Asia and pre-Columbian America expand the breadth of the gallery's collections, along with a regularly changing calendar of touring international exhibitions. The gallery also has a glistening sculpture garden overlooking Lake Burley Griffin.

Australian Capital Territory

Canberra Transport

 Airport: Canberra International Airport; Brindabella Circuit, Pialligo; tel: 02-6275 2222; **www.canberraairport.com.au**

 Trains: Canberra Railway Station; Wentworth Avenue, Kingston. Main operators: Country Link; tel: 02-6208 9708; **www.countrylink.info**. V/Line; tel: 136 196, **www.vline.com.au**

Buses: Interstate Bus Terminal; Jolimont Centre, 65–67 Northbourne Avenue, Civic. Main operators: Greyhound Australia; tel: 131 499; **www.greyhound.com.au**. Murrays; tel: 132 251; **www.murrays.com.au**

Taxis: Canberra Elite Taxis; tel: 13 2227; **www.canberracabs.com.au**

Canberra's arts precinct also includes the adjacent **National Portrait Gallery** (King Edward Terrace; www.portrait.gov.au; daily 10am–5pm; free), which highlights the changing face of Australia and Australians over the centuries. More intimate in scale than its cavernous concrete neighbour, the portrait gallery hosts a lively and creative calendar of exhibitions.

North of the Lake

On the opposite side of Lake Burley Griffin on Acton Peninsula, the **National Museum of Australia G** (Lawson Crescent; www.nma.gov.au; daily 9am–5pm; free M) houses an eclectic collection of artefacts. Highlights include convict clothing and leg irons and the world's largest collection of Aboriginal bark paintings. Lovers of cinema and TV can head to the nearby **National Film & Sound Archive** (McCoy Circuit; www.nfsa.gov.au; daily 9am–5pm; free M), a treasure trove of popular culture celebrating 100 years of Australian film, TV and recorded sound.

Away from the lake to the east, the Canberra skyline is pierced by the dome of the **Australian War Memorial Museum G** (Treloar Crescent; www.awm.gov.au; daily 10am–5pm; free). The museum's collection of relics, weapons, documents and photographs is one of the best of its kind in the world. It's hard to avoid being swept up in the sombre mood of the place as you walk past walls inscribed with the names of more than 100,000 Australian war dead. Beyond the statues and murals, the memorial is the most-visited museum in Australia. Items displayed in its 20 galleries include uniforms through the years, battle maps,

The National Museum of Australia

and plenty of hardware – from rifles to a World War II Lancaster bomber.

Not far away, on Regatta Point, is the **National Capital Exhibition** ❶ (www.nationalcapital.gov.au; Mon–Fri 10am–5pm, Sat–Sun 10am–4pm; free). Essential if you want to make sense of the layout of Canberra, the exhibition offers fine views of the city and highlights curious facts about the shaping of the capital. According to the original plan, the surrounding hills were to be planted with flowering shrubs in different coloured vegetation. The plan was never implemented with any enthusiasm, but if you'd like to immerse yourself in the beauty of Australia's flora, visit Canberra's beguiling **National Botanic Gardens** ❶ (Clunies Ross Street; www.anbg.gov.au; daily 8.30am–5pm; free). Walter Burley Griffin was so fascinated by the native trees and plants of Australia that he included the gardens, located on the eastern slopes of Black Mountain and devoted to plant life from across the country, in his original plan for Canberra. Every January and February they play host to a series of summertime outdoor, jazz, funk, folk and blues concerts on Saturday and Sunday evenings (for more details, call the gardens' visitor centre on tel: 02-6250 9540).

Head northwest of the botanic gardens to explore Australia's love affair with the sporting life at the **Australian Institute of Sport** (Leverrier Crescent; www.ausport.gov.au/ais; daily tours at 10am, 11.30am, 1pm and 2.30pm; charge 🅜) in the suburb of Bruce. Guided by top athletes, the 90-minute tours take you behind the scenes of Australia's premier sporting precinct.

What's in a Name?

The name of Australia's new capital city, which is said to be derived from 'meeting place' in an Aboriginal tongue, was officially chosen in 1913 from among a huge outpouring of suggestions. Some of the more serious citizens wanted to have a name as uplifting as Utopia or Shakespeare. Others devised classical constructions such as Auralia and Austropolis. The most unusual proposal was a coinage designed to soothe every state capital: Sydmeladperbrisho. Fortunately, this one wasn't adopted!

Australian Capital Territory

ACCOMMODATION

While most hotels are close to the shopping and business district, a smaller selection is within walking distance of the National Gallery of Australia and Parliament House.

South of the Lake

Diplomat Boutique Hotel
Corner Canberra Avenue and Hely Street, Griffith
Tel: 02-6295 2277
www.diplomathotel.com.au
With large rooms and extensive facilities, the Diplomat is one of Canberra's premier boutique hotels. **$$$**

Forrest Inn and Apartments
30 National Circuit, Forrest
Tel: 02-6295 3433
www.forrestinn.com.au
This reliable choice is set in leafy surrounds close to Parliament House and the Australian National Gallery. **$$$**

Hotel Heritage
203 Goyder Street, Narrabundah
Tel: 02-6295 2944

The elegant lobby of the
Rydges Lakeside Canberra

Accommodation Price Categories

Prices are for one night's accommodation in a standard double room (unless otherwise specified)

$ = below A$35 (per dorm bed or camp site)
$$ = A$35–120
$$$ = A$120–250
$$$$ = A$250–400
$$$$$ = over A$400

www.hotelheritage.com.au
The Heritage offers hotel rooms and family apartments in Narrabundah, 12 minutes from the city centre. **$$**

Hyatt Hotel Canberra
Commonwealth Avenue, Yarralumla
Tel: 02-6270 1234
www.hyatt.com
A Canberra landmark, this refurbished luxury hotel is an elegant example of Australian Art Deco style. **$$$$**

North of the Lake

Canberra City YHA Hostel
7 Akuna Street, Civic
Tel: 02-6248 9155
www.yha.com.au
One of the best YHA hostels in Australia, the Canberra City hostel is within walking distance of shops, restaurants, nightclubs and the Jolimont Centre transport depot. **$$**

Canberra Rex Hotel
150 Northbourne Avenue, Braddon
Tel: 02-6248 5311
www.canberrarexhotel.com.au
A reliable four-star hotel, popular with both holiday-makers and business travellers. **$$$**

Rydges Lakeside Canberra
London Circuit, Civic
Tel: 1800 857 922
www.rydges.com
Rooms here have great views of the lake and surrounding mountains. **$$$**

RESTAURANTS

Canberra has a wide range of restaurants featuring all manner of international cuisines. For the best selection, head to Civic north of Lake Burley Griffin, or Manuka and Kingston south of the lake.

Capital Hill

The Ginger Room
Old Parliament House (enter by Queen Victoria Terrace), Capital Hill
Tel: 02-6270 8262
www.gingercatering.com.au
Dine in the rarefied atmosphere of Old Parliament House, where the cuisine is inspired by Pacific Rim flavours. **$$$$**

South of the Lake

Artespresso
31 Giles Street, Kingston
Tel: 02-6295 8055
www.artespresso.com.au
Café meets bistro meets restaurant at this much-loved modern Australian eatery. **$$$**

Aubergine
18 Barker Street, Griffith
Tel: 02-6260 8666
www.auberginerestaurant.com.au
A favourite for fine dining in Canberra, showcasing French and Italian flavours. **$$$**

Ottoman Cuisine
9 Broughton Street (corner Blackall Street), Barton
Tel: 02-6273 6111
www.ottomancuisine.com.au
Ottoman serves an extensive range of superbly executed Turkish dishes, including degustation and banquet menus. **$$$**

Silo Bakery
36 Giles Street, Kingston
Tel: 02-6260 6060
www.silobakery.com.au
A popular destination for coffee aficionados, this warm, wonderful bakery-café is known for its pastries and quality sourdoughs. **$$**

Waters Edge
40 Parkes Place, Parkes
Tel: 02-6273 5066
www.watersedgecanberra.com.au
This place offers panoramic lakeside views plus excellent modern cuisine and wines. **$$$**

North of the Lake

Blue Olive Café
56 Alinga Street, Civic
Tel: 02-6230 4600
In the lovely old Melbourne Building in the city centre, the Blue Olive serves up hearty home-baked bread and delicious cakes. **$**

Courgette
54 Marcus Clarke Street, Civic
Tel: 02-6247 4042
www.courgette.com.au
The decor is simple but stylishly modern at this classy restaurant, which serves imaginative modern European cooking. **$$$**

Fekerte's
74/2 Cape Street, Dickson
Tel: 02-6262 5799
www.fekertes.com.au
Ethiopian chef Fekerte Tesfaye cooks up a wonderful range of flavoursome dishes, including plenty of vegetarian options. **$$**

Mezzalira
Melbourne Building, 20 West Row, Civic
Tel: 02-6230 0025
www.mezzalira.com.au
The atmosphere is buzzy and the regional Italian cooking is exquisite. **$$$**

Milk and Honey
Center Cinema Building, 29 Garema Place, Civic

Tel: 02-6247 7722
www.milkandhoney.net.au
The ambience is relaxed and the cuisine is modern Mediterranean at this popular café-restaurant. **$$**

Tasuke
Sydney Building, 122 Alinga Street, Civic
Tel: 02-6257 9711
Savour some of Canberra's finest and freshest Japanese food at tiny Tasuke. **$**

NIGHTLIFE AND ENTERTAINMENT

Consult the 'Fly' section in the Thursday edition of the *Canberra Times* or the free monthly magazine *BMA* for a rundown of what's on in town.

South of the Lake
bbar
21 Kennedy Street, Kingston
Tel: 02-6295 1949
A sleek bar for a quiet drink and tasty bar snack. Bring your dancing shoes Thur–Sat.

The Julep Lounge
8 Franklin Street, Manuka
Tel: 02-6239 5060
www.thejuleplounge.com
This dimly lit velvet hideaway serves classic and contemporary tapas and cocktails.

North of the Lake
Antigo Café and Bar
131 London Circuit, Civic
Tel: 02-6249 8080
Drop in for a tipple if you're coming or going from the Canberra Theatre.

ANU Bar
Australian National University, Acton
Tel: 02-6125 3660
www.anuunion.com.au
Students and music-lovers alike head to this university bar for gigs by Australian bands.

Benchmark Wine Bar
65 Northbourne Avenue, Civic
Tel: 02-6262 6522
www.benchmarkwinebar.com.au
Join civil servants at this wine bar and choose from 100 wines available by the glass.

Canberra Symphony Orchestra
Llewellyn Hall, Childers Street, Acton

Tel: 02-6125 4993
www.cso.org.au
Canberra's symphony orchestra performs at the ANU School of Music's Llewellyn Hall. The Proms concert takes place in February in the grounds of Government House in Yarralumla.

Canberra Theatre Centre
Civic Square, Civic
Tel: 02-6243 5711
www.canberratheatre.org.au
Canberra's theatre and performing arts hub contains a theatre, playhouse and gallery, and programmes a lively calendar of events.

Cube
33 Petrie Plaza, Civic
Tel: 02-6257 1110
www.cubenightclub.com.au
Gay and lesbian Cube is hetero-friendly, and hosts themed nights and plenty of all-night action on the dance floor.

Hippo Lounge Bar
17 Garema Place, Civic
Tel: 02-6257 9090
www.hippobar.com.au
Laid-back yet sophisticated, the Hippo bar above Garema Place hosts a varied music line-up of live jazz and DJ-spun fusion.

The Phoenix
23 East Row, Civic
Tel: 02-6247 1606
www.lovethephoenix.com
This cosy, convivial Irish pub has a friendly atmosphere and occasional live music.

TOURS

As well as being the nation's cycling capital, tours here cover everything from hot-air ballooning to water cruises.

Aquila Helicopters
16 Alanson Place, Isaacs
Tel: 0418 323 777
Choose from a range of scenic flights over Canberra, the ACT and the Snowy Mountains.

Balloon Aloft
7 Irving Street, Phillip
Tel: 02-6285 1540
www.canberraballoons.com.au
For a different view of Canberra, take in the lie of the land from above with a hot-air balloon flight across the city.

Balloon Aloft offer a great way to see Canberra

Mr Spokes
Barrine Drive, Acton
Tel: 02-6257 1188
www.mrspokes.com.au
Bikes, gear, maps and routes for self-guided cycle tours around Lake Burley Griffin.

Go Bush Tours
128 Marconi Crescent, Kambah
Tel: 02-6231 3023
www.gobushtours.com.au
A range of guided tours covering city sights, national parks, nature reserves and wineries.

Southern Cross Cruises
Mariner Place Lotus Bay, Yarralumla
Tel: 02-6273 1784
www.cscc.com.au
A one-hour cruise of Lake Burley Griffin.

Listings

FESTIVALS AND EVENTS

Canberra hosts some of the country's major public events and festivals.

January
Australia Day in the Park
www.events.act.gov.au
Celebrate Australia's national day (26 January) in Commonwealth Park.

February
National Multicultural Festival
www.multiculturalfestival.com.au
Free performances around the city.

March
Canberra Festival
www.events.act.gov.au
Fireworks, hot-air ballooning and more than 60 cultural extravaganzas and events.

April
National Folk Festival
www.folkfestival.asn.au
Folk and world music performances, dance and poetry on Easter weekend.

September
Floriade
www.floriadeaustralia.com
Australia's biggest flower show.

October
Stonefest
www.stonefest.com.au
Canberra's best music festival, held at the University of Canberra at the end of October.

Queensland

Queensland offers everything that makes Australia such a desirable destination, plus some truly spectacular attractions of its own. The sun-soaked state boasts a swag of beach resorts, historic towns, pristine rainforests and a lively modern metropolis. But the most amazing attraction of all is Queensland's Great Barrier Reef – the longest coral reef in the world.

Brisbane

Population: 2 million

Local dialling code: 07

Tourist office: Brisbane Visitor Information Centre; Queen Street Mall; tel: 07-3006 6290; www.visitbrisbane.com.au

Main police station: 46 Charlotte Street; tel: 07-3258 2582

Main post office: 261 Queen Street

Hospital: Royal Brisbane and Women's Hospital; corner Butterfield Street and Bowen Bridge Road, Herston; tel: 07-3636 8111; www.health.qld.gov.au/rbwh

Local newspapers: *Courier Mail*; www.couriermail.com.au. *Brisbane Times*; www.brisbane times.com.au

Time zone: Eastern Standard Time (GMT plus 10 hours)

Queensland was founded in 1824 as a colony for incorrigible convicts, for whom not even the rigours of New South Wales were a sufficient deterrent. In an effort to quarantine criminality, free settlers were banned from an 80km (50-mile) radius. But Queensland's pastureland attracted many eager squatters along with adventurers, missionaries and hopeful immigrants. In 1867 the state joined the great Australian gold rush with a find of its own.

While mining still contributes generously to Queensland's economy, tourism is one of the biggest money-spinners. Queensland is Australia's vacation state, with wild tropical adventurelands in the far north, and the sophistication of the Gold Coast in the south. Tourism was hit, however, by the massive floods that engulfed the state in December 2010 and January 2011, followed almost immediately by Cyclone Yasi, which smashed into the coast between Cairns and Townsville in February. Recovery, however, was swift; within weeks most infrastructure was up and running and even the devastated resorts on Dunk and Bedarra Islands were due to reopen by 2012.

Brisbane and Around

As befits a subtropical city with palm trees and back-garden swimming pools, **Brisbane** ❶ has a pace so relaxed you'd hardly imagine its population is over 2 million. The skyscrapers, some quite audacious, have gone a long way towards overcoming the 'country-town' image, and despite the depredations of town planners and politicians enough of the elegant, low-slung buildings of earlier days remain. As well as having its own attractions, Brisbane is also a handy gateway to nearby tourist sites such as the Gold Coast and Fraser Island.

Central Business District (CBD)

Brisbane's CBD, in an area cupped by the river, is a mixture of stately colonial buildings and eye-catching modern architecture, with lungs provided by the City Botanic Gardens at one end and Roma Street Parkland at the other.

Queen Street Mall is bursting with shops and cafés

The heritage-listed **Brisbane City Hall** ❷ in King George Square closed its doors for extensive renovations and won't reopen until 2013. The **Museum of Brisbane** (www.museumofbrisbane.com.au; daily 10am–5pm; free **M**), formerly housed in the City Hall and temporarily relocated to 157 Ann Street, offers an overview of the city's history and its culture as well as a continually changing programme of exhibitions and events.

King George Square, opposite the City Hall, and nearby **Anzac Square**, are typical of the city's open spaces. Pedestrian-only **Queen Street Mall** is flanked by large stores and interspersed with shady refuges and cafés. Here, on a fine day, visitors from cooler climes should take a seat to enjoy the warm sun and watch the passers-by, or take a stroll along Albert Street, from King George Square to the City Botanic Gardens.

Where central Brisbane fits into the bend in the river, the **City Botanic Gardens** ❸ (www.brisbane.qld.gov.au; Mon–Sat free guided tour 11am and 1pm) turn the peninsula green with

Heritage-listed Brisbane City Hall and King George Square opposite

countless species of Australian and exotic trees, plants and flowers. **Parliament House** (corner George and Alice Streets; www.parliament.qld.gov.au; Mon–Fri 9am–5pm; free), built in the 19th century in Renaissance style, overlooks the gardens and is the headquarters of the state's legislative assembly.

Roma Street Parkland (1 Parkland Boulevard; www.romastreetparkland. com; daily; free 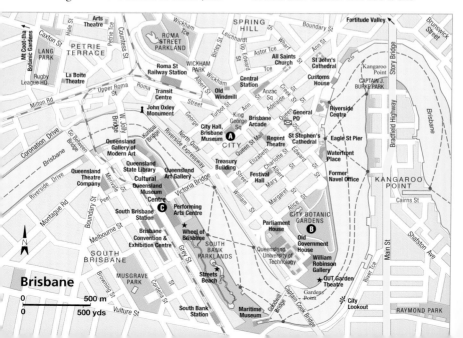), built on the old Roma Street railway shunting yards, has been transformed into a diverse area of waterfalls, lakes, misty crannies of tropical vegetation and floral displays with their own ecosystem of insects and birds.

South Bank

A stroll across the Goodwill footbridge from the Botanic Gardens or Victoria Bridge from the centre of town (and also accessible by ferry) is one of the city's main focal points, **South Bank** (www.visitsouthbank.com.au), a recreational precinct of parks, gardens, restaurants, cafés and many other attractions stretching along the southern bank of the Brisbane River.

At its northern end is the **Queensland Cultural Centre** ●, which puts most of Brisbane's cultural eggs in one lavish, modern basket. The centre includes the **Queensland Art Gallery/Gallery of Modern Art** (http://qag. qld.gov.au; Mon–Fri 10am–5pm, Sat–Sun 9am–5pm; free), the **Queensland Museum** (www.southbank. qm.qld.gov.au; daily 9.30am–5pm; free) and its offshoot **Sciencentre** (www.southbank.qm.qld.gov.au/sciencentre; daily 9.30am–5pm; free), an interactive science museum aimed at kids and teens. Here too is the

The Wheel of Brisbane is one of many attractions at South Bank Parklands

Queensland Performing Arts Centre (www.qpac.com.au), with several performance spaces for drama, dance, music and comedy.

To the south of the Cultural Centre, and linked to it by a beautiful bougainvillea-clad arbour, are the **South Bank Parklands**. The attractions here include the **Wheel of Brisbane** (Mon–Thur 10am–10pm, Fri–Sat 9am–midnight, Sun 9am–10pm; charge), a 60m (196ft) -high rotating wheel with enclosed gondola-style air-conditioned capsules affording 360-degree views over the city. The **Queensland Maritime Museum** (www.maritimemuseum.com.au; daily 9.30am–4.30pm; charge) features a varied collection celebrating all things nautical. The main attraction is the restored

Brisbane Transport

✈ **Airports:** Brisbane Airport (tel: 07-3406 3000; **www.bne.com.au**) is 13km (8 miles) northeast of the city centre. Transport to Brisbane: taxi (15–20 minutes; A$35). Coachtrans (tel: 07-3358 9700; **www.coachtrans.com.au**; every 30 minutes to Brisbane transit centre or hotels if pre-booked; adults A$15 one way, A$30 return). Airtrain (tel: 1800 119 091; **www.airtrain.com.au**; every 15 minutes during peak hours to Roma Street transit centre and Central Station; adults A$14.50 one way, A$27 return)

 Buses: Run by Translink (tel: 131 230; **www.translink.com.au**) from 5am–11pm. Tickets: the reusable *go* card (A$5 deposit), which offers discounted travel on all forms of public transport, is available at the Translink website, train stations, information centres and convenience stores. You can also purchase a daily, off-peak daily or weekly ticket at bus, train and ferry stations

 Trains: Run by Translink from 5am–midnight

 Ferries: Run by Translink from 5.50am–10.30pm

 Taxis: Yellow Cabs (tel: 131 924; **www.yellowcab.com.au**), Black & White Cabs (tel: 133 222; **www.blackandwhitecabs.com.au**)

 Parking Road parking is metered; there are plenty of paid car parks in the city centre

Diamantina, a Royal Australian Navy frigate built in 1945.

South Bank Market (Fri 5–10pm, Sat 10am–5pm, Sun 9am–5pm ) offers a range of crafts, homewares and collectibles. If the heat gets too much for you, the nearby **Streets Beach** (free ), an artificial beach complete with lagoon and sandy beaches, is the perfect way to cool off. There is also a diverse array of restaurants in South Bank for a relaxing outdoor meal.

Fortitude Valley and New Farm

Just outside the CBD, **Fortitude Valley** is one of the city's most lively precincts. Brunswick Street, the valley's main thoroughfare, is lined with clubs, street cafés, ethnic restaurants and specialist stores and galleries. This suburb is also the location of Brisbane's busy Chinatown. The Valley has a thriving nightlife, but some of its more insalubrious character remains, so it's wise to take a taxi home after dark. Linking Fortitude Valley to Kangaroo Point is the cantilevered **Story Bridge** (www.storybridgeadventureclimb.com.au; charge ), a city landmark lit up at night.

Continuing down Brunswick Street towards the river, New Farm is a more gentrified suburb than its slightly grungy neighbour. **New Farm Park** attracts a mixed bunch of walkers, picnickers and culture vultures. **Brisbane Powerhouse** (119 Lamington Street; www.brisbanepowerhouse.org), a former power station, has morphed into a contemporary arts centre showcasing local visual arts, music and comedy acts. Bars and restaurants ensure that the waterfront views are maximised.

It's only about 11km (7 miles) to **Lone Pine Koala Sanctuary** (708 Jesmond Road, Fig Tree Pocket; www.koala.net; daily 8.30am–5pm; charge ), which hosts one of the country's

Climbing Story Bridge is the best way to appreciate the city skyline

Dozing in a tree at the Lone
Pine Koala Sanctuary

best-known collections of native animals. The stars of the show, of course,
are the koalas, mostly sleeping like
babies while clinging to their eucalyptus branches. You can get there by
bus or by taking the scenic river cruise
operated by **Mirimar Cruises** (on the
boardwalk outside the State Library;
www.mirimar.com; daily 10am, returns
1.45pm; adults A$55, children A$33).

North Stradbroke Island

'Straddie' is a popular island getaway
close to Brisbane with spectacular
swimming and surf beaches. At 38km
(24 miles) long and 11km (7 miles)
wide, it's the world's second-largest
sand island. Home to the Nunu-
kul, Nughie and Goenpul tribes,
who know it as Minjerribah, it was

colonised by Europeans in the 1820s.
For information on exploring the
island by four-wheel-drive, *see p.124.*

The Gold Coast

South of Brisbane (a day-trip distance
if you're rushed) is the **Gold Coast ❷**,
a Down Under impression of Miami
Beach. More than 20 Gold Coast surfing beaches patrolled by lifesavers
form the backdrop for activities such as
swimming, sailing, boating, surfboard-
ing and windsurfing.

The trip down the Pacific Highway
to the Gold Coast south from Brisbane
lures fun-seekers with attractions for all
the family. Huge theme park **Dreamworld** (www.dreamworld.com.au;
daily 10am–5pm; charge 🎫) operates
an attraction claimed to be 'one of the
fastest rides in the world', the Tower
of Terror. **Warner Bros Movie World**
(http://movieworld.myfun.com.au;
daily 10am–5pm charge 🎫) offers a
Hollywood-style experience, including
stunt shows and amusement rides.

Sea World (http://seaworld.myfun.
com.au; daily 10am–5pm; charge;
🎫) is noted for its marine attractions,

Head for the Hills

To escape the heat and rush of the city,
escape to **Brisbane Botanic Gardens
Mount Coot-tha** (Mount Coot-tha Road;
www.brisbane.qld.gov.au; Apr–Aug
daily 8am–5pm; free) in Toowong,
7km (4 miles) west of the city centre.
Covering 52 hectares (128 acres),
these tropical and subtropical gardens
are the largest in Australia and feature
a giant modern dome enclosing 200
species of tropical plants.

'Straddie' has long been Brisbane's favourite escape. This full-day four-wheel-drive tour takes in white-sand beaches, freshwater lagoons and scenic lookout points.

Disembark from the ferry at the small fishing township of **Dunwich**. A Heritage Walking Trail covers many buildings dating from the start of white settlement here, winding through convict relics and graves dating back to shipwrecks in the 1800s. The **North Stradbroke Island Historical Museum** (15–17 Welsby St; www.stradbrokemuseum.com; Tue–Sat 10am–2pm; charge) offers an impressive display of photographs and items retrieved from shipwrecks, as well as information about the island's Aboriginal and pioneer settlements.

From Dunwich, drive 20km (12 miles) northeast to the township of **Point**

A glorious sunset seen from the Dunwich ferry terminal

Lookout ('The Point'), Queensland's most easterly point. From here, make sure you do the spectacular **North Gorge Walk**, which is only about 1km (half a mile) and offers superb views. You're almost guaranteed to see dolphins and turtles frolicking in the surf.

For lunch, consider the **Stradbroke Island Beach Hotel** (East Coast Road, Point Lookout; tel: 07-3409 8188; www.stradbrokehotel.com.au; $$–$$$), known to locals as the 'Straddie Pub'. Between June and November you can sit and eat your meal while watching humpback whales breach and splash in the waters of Moreton Bay below. Not far west of the Straddie Pub there

---

Tips

- Distance: 71km (44 miles), not including drive on Main Beach
- Time: A full day
- Vehicle ferries and water taxis access the island from Cleveland Ferry Terminal, 35km (22 miles) southeast of Brisbane's CBD. To catch a 9am ferry, leave Brisbane by 7.45am. The ferry crossing takes 45 minutes.
- Ferry operators include Sea Stradbroke Car & Passenger Ferries, aka **The Big Red Cat** (tel: 07-3488 9777; www.seastradbroke.com; 8 services daily), and **Stradbroke Ferries** (tel: 07-3488 5300; www.stradbrokeferries.com.au; 9–11 services daily).
- It's essential to book your fare in advance and obtain a beach access (driving) permit – these are available on board the ferry or at the terminal offices in Cleveland.

is a turn-off to the south onto George Nothling Drive, with signposts indicating access to **Main Beach**. Before heading down there, consult the tide chart that came with your driving permit – beach driving is best an hour or so either side of low tide and prohibited an hour either side of high tide. Driving along the 36km (22-mile) stretch of pristine white beach to **Jumpinpin**, the tidal channel between North and South Stradbroke Islands, is legendary with Stradbroke regulars.

From Main Beach it's a 16km (10-mile) drive west to Amity Point for a look at this down-to-earth fishing village on the island's northwestern tip. Next, retrace your drive back out onto the East Coast Road and turn right for Dunwich, keeping an eye on the time now for your return ferry journey. If you

From Point Lookout, be sure to do the magnificent North Gorge Walk

have time to spare, Brown Lake is only 4km (2 miles) east of Dunwich. Stained tea-brown from the surrounding trees, reeds and organic matter, it's a tranquil spot for a swim or a wander around the shore. Alternatively, Blue Lake is a 10km (6-mile) drive east of Dunwich (with a 30-minute walk from the car park). Wildlife, including swamp wallabies and sand goannas, abounds here, especially in the early morning or late afternoon.

Driving Tour of North Stradbroke Island

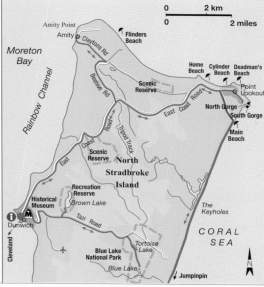

including dolphins, sharks and polar bears; while **Wet 'n' Wild** (http://wetnwild.myfun.com.au; daily from 10am, closing times vary; charge 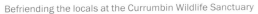) is a huge aquatic park containing a giant wave pool, whitewater ride and a seven-storey speed slide.

For something more sedate, **Currumbin Wildlife Sanctuary** (www.currumbin-sanctuary.org.au; daily 8am–5pm; charge; 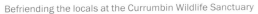) features koalas, kangaroos, Tasmanian devils, snakes and crocodiles; **David Fleay Wildlife Park** (www.fleayswildlife.com.au; daily 9am–5pm; charge; 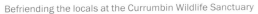) is a conservation park and the only place on the Gold Coast where you can see a platypus.

The essence of the Gold Coast is **Surfers Paradise**, as lively as any seaside resort in the world and much addicted to high-rise living. When you're not sunbathing, swimming or surfing, you can go bungy jumping or just window-shop, eat out, socialise or wander through the malls. **Skypoint**

(Q1 Surfers Paradise Boulevard; www.skypoint.com.au; Sun–Thur 9am–9pm, Fri–Sat 9am–midnight; charge) is one of the Gold Coast's essential attractions. Ascend to Level 77 of the world's tallest residential building, rising 322m (1056ft) into the sky for breathtaking 360-degree views along the coast.

To unwind, take a leisurely boat cruise along the **Southport Broadwater** or canals of Surfers Paradise. Another Surfers Paradise landmark, not far from Sea World, is **Palazzo Versace** (www.palazzoversace.com), the world's first Versace Hotel, billed as 'six star' and filled with all kinds of designer chic.

The lush green backdrop to the Gold Coast is known as the **Hinterland**. The area encompasses luxuriant subtropical rainforests, waterfalls and bushwalking tracks, mountain villages and guesthouses, craft galleries and farm-stay accommodation. World Heritage-listed **Lamington National Park** (www.derm.qld.gov.au/parks/

Befriending the locals at the Currumbin Wildlife Sanctuary

Laid-back Noosa boasts an excellent beach

lamington) is home to a diverse collection of flora and fauna. There are several half- or full-day walks to choose from and the park is an easy day trip from Surfers Paradise.

Sunshine, Fraser, Capricorn and Whitsunday Coasts

For the beachy perfection of the Gold Coast with less commercialism (although they're working on it), try the resorts of the Sunshine, Fraser, Capricorn and Whitsunday coasts, stretching for golden kilometres north of Brisbane and into the tropics. Some of Australia's best surfing waves pound this stretch of coast.

The Sunshine Coast

The **Sunshine Coast ❸** is home to some of Queensland's most gorgeous coastline, with beaches such as those fronting the towns of **Maroochydore** and **Coolum** particular gems. The resort closest to Brisbane is **Caloundra**, with a beach for every tide. The northernmost town on the Sunshine Coast is **Noosa**, a laid-back and relaxed

town with luxury resorts and great restaurants and cafés. **Noosa National Park**, a sanctuary of rainforest and underpopulated beaches, occupies the dramatic headland. Fraser Island is easily reached from here.

Inland, the Hinterland is laden with plantations of sugar cane, bananas, pineapples and passion fruit. The area is also a centre of production of the macadamia nut. Above **Nambour**, the principal town of the Hinterland, is the **Blackall Range**, a remnant of

Highway 1

Highway 1, the main coastal route from Brisbane to Cairns, stretches for 1,703km (1,058 miles). Although it is being continually improved, don't think of it as a 'highway' in the American or European sense; much of it is just a good-quality undivided two-lane road. Diversions from the route north will reveal magnificent uncrowded beaches, pristine rainforests, tropical islands (from uninhabited to luxurious resorts), authentic country pubs and splendid fishing and diving.

Lady Elliot Island is part of the Great Barrier Reef

ancient volcanic activity. Attractive towns in the area include **Montville** and **Maleny**, which are home to crafts shops, cafés and tearooms.

To the south, just off the Bruce Highway near Beerwah, is **Australia Zoo** (www.australiazoo.com.au; daily 9am–4.30pm; free ). Made famous by the late Steve Irwin, the zoo has a wide variety of Australian wildlife, as well as many exotic species, including elephants and tigers.

Fraser Coast

Gympie, a one-time gold-mining town, kick-starts your trip along the Fraser Coast, where a week-long Gold Rush Festival is held every October. Atmospheric **Maryborough** ❹ is an old-world charmer of a town with many fine Victorian colonial buildings. Nearby, **Hervey Bay** is an attractive holiday destination and another jumping-off point for Fraser Island.

Childers, on the highway to the north, is a National Trust–listed town surrounded by rolling hills covered in sugar cane. The town encapsulates the region's early architecture. Turn off to Woodgate Beach and **Woodgate National Park**, about 40km (25 miles) down the side road, for one of the region's most beautiful beaches. The next major town north is **Bundaberg** ❺ on the coast, 45km (28 miles) from Highway 1. For millions of Australians 'Bundy' is synonymous with rum, and here, in the heart of sugar country, is the distillery that put the town on the map. The **Bundaberg Rum Distillery** (www.bundabergrum.com.au; Mon–Fri 10am–3pm, Sat–Sun 10am–2pm; charge) operates self-guided and guided tours that provide insights into the production process, a visit to the museum and a taste of the product.

Capricorn Coast and Hinterland

On the Tropic of Capricorn, the Capricorn Coast is often described as

Queensland

0   200 km
0   200 miles

Badu I.   Moa I.
Torres Strait
Thursday I.   Horn I.
Prince of Wales I.   Cape York
Bamaga

Jardine River N.P.

Cape Grenville

Iron Range N.P.

Weipa

Coral Sea

Cape

Coen

Princess Charlotte Bay
Cape Melville

PACIFIC

OCEAN

Gulf of Carpentaria

York

Kowanyama

Lakefield National Park

Laura   Cooktown ⑭

Quinkan Reserve   Helenvale
Daintree N.P.
Lakeland Downs   Cape Tribulation
Kuranda   Mossman
Port Douglas ⑬
Cairns ⑫

Mornington I.

Wellesley Is
Bentinck I.

Burketown

Karumba

Normanton

George Town

Chillagoe

Mareeba

Atherton Tableland
Atherton
Innisfail

Mt Surprise   Ravenshoe

Tully
Mission Beach
Hinchinbrook I. ⑪
Ingham

Boodjamulla N.P. ⑯
Lawn Hill Gorge

Croydon

Undara Volcanic N.P. ⑮
Undara Lava Tubes ★
Greenvale

Paluma Range N.P.
Magnetic I.

Townsville ⑩

Riversleigh

Camooweal

Lake Moondarra

Mount Isa ⑰

Cloncurry

Flinders Hwy

Julia Creek

Flinders

Norman

Gregory Range

Great

Charters Towers

Ayr
Bowen
Whitsunday Islands ⑨

McKinlay   Kynuna

Richmond   Hughenden

Porcupine Gorge N.P.

Proserpine

Dajarra

Matilda   Highway

Middleton

Boulia

Winton

Muttaburra

Clermont

Mackay ⑧
Sarina
Broad Sound

Dividing

Lark Quarry Dinosaur Trackways ★

Longreach ⑱

Barcaldine

Emerald

Rockhampton ⑥
Yeppoon
Great Keppel I.
Heron I.

Bedourie

Diamantina

Capricorn Hwy

Dingo

Tropic of Capricorn

Gladstone

Barcoo

Blackall

Yaraka

Carnarvon National Park

Carnarvon Gorge ⑦

Biloela

1770
Agnes Water

Range

Bundaberg ⑤

Birdsville

Windorah

Augathella

Taroom

Great Sandy National Park

Hervey Bay

Fraser Island

Clifton Hills

Charleville

Quilpie ⑲

Mitchell
Roma
Miles

Childers
Gympie

Maryborough ④
Noosa Heads
Coolum
Maroochydore
Caloundra
Sunshine Coast

South Australia

Innamincka

The Dig Tree ⑳

Thargomindah

Warrego Hwy

Murgon
Nanango

Nambour
Australia Zoo ★

Moreton I.

Sturt Desert

Cunnamulla

St George

Moonie

Dalby

Caboolture

Lone Pine
Koala Sanctuary ★

Brisbane ①

Grey   *Range*

Hungerford

Bollon

Dirranbandi

Goondiwindi

Toowoomba

Ipswich

Surfers Paradise

Gold Coast ②

Darling Downs

Lamington N.P.

Lyndhurst

Leigh Creek

Flinders Ranges

Lake Frome

Wompah
Milparinka

Wanaaring

Barringun

Goodooga

Warwick
Stanthorpe

Lismore

Murwillumbah

Ballina

New South Wales

Packsaddle

Bourke

Brewarrina

Collarenebri

Walgett

Narrabri

Moree

Glen Innes

Tenterfield

Grafton

Fraser Island

About 120km (75 miles) long, Fraser is considered to be the largest sand island in the world, and is listed as a World Heritage Site. This is an unspoilt island for fishing, beachcombing and four-wheel-drive trekking, not forgetting swimming or coral dives. You can take excursions and flights to the island from Hervey Bay, or stay overnight at resorts, lodges, cabins or campsites.

undiscovered. Admittedly, it is a little less touristy than the rest of North Queensland – but only just. **Lady Elliot Island** (www.ladyelliot.com.au), south of the Tropic of Capricorn, is part of the Barrier Reef. Activities centre on diving, swimming and windsurfing. The twin coastal resorts of **Agnes Water** and **Town of 1770** have become popular fishing and boating centres, as well as being the departure point for visits to **Eurimbula** and **Deepwater National Parks** with their pristine coastal landscapes.

Rockhampton ❻ is the commercial heart of central Queensland, with a population of about 65,000. It's a mix of the old and new, with plenty of pubs and modern office blocks interspersed among older buildings. The National Estate lists **Quay Street** in its entirety on its heritage register, and superb colonial homes are found in **Agnes Street**. Pick up a heritage guide from the **Rockhampton Visitor Information Centre** (208 Quay Street; tel: 07-4922 5339) in the old Customs House.

Great Keppel Island is one of the larger resort islands in both area and in tourist population (there's even a youth hostel). The white beaches are gorgeous. The coral-fringed island is a vast bushland, with plenty of walking tracks to explore.

Carnarvon Gorge

The Dawson Highway, heading west from Gladstone, is the route to one of Queensland's most outstanding national parks at **Carnarvon Gorge ❼**. This 30km (16-mile) sandstone

Lush vegetation with beach and sea beyond in the Whitsundays

The Great Barrier Reef is home to infinite varieties of marine life

gorge has a profusion of palm trees, cycads, ferns and mosses as well as fine examples of Aboriginal rock paintings.

The Great Barrier Reef

Australia's largest and most wonderful sight, the **Great Barrier Reef** lies just below the ocean waves. The world's largest living phenomenon, the reef is home to 400 different types of coral and more than 2,900km (1,430 miles) of submerged tropical gardens. The giant reef was proclaimed a marine park by the Australian Government in 1975, and placed on the World Heritage list in 1981, becoming the biggest World Heritage area in existence. It is now managed by the **Great Barrier Reef Marine Park Authority**; *see p.22* for more information.

Whitsunday Coast

A tropical paradise of sun-drenched islands and heavenly beaches makes the Whitsunday Coast one of the country's key holiday destinations. Fanned by tropical breezes and surrounded by a rustling sea of sugar cane, **Mackay ❽** is a pleasant city of wide streets and elegant old hotels. A stroll through the centre reveals an assortment of Victorian buildings interspersed with several displaying the sleek lines of 1930s Art Deco. North of the centre there are some fine beaches, including Black Beach stretching 6km (4 miles) along the coast.

Whitsunday Islands

At the southern end of the **Whitsunday Islands ❾** archipelago, **Lindeman Island** (www.clubmed.com.au) is Australia's first Club Med, and beyond the buildings it has retained the beauty of its natural setting. You can play tennis, swim or fish, and 20km (12 miles) of bushwalking trails wind through 500 hectares (1,230 acres) of national park. Access is from Mackay, Hamilton Island and Proserpine.

Three very different resorts coexist on **Long Island** (www.longisland resort.com.au), only a short boat trip from Shute Harbour. Club Crocodile is for all ages, but is particularly popular with the young. Peppers Palm Bay is ideal for a back-to-nature holiday with lovely beaches, clear water and coral, and solitude. The self-catering Whitsunday Wilderness Lodge provides camping cabins.

Hamilton Island (www.hamilton island.com.au), the largest, most aggressively marketed Whitsunday resort, has a high-rise hotel, a floating marina, an airstrip with direct flights to major cities and a sports complex. With a pseudo-South Seas main street once described as 'Daiquiri Disneyland', this is not the place for a quiet sojourn.

The largest of the group, covering 109 sq km (42 sq miles), is **Whitsunday Island**. There's no resort here, but the fabulous Whitehaven Beach is a great option for campers (with permits).

South Molle Island (www.south molleisland.com.au ⓜ) offers a self-contained resort (Koala Adventure Island) on a large, hilly island and is popular with families. Diving, swimming, sailing, golf, fishing and shopping are all offered. Travel is from Shute Harbour or Hamilton Island.

A popular family resort, **Daydream Island** (www.daydreamisland.com ⓜ) has all the essentials for a good time at a reasonable all-inclusive tariff. Great beaches and a wide range of activities including memorable crazy golf are all just 15 minutes from Shute Harbour or Hamilton Island.

The second-largest island in the Whitsundays, **Hook Island** (www. hookislandresort.com) provides budget camping and cabins as well as services for visiting yachts. There

A pair of humpback whales off the coast of the Whitsunday Islands

Most of Magnetic Island is a national park

is an excellent underwater observatory here and an Aboriginal cave painting at Nara Inlet.

The exclusive five-star **Hayman Island Resort** (www.hayman.com.au) is set in a coral-trimmed lagoon, near the Outer Reef. A favourite with honeymooners, Hayman's fine beaches and fishing are complemented by lavish resort facilities. Access is from Hamilton Island, Proserpine, Shute Harbour and Townsville.

North Coast and the Far North

The stretch of coast between Townsville and Cooktown is home to thriving townships, a necklace of tropical islands, pristine rainforests, mountainous regions and, of course, the headlining act, the majestic Great Barrier Reef. Backpackers on a penny-pinching budget and the seriously moneyed luxuriating in Port Douglas's exclusive resorts are all here to enjoy the region's bountiful natural attractions.

Townsville

Townsville ⑩ is the hub of the mining and cattle industries of Queensland's interior and one of the gateways for islands of the Reef, including neighbouring Magnetic Island. In the historic town centre,

Above and Below

Seeing the Great Barrier Reef up close and personal by either diving or snorkelling is a must for any Queensland holiday-maker. As a starting point for planning a trip have a look at the **Dive Queensland** website (www.dive-queensland.com.au).

Boating enthusiasts will find that Queensland offers plenty of opportunities to indulge in their sport. Most are drawn to the islands of the Whitsundays, where dozens of operators hire yachts, catamarans, tall ships and sea kayaks at Airlie Beach and Shute Harbour. To arrange boat charter before leaving home, visit the **Whitsunday Tourism** (www.whitsundaytourism.com) website.

along the river, are some photogenic old buildings with filigreed iron balconies and stately columns and arches.

One of Townsville's top attractions is **Reef HQ** (2-68 Flinders Street East; www.reefhq.com.au; daily 9.30am–5pm; charge ), with a superb simulation of the Great Barrier Reef, an Imax cinema and a colossal aquarium. Next door, the **Museum of Tropical Queensland** (www.mtq.qm.qld.gov.au; daily 9.30am–5pm; charge ) combines maritime archaeology and the natural history of North Queensland. There's also a beachside playground along the 5km (3-mile) Strand, adjoining Jupiters Casino.

Reef Islands

Magnetic Island is virtually a suburb of Townsville, with many of the island's 2,000 or so permanent residents commuting to work on the mainland by ferry. Being so easy to reach, it's a busy day-trip destination. Most of the island is a national park, busy with birds and other animals (including koalas in the eucalyptus trees), and the choice of beaches is enticing.

The **Great Barrier Reef** runs close to shore in the north of Queensland. Hundreds of islands are scattered across the protected waters between the coral barrier and the mainland, and more than a dozen have been developed into resorts, ranging from spartan to sybaritic. Only two resort islands – **Heron Island** (www.heronisland.com) and **Green Island** (www.greenislandresort.com.au) – are right on the reef itself.

Hinchinbrook Island ⑪ basks in a superlative of its own: 'the world's largest island national park.' A continental rather than coral island, but only 5km (3 miles) from the reef, it encompasses smooth sand beaches, mountains well worth climbing, rainforest, waterfalls and bushland. Day trips to the island depart from Cardwell.

Cairns

The landscape changes from dry to lush as you head north to **Cairns** ⑫,

Tropical Cairns is an ideal base for exploring the Great Barrier Reef

The Kuranda Scenic Railway makes for a charming day trip from Cairns

Townsville's regional rival as Australia's largest tropical city. A port laid out in grid style with huge blocks and extra-wide streets, Cairns has benefited economically from Australia's tourist boom and grown dramatically over the past couple of decades.

In a prominent position on Trinity Inlet is **The Pier** (a shopping and leisure complex), which fronts a large marina from which reef cruises and game-fishing excursions depart. The centrepiece of the waterfront, called the **Esplanade**, is a huge landscaped swimming lagoon. **Cairns Museum** (corner Lake and Shields streets; www.cairnsmuseum.org.au; Mon–Sat 10am–4pm; charge 🏛) has exhibits on the more rough-and-ready past of the area.

Cairns makes an ideal base for diving and cruising the Great Barrier Reef and the city has become Australia's centre for adventure tourism. From hot-air balloon and bungy jumping to skydiving and whitewater rafting, you can do it here.

Kuranda

The mountain town of **Kuranda** is a short distance northwest of Cairns. It is very tourist oriented, with numerous craft shops, galleries, restaurants and markets. The **Original Kuranda Rainforest Market** (daily 9am–3pm; free 🏛) has a wide and varied range of locally designed crafts and artefacts on sale. Kuranda is linked to Cairns by two fascinating transport systems: the wonderfully quaint and picturesque **Kuranda Scenic Railway** (www.ksr.com.au) and the **Skyrail Rainforest Cableway** (www.skyrail.com.au), which transports visitors to Kuranda in six-person aerial gondolas over dense, tangled rainforest.

Port Douglas is the nearest thing to a tropical paradise

The **Tjapukai Aboriginal Cultural Park** (www.tjapukai.com.au; daily 9am–5pm; charge 🅼) at the base of Skyrail is home to the renowned Tjapukai Aboriginal Dance Theatre, which showcases the culture of the rainforest people of Tropical North Queensland.

Port Douglas and Around
Beautiful coastal scenery is the reward along the highway north from Cairns to **Port Douglas** ⑬. The town's palm-fringed **Four Mile Beach** is most people's idea of a tropical paradise. Once a little fishing village, Port Douglas has climbed on the tourism bandwagon, but it's more relaxed than Cairns. **Quicksilver** (www.quicksilver-cruises. com) runs catamaran services to the islands and outer reef.

Popular destinations near Port Douglas are the sugar-milling town of **Mossman**; **Daintree National Park**, with its World Heritage-listed rainforests; and

lovely **Cape Tribulation**, where 'the rainforest meets the reef'. There are also crocodile-spotting boat tours on the Daintree River. The complete packaged rainforest experience can be enjoyed at the **Daintree Discovery Centre** (www. daintree-rec.com.au) a short distance north of the Daintree ferry. Boardwalks wend along the forest floor, and a steel walkway through the canopy provides an entirely different perspective on life as the birds see it.

Cooktown and Cape York
From Mossman it's about 100 hot kilometres (60 miles) north to the like-able river port of **Cooktown** ⑭, where Captain Cook's battered *Endeavour* was beached in 1770. The well-regarded **James Cook Memorial Museum** (corner Helen and Furneaux streets; daily 9.30am–4pm; charge 🅼) exhibits the original anchor of the *Endeavour*, retrieved from the Reef. The Cooktown

cemetery, just north of town, is full of its own stories of the old pioneers.

Beyond Cooktown sprawls the **Cape York Peninsula**, a popular destination for four-wheel-drive expeditions in the dry season. It can take several days to get to Australia's northernmost point, the tip of Cape York, and experience in serious off-road driving is essential. The tiny township of Laura at the southern tip of the **Lakefield National Park** is one of the last accessible spots without a four-wheel-drive vehicle as long as you stay outside the park.

The Queensland Outback

Most of Queensland's key tourist destinations and the majority of the population are to be found on the coast, but it's impossible to get a real handle

In the Mossman rainforest

on the state until you've headed off into the Outback. The **Savannah Way** winds inland from Cairns to Broome in northern Western Australia. The land is vast and there may be hundreds of kilometres between destinations, so keep a keen eye on the fuel gauge.

At **Undara Volcanic National Park** ⓑ you'll find the subterranean wonders of the Undara lava tubes a few kilometres south of the Savannah Way, one of the best examples of lava tube formation anywhere on the planet. The Savannah Way continues on through **George Town**, where there are some significant buildings. The **Terrestrial Centre** (Low Street; www.etheridge.qld.gov.au/web/guest/terrestrial; Apr–Sept daily 9am–5pm, Oct–Mar Mon–Fri 8.30am–4.30pm; charge 🅜) highlights the importance of minerals to the area.

It's another 148km (92 miles) to **Croydon**, a friendly township with a well-preserved timber pub and an interesting historic precinct. From here, an old railway service, the Gulflander, runs through to **Normanton**, just a short distance from the Gulf of Carpentaria.

Towards the border with the Northern Territory, where the terrain is drier and less hospitable, **Lawn Hill Gorge** ⓰ provides a green oasis and stakes a claim to be one of the most spectacularly beautiful locations in the state. Not many get out this far but, for those who do, there are kayaks to paddle between sheer red sandstone cliffs, and easy hikes through the surrounding **Boodjamulla National Park**. A half-hour drive away is the World Heritage-listed Riversleigh Fossils site.

Mining Towns

At **Mount Isa** , learn about mining heritage at **Outback at Isa** (19 Marian Street; www.outbackatisa. com.au; daily 8.30am–5pm; charge), which features various galleries including the **Riversleigh Fossil Centre**. Mount Isa is a mining city truly in the middle of nowhere. A rich lode of lead, silver, copper and zinc was discovered here in 1923, and a tiny tent settlement rapidly developed into Australia's largest company town, dominated by the looming presence of the mine and its tailings.

Cloncurry is also a mining town, and among the attractions in town is **John Flynn Place** (corner Daintree and King streets; www.cloncurry.qld. gov.au/tourism; Mon–Fri 8.30am–4.30pm, May–Sept Sat–Sun 9am–3pm; charge), with a museum devoted to the Royal Flying Doctor Service and its founder *(see p. 154)*.

Matilda Highway

The Matilda Highway heads southeast through **McKinlay**, home of the pub used in the *Crocodile Dundee* films and now rechristened the **Walkabout Creek Hotel**. Some 241km (150 miles) further on sits **Winton**, a town full of character and home to the **Waltzing Matilda Centre** (50 Elderslie Street; www.matildacentre. com.au; daily 9am–5pm; charge), which celebrates the song, its composer 'Banjo' Paterson and all aspects of Outback life. This is also dinosaur country *(see box, right)*.

From Winton the Matilda Highway continues to **Longreach** , home of the **Australian Stockman's Hall of Fame** (Landsborough Highway; www. outbackheritage.com.au; daily 9am–5pm; charge), a fascinating tribute to the cattle drovers, shearers, jackaroos and entrepreneurs who opened up Australia to European settlement.

The Walkabout Creek Hotel shot to fame in *Crocodile Dundee*

Queensland

Barcaldine to the east is notable for its collection of fabulous vintage hotels and pubs, and for the **Workers' Heritage Centre** (www.australianworkers heritagecentre.com.au; Mon–Sat 9am–5pm, Sun 10am–4pm; charge), where heritage structures commemorate the role played by workers in the social and political development of Australia.

The Matilda Highway continues south all the way to **Charleville** ⑲. The usual assortment of historic buildings is worth a look but the points of difference are the **Cosmos Centre** (Qantas Drive; www.cosmos-centre.com; daily 10am–5pm; charge Ⓜ), an observatory and museum which makes the most of clear night skies to host astral viewing sessions, and the **Steiger Gun**, a bizarre device designed in 1902 to fire hot air into the sky in order to create rain.

Heading east through Roma and Miles, with its charming **Miles Historical Village** (Murilla Street; www.mhv.org.au; daily 8am–5pm; charge Ⓜ), would eventually lead you back to the east coast. But that would be to ignore two of Queensland's iconic sites. The **Dig Tree** ⑳, right on the border with South Australia, is the location of the famous base camp of the Burke and Wills expedition, where the two explorers just missed a rendezvous with the men who could have rescued them from starvation and death. The other attraction is the legendary Outback town of **Birdsville**, host of the annual Birdsville races *(see p.147).*

(see p.147).

139

Queensland

Dinosaur Country

Detour south from Winton to **Lark Quarry Dinosaur Trackways** (www.dinosaurtrackways.com.au; tours at 10am, noon, 2pm; charge Ⓜ), where petrified footprints denote a dinosaur encounter millions of years ago.

The theme is maintained in two towns to the north: Richmond has **Kronosaurus Korner** (www.kronosauruskorner.com.au; daily 8.30am–4.45pm; charge Ⓜ), a marine fossil museum; and Hughenden features the **Flinders Discovery Centre** (daily 9am–5pm; charge Ⓜ), with a replica of a dinosaur skeleton found locally. A concrete dinosaur in the middle of town presses the point home. Nearby is the majestic Porcupine Gorge with its 120m (400ft) walls.

ACCOMMODATION

Queensland's coastline is a near-continuous strip of excellent beaches studded with hundreds of holiday resorts. While Brisbane itself has no natural beaches, it is a great base or jumping-off point for exploring the south of Queensland. Cairns in the far north is the direct arrival point for visitors to the Great Barrier Reef and Cape York.

Brisbane

Acacia Inner City Inn
413 Upper Edward Street
Tel: 07-3832 1663
Continental breakfast is inclusive at this friendly inner-city facility with its range of accommodation choices and sociable environment. **$$**

Base Brisbane Central
308 Edward Street
Tel: 07-3211 2433
www.stayatbase.com
Smack-bang opposite Central Station and with everything you need, including the famous Down Under Bar. **$$**

Bowen Terrace
365 Bowen Terrace
Tel: 07-3254 0458
www.bowentceaccommodation.com
With very affordable, quiet and clean budget accommodation, this is a good opportunity to stay in an original timber Queenslander home. **$$**

Brisbane City YHA Hostel
392 Upper Roma Street
Tel: 07-3236 4999
www.yha.com.au
This backpacker-orientated youth hostel in trendy Paddington, close to the city, has excellent facilities. **$$**

Conrad Treasury
William and George streets
Tel: 07-3306 8888
www.conradtreasury.com.au
The Treasury building – which houses Brisbane's casino – is one of the finest 19th-century structures in the city. Choose from a range of rooms and individually decorated suites. **$$$$**

Explorers Inn
63 Turbot Street
Tel: 07-3211 3488
www.explorers.com.au
Budget-style accommodation in the Brisbane CBD, just metres from the Queen Street Mall and a range of bars and restaurants. **$$**

Il Mondo Boutique Hotel
25–35 Rotherham Street, Kangaroo Point
Tel: 07-3392 0111
www.ilmondo.com.au
The rooms and self-contained units at this boutique hotel have been stylishly decorated. **$$$**

The Conrad Treasury occupies one of Brisbane's finest 19th-century buildings

Kangaroo Point Apartments
819 Main Street, Kangaroo Point
Tel: 07-3391 6855
www.kangaroopoint.com
Architect-designed fully self-contained apartments have well-appointed rooms and excellent facilities. **$$$**

The Marque Hotel Brisbane
103 George Street
Tel: 07-3221 6044
www.marquehotels.com
A refurbished 99-room hotel with a distinctive casual elegance, the Marque is a five-minute walk to the Southbank Parkland across the river. **$$$**

Mercure Brisbane
85–87 North Quay
Tel: 07-3237 2300
www.mercurebrisbane.com.au
Perfect if you're looking for comfortable accommodation just a few minutes' walk from the city centre and casino. **$$$**

Quay West Suites Brisbane
132 Alice Street
Tel: 07-3853 6000
www.mirvachotels.com.au
The one- and two-bedroom apartments have balconies for views of the city centre and Botanic Gardens. **$$$$**

Stamford Plaza Hotel
Corner Margaret and Edward Streets
Tel: 07-3221 1999
www.stamford.com.au
Brisbane's finest luxury hotel is in the city centre beside the historic Botanic Gardens. Elegant rooms of generous country-style proportions overlook the winding Brisbane River. **$$$$**

Watermark Hotel Brisbane
551 Wickham Terrace, Spring Hill
Tel: 07-3058 9333
www.watermarkhotelbrisbane.com.au
This up-market hotel with European-style decor is near Roma Street Parkland and the Transit Centre. **$$$$**

Il Mondo Boutique Hotel

The Gold Coast and Hinterland

Binna Burra Mountain Lodge
Beechmont, Lamington National Park
Tel: 07-5533 3622
www.binnaburralodge.com.au
This award-winning eco-accredited lodge is in a World Heritage area with over 160km (100 miles) of hiking tracks. **$$$**

Broadwater Keys Holiday Apartments
125 Frank Street, Labrador
Tel: 07-5531 0839
www.broadwaterkeys.com.au
A skip from the Broadwater, self-contained units here are available on daily and weekly rates. **$$$**

O'Reilly's Rainforest Guest House
Lamington National Park Road, via Canungra
Tel: 07-5502 4911
www.oreillys.com.au
This friendly family-run guesthouse has been providing accommodation, naturalist guide services, touring and special events in this beautiful World Heritage region for over 80 years. **$$$$**

Palazzo Versace
94 Sea World Drive, Main Beach
Tel: 07-5509 8000

Palazzo Versace

www.palazzoversace.com
The world's first hotel designed by Versace – to describe it as over the top would be an understatement. **$$$$$**

Sheraton Mirage Resort and Spa
Sea World Drive, Main Beach
Tel: 07-5591 1488
www.sheraton.com
A low-rise luxury resort with comprehensive health-club facilities. The restaurant here is highly rated. **$$$$**

Vibe Hotel
42 Ferny Avenue, Surfers Paradise
Tel: 07-5539 0444
www.vibehotels.com.au
On the Nerang River, right in the thick of Surfers, Vibe is a refurbished high-rise with a modern makeover. It's spacious, clean and great value for money. **$$$**

Sunshine, Fraser, Capricorn and Whitsunday Coasts

Carnarvon Gorge Wilderness Lodge
Carnarvon Gorge, via Rolleston
Tel: 07-4984 4503
www.carnarvon-gorge.com
Unique timber and canvas safari cabins have their own Outback charm, and make a good base for exploring the gorge with its ancient plant life and fossilised Aboriginal rock art. **$$$$**

Great Keppel Island Holiday Village
Great Keppel Island

Tel: 07-4939 8655
This YHA site offers camping, safari tents and on-site cabins. Book well ahead for this popular location. Facilities include café and shop. **$$$**

Heron Island Resort
Via Gladstone
Tel: 07-4972 9055
www.heronisland.com
A coral cay located right on the Great Barrier Reef and one of the world's top dive sites, the island is a pristine national park, bird sanctuary and turtle rookery. **$$$$$**

Hyatt Regency Coolum Golf Resort & Spa
1 Warran Road, Coolum
Tel: 07-5446 1234
www.coolum.hyatt.com
About 90 minutes' drive north of Brisbane, this championship golf-course resort set in natural bushland with ocean beachfront has its own lifeguard on duty. **$$$$**

Kingfisher Bay Resort and Village
North White Cliffs, Fraser Island
Tel: 07-4194 9300
www.kingfisherbay.com
The only deluxe property on this stunningly beautiful World Heritage-listed island. There are tours to scenic sites, or you can rent a four-wheel drive. **$$$$**

Lady Elliot Island Eco Resort
Tel: 07 5536 3644
www.ladyelliot.com.au
Accessed by light plane only within the Great Barrier Reef Marine Park, Lady Elliot is a take-your-breath-away destination. The range of accommodation includes eco cabins, reef rooms and island suites. **$$$$**

Noosa Blue Resort
16 Noosa Drive, Noosa
Tel: 07-5447 5699
www.noosablue.com.au
A stylish boutique resort perched high on Noosa Hill, with sweeping views of the town's coastline and hinterland. **$$$$**

Whitsunday Islands

Daydream Island Resort and Spa
Tel: 07-4948 8426
www.daydreamisland.com
Family-style resort on a smallish, pretty trop-ical island with a wide range of free activities including an outdoor cinema.  **$$$$**

Hamilton Island
Tel: 07-4946 9999
www.hamiltonisland.com.au
There is a range of room types to choose from at this family-friendly Whitsunday base, which has plenty of facilities and activities. **$$$$**

Hayman Island Resort
Tel: 07-4940 1234
www.hayman.com.au
Hayman Island is a 'total luxury' resort whose modern, three-level complex over-looks a vast pool and the sea. **$$$$$**

Long Island Resort
Tel: 07-4946 9400
www.longislandresort.com.au
Relaxed resort on its own bay with the emphasis on water sports and fun, but offer-ing quiet woodland walks if you want to get away from it all. **$$$$**

North Coast and the Far North

Archipelago Studio Apartments
72 Macrossan Street, Port Douglas
Tel: 07-4099 5387
www.archipelago.com.au
Self-contained apartments right on Macros-san Street and only minutes from Four Mile Beach. **$$$**

Bloomfield Lodge
Tel: 07-4035 9166
www.bloomfieldlodge.com.au
In this remote and beautiful location abut-ting Cape Tribulation National Park, private cabins hidden in the rainforest overlook the Coral Sea. **$$$$**

Cape Trib Beach House
Cape Tribulation Road, Cape Tribulation
Tel: 07-4098 0030

www.capetribbeach.com.au
Dormitory and family cabins as close to the beach as the National Parks Authority will allow. There are kitchen/laundry facilities, a swimming pool and a bistro/bar. **$$$**

Daintree Eco Lodge & Spa
20 Daintree Rd, Daintree
Tel: 07-4098 6100
www.daintree-ecolodge.com.au
Fifteen tranquil villas are on offer in this lux-urious compound set deep in the rainforest. It's a regular fixture on international 'best spa resort' lists. **$$$$$**

Dunk Island
Tel: 07-4047 4740
www.dunk-island.com
Almost completely rainforested, Dunk is good for families, it has a full range of activi-ties, four levels of accommodation and a child-minding facility. Repairs after Cyclone Yasi will see Dunk reopen in 2012.  **$$$**

The Elandra Mission Beach
Tel: 07-4068 8154
www.elandraresorts.com
South of Cairns and surrounded by rainfor-est, with commanding views of Dunk and Bedarra Islands. The spacious verandas look out to sea and a short stroll leads to a private beach. Cyclone Yasi landed here but normality returned within weeks. **$$$$**

Gilligan's Backpackers Hotel & Resort
57–89 Grafton Street, Cairns

Hayman Island Resort

Tel: 07-4041 6566
www.gilligansbackpackers.com.au
This large backpacker resort has plenty of party-style activities to keep you busy, plus comfortable rooms with air conditioning, en suites and balconies. **$$**

Green Island Resort
PO Box 898, Cairns
Tel: 07-4031 3300
www.greenislandresort.com.au
Forty-five minutes by fast catamaran from Cairns, Green Island Resort is a luxury eco-tourist development built on a coral cay. **$$$$**

Hinchinbrook Island Wilderness Lodge
Tel: 07-4066 8270
www.hinchinbrooklodge.com.au
Choose from either the modest cabins located behind the beach or the much more designer-friendly rainforest treetop bunga-lows. **$$$$**

The Lakes Cairns Resort & Spa
2 Greenslopes Street, Cairns
Tel: 07-4053 9411
www.thelakescairns.com.au

Dunk Island

Adjoining the Botanical Gardens and close to the action, Lakes is a well-designed resort in natural surroundings. **$$$**

Island Leisure Resort
Tel: 07-4778 5000
www.islandleisure.com.au
A short ferry ride from Townsville, this family-style resort on Magnetic Island comprises 17 self-contained units in a tropical village garden setting only minutes from the beach. **$$$**

Port O'Call Eco Lodge
Tel: 07-4099 5422
Corner Port Street and Craven Close, Port Douglas
www.portocall.com.au
A good option for budget accommodation, located about 1km (¾ mile) from town. There are four-share and private rooms, cooking facilities, a pool, bar and bistro, and a courtesy bus to and from Cairns. **$$**

Red Mill House
11 Stewart Street, Daintree Village
Tel: 07-4098 6233
www.redmillhouse.com.au
An excellent B&B in an old Queenslander house set in spacious gardens near the Daintree River. **$$$**

Sheraton Port Douglas
Davidson Street, Port Douglas
Tel: 07-4099 5888
www.sheraton-mirage.com.au
The glitziest resort in Port Douglas has all the five-star luxury you can imagine, includ-ing swimmable blue lagoons and an 18-hole international-standard golf course. **$$$$**

Silky Oaks Lodge and Healing Waters Spa
Finlayvale Road, Mossman River Gorge
Tel: 07-4098 1666
www.silkyoakslodge.com.au
Some 27km (17 miles) from Port Douglas, the treehouses and river houses here have all the creature comforts you need, plus a spa and restaurant. **$$$$$**

The Sovereign Resort Hotel
128 Charlotte Street, Cooktown
Tel: 07-4043 0500
www.sovereign-resort.com.au
A relaxed 'plantation-style' resort hotel. The
balcony restaurant and air conditioning are
welcome at the end of a warm day. **$$$**

Yungaburra Pub
6–8 Kehoe Place, Yungaburra
Tel: 07-4095 3515
www.yungaburrapub.com.au
A comfortable base for exploring the rolling
hills of the Atherton Tablelands, the rooms at
this pub are simple but pleasantly decorated.
There's good nosh and friendly staff. **$$**

The Queensland Outback

Albert Park Motor Inn
Matilda Highway, Longreach
Tel: 07-4658 2411
Very comfortable with modern facilities, the
motor inn is within walking distance of the
Stockman's Hall of Fame and the Qantas
Founders' Outback Museum. **$$$**

Undara Lava Lodge
Mount Surprise
Tel: 07-4097 1900
www.undara.com.au
Accommodation is in quaint refurbished
railway carriages on the edge of the Undara
Volcanic National Park. **$$**

RESTAURANTS

Imaginative chefs and terrific local
produce are highlights of Queensland's
dining scene – Brisbane, Noosa and
Port Douglas are home to some of the
country's top fine-dining locations.

> **Restaurants Price Categories**
>
> Prices are for a two-course meal
>
> **$** = below A$20
> **$$** = A$20–45
> **$$$** = A$45–75
> **$$$$** = over A$75

Brisbane

1889 Enoteca
10–12 Logan Road, Woolloongabba
Tel: 07-3392 4315
www.1889enoteca.com.au
Gorgeous Italian food served in a refurbished
shopfront of an 1889 heritage building. **$$$**

Beccofino
10 Vernon Terrace, Newstead
Tel: 07-3666 0207
www.beccofino.com.au
This buzzing Italian restaurant has a great
selection of perfect thin-crust pizzas and
pasta dishes. **$$$**

Buffalo Club
Level 1, corner Wickam and Brunswick
streets, Fortitude Valley
Tel: 07-3216 1323
www.thebuffaloclub.com.au
Abandon yourself to the degustation menu
concocted by chef Ashly Hicks. **$$$$**

Chouquette
19 Barker St, New Farm
Tel: 07-3358 6336
www.chouquette.com.au
A wonderful French boulangerie patisserie
with deliciously authentic flavours. **$**

E'cco
100 Boundary Street (corner Adelaide
Street East)
Tel: 07-3831 8344
www.eccobistro.com
One of Brisbane's finest bistros. Owner-chef
Philip Johnson stresses simplicity, fresh ingre-
dients and unfussy preparation. **$$$$**

Gold Coast

Absynthe
Q1 complex, 9 Hamilton Avenue, Surfers
Paradise
Tel: 07-5504 6466
www.absynthe.com.au
Celebrated French chef Meyjitte Boughenout

Listings

creates taste sensations that are as beguiling as they are unexpected. **$$$$**

Ristorante Fellini
Marina Mirage, Seaworld Drive, Main Beach
Tel: 07-5531 0300
www.fellini.com.au
Brothers Carlo and Tony Percuoco dish up superb Italian cuisine. **$$$**

Sunshine, Fraser, Capricorn and Whitsunday Coasts
Berardo's on the Beach
Hastings Street, Noosa
Tel: 07-5448 0888
www.berardos.com.au
A delightful location for acclaimed chef Bruno Loubet's version of Noosa cuisine. **$$$**

North Coast and the Far North
C Bar Café
Gregory Street Headland, The Strand, Townsville
Tel: 07-4724 0333

Attractively situated on the beachfront, C Bar offers open-air dining with great sea views. **$$**

Nautilus Restaurant
17 Murphy Street, Port Douglas
Tel: 07-4099 5330
www.nautilus-restaurant.com.au
Soak up the tropical ambience and dine under palm trees. **$$$$**

Ochre Restaurant
43 Shields Street, Cairns
Tel: 07-4051 0100
www.ochrerestaurant.com.au
Renowned for its innovative handling of bush tucker and native species; expect smoked wild kangaroo and emu pâté. **$$$**

Sebel Reef House Restaurant
99 Williams Esplanade, Palm Cove
Tel: 07-4055 3633
www.reefhouse.com.au
By day, feast on meze plates; by night, complex cosmopolitan feasts. **$$$$**

NIGHTLIFE AND ENTERTAINMENT

Brisbane has embraced the café/bar scene, with Fortitude Valley and New Farm the hotspots.

The Bowery
676 Ann Street, Fortitude Valley, Brisbane
Tel: 07-3252 0202
Craggy walls and plush banquettes make this converted terrace a cosy place for a drink.

Bar Alto
The Powerhouse, 119 Lamington Street, New Farm
Tel: 07-3358 1063
www.baralto.com.au
Eat, drink and soak up some culture at this multifunction arts venue, which hosts plays, dance, music and art exhibitions at the edgy end of the scale.

Cru Bar and Cellar
22 James Street, Fortitude Valley
Tel: 07-3252 2400
www.crubar.com
Sweeping gold curtains, open-air seating, stellar wine list and great tapas.

Bar Alto

TOURS

There's a huge range of tour operators in Queensland, particularly around the Great Barrier Reef. For more recommended operators, see the Aboriginal Australia and Great Barrier Reef Unique Experience spreads at the front of the book.

Down Under Tours
Tel: 07-4035 5566
www.downundertours.com
Offers a huge range of tours throughout North Queensland, including Cairns day tours, the Atherton Tablelands, Kuranda and Cape Tribulation.

Quicksilver
Tel: 07-4087 2100
www.quicksilver-cruises.com
A fleet of catamarans with cruises to both the Low Isles and the outer edge of the Great Barrier Reef, departing daily from Port Douglas and Cairns.

Undara Experience
Tel: 1800-990 992

Exploring the Great Barrier Reef

www.undara.com.au
A range of Savannah outback tours including a visit to the spectacular Undara National Park lava tubes and the chance to sleep in a restored railway carriage.

Wavelength
Tel: 07-4099 5031
www.wavelength.com.au
Ecotourism operator specialising in small-group snorkelling tours.

FESTIVALS AND EVENTS

Queensland isn't as festival-focused as its southern neighbours – the locals are too busy enjoying the year-round sun and surf to take time out for too many cultural activities. That said, there are still a few headline events.

June
Brisbane Pride Festival
www.pridebrisbane.org.au
Gay and lesbian cultural festival.

August
Australian-Italian Festival
www.australianitalianfestival.com.au
One of northern Queensland's biggest events, held in Ingham near Townsville.

Cairns Festival
www.festivalcairns.com.au

Arts, music, dance and theatre take centre stage at this annual festival.

September
Brisbane Festival
www.brisbanefestival.com.au
A three-week arts and culture festival, with music, dance, theatre and visual events.

Birdsville Races
www.birdsvilleraces.com
Annual racing event held to raise money for the Royal Flying Doctor Service.

Northern Territory

The Northern Territory is Australia in epic mode. Everything here is huge – the sky, the temperatures, the distances, the natural features. Even the locals are larger than life: weather-beaten, tough as old boots (as a local saying goes), laconic, egalitarian and true believers that humour is the most important human virtue (the ability to sink a few stubbies – local parlance for enjoying a few beers – comes in a close second).

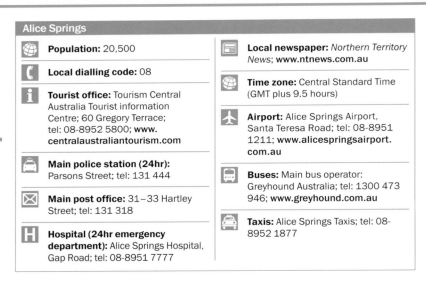

Alice Springs

Population: 20,500

Local dialling code: 08

Tourist office: Tourism Central Australia Tourist information Centre; 60 Gregory Terrace; tel: 08-8952 5800; www.centralaustraliantourism.com

Main police station (24hr): Parsons Street; tel: 131 444

Main post office: 31–33 Hartley Street; tel: 131 318

Hospital (24hr emergency department): Alice Springs Hospital, Gap Road; tel: 08-8951 7777

Local newspaper: *Northern Territory News*; www.ntnews.com.au

Time zone: Central Standard Time (GMT plus 9.5 hours)

Airport: Alice Springs Airport, Santa Teresa Road; tel: 08-8951 1211; www.alicespringsairport.com.au

Buses: Main bus operator: Greyhound Australia; tel: 1300 473 946; www.greyhound.com.au

Taxis: Alice Springs Taxis; tel: 08-8952 1877

Despite its size, the Northern Territory ('The Territory' or NT) fits neatly into a travel itinerary. There is the 'Red Centre' – Alice Springs and the stunning hinterland in the Territory's south; various points along 'The Track' (the Stuart Highway) heading north; and the 'Top End', Darwin, Kakadu and surroundings. The distance between points of interest can be intimidating – roughly 1,600km (1,000 miles) from Alice to Darwin – but only by driving through the Territory do you get a true sense of its grand and ancient terrain.

Alice Springs and the Red Centre

Australia's Red Centre is the heart of the country in more ways than one. Owing its name to the local sand and rock, coloured red by naturally occurring iron oxides, it is home to the continent's greatest natural feature, Uluru (Ayers Rock), as well as the fabled Outback town of Alice Springs ('Alice').

Uluru (Ayers Rock)

Australia's great Outback icon, **Uluru** ❶ was World Heritage-listed for its natural significance in 1987, and for its cultural significance in 1994. Located in the **Uluru-Kata Tjuta National Park** (www.environment.gov.au/parks/uluru; daily dawn–dusk; charge for a three-day pass), its name means 'meeting place', and many Aboriginal Dreaming tracks or 'songlines' intersect here. The rock's traditional owners are the Anangu people, who believe that the rock is too sacred to climb and ask visitors not to do so.

An alternative to climbing is the 10.6-km (6½-mile) Uluru Base Walk around the rock, which is well marked. A self-guiding brochure is available from the cultural centre and numerous interpretive signs are displayed.

Kata Tjuta has a number of excellent trails

World Heritage-listed Uluru is Australia's great Outback icon

While more walks in the rock's vicinity are scheduled, **Kata Tjuta (The Olgas)** ❷ has a number of excellent trails, including the three-hour Valley of the Winds circuit. Climbing Kata Tjuta (which means 'many heads', referring to the 36 domes) is not permitted and, just in case you get the urge to take home any souvenir rocks or sand, bear in mind that it is disrespectful to Aboriginal beliefs and that park authorities receive, on average, two letters a week from visitors returning rocks they had taken, claiming that their luck has been bad ever since their stay in Uluru.

Visitors to the national park are serviced by the award-winning **Yulara Resort**. A wide range of tours and activities is available from the resort (see p.167).

Uluru to Alice

Travelling north along the Stuart Highway to Alice Springs offers a number of worthwhile detours, including kaleidoscopic **Rainbow Valley** (www.nt.gov.au/nreta/parks/find/rainbowvalley.html), a stunning

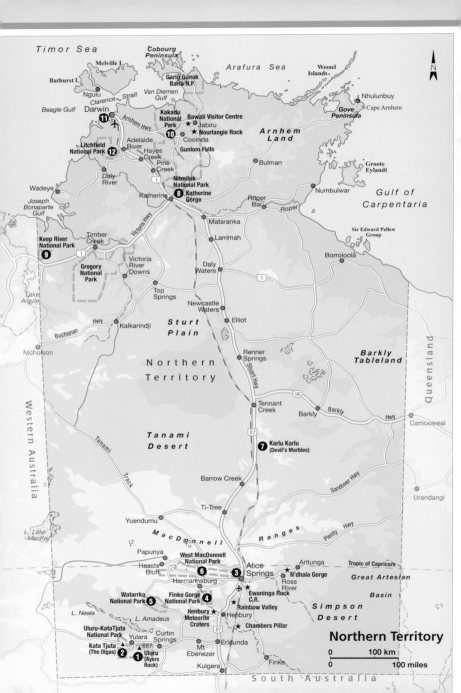

was caused by four meteors, each the size of a 200-litre (44-gallon) drum. The craters have become occasional pools, sprouting plants and attracting a variety of animal life.

Alice Springs

The natural base for exploring the Red Centre is **Alice Springs** ❸. It is a grid-patterned, sun-scorched town of squat, mostly modern buildings, which crouches in one of many gaps (or Outback oases) in the rugged Mac-Donnell Ranges. These hills – which turn an intense blue at sunset, as if lit internally – act like a wagon train, a protective ring that might just keep the expanse of the Outback at bay.

By no means a picture-postcard town, Alice none the less has strange powers of attraction: visitors find themselves drawn again and again to this incongruous outpost, and many who come here for short-term work wake up 10 years later and wonder what happened.

White settlement began here in 1871 in the form of a repeater station on the Overland Telegraph Line, constructed beside the permanent freshwater springs. The telegraph line ran from Adelaide through Alice and up to Darwin, linking the cities of Australia's south and southeast with the rest of the world, as it continued from Darwin through Indonesia to Singapore, Burma, British India and across Asia and Europe to colonial headquarters in London. It's still possible to see some of the

151

Northern Territory

rock formation, and **Chambers Pillar** (www.nt.gov.au/nreta/parks/find/chamberspillar.html), a solitary upstanding red ochre outcrop inscribed with the names and dates of early explorers, who used it as a convenient landmark.

The Aboriginal rock carvings at **Ewaninga** (www.nt.gov.au/nreta/parks/find/ewaningarock.html) are of undetermined age. Cryptic and alluring, they are best viewed in early morning or late afternoon.

The **Henbury Meteorite Craters** (www.nt.gov.au/nreta/parks/find/henbury.html), just off the highway, consist of 12 indentations, about 5,000 years old, the biggest of which (180m/590ft wide by 15m/49ft deep)

original telegraph posts, now disused, rising from the hard earth at the **Telegraph Station Historical Reserve** (www.nt.gov.au/nreta/parks/find/astelegraphstation.html; daily 8am–5pm; tours daily; tel: 08-8952 3993 for times). The township owes its name to a small spring near the station buildings.

Alice developed slowly; in 1925, it had just 200 residents. Four years later, the arrival of the *Ghan* train service – which at that time ran from Adelaide via Oodnadatta to Alice and is named after Afghan camel drivers who pioneered transport in these parts – saw things pick up, but the trip was fraught with hazards. In the mistaken belief that the Outback never flooded, the track was routed across low-lying terrain; consequently, the train was often stranded in nowheresville, with additional supplies having to be parachuted in to the hapless passengers. A new, flood-proof route was completed in 1980, and the *Ghan* remains one of Australia's great rail journeys (see p.51). In 2004 an Alice–Darwin 1,420-km (880-mile) extension to the line was completed.

In Alice, most visitors spend their first sunset on Anzac Hill to get the lie of the land. Popular tourist attractions include the **Royal Flying Doctor Service Visitors' Centre** (see p.155) and the **Alice Springs School of the Air** (80 Head Street; www.assoa. nt.edu.au; Mon–Sat 8.30am–4.30pm, Sun 1.30–4.30pm; charge). The school, unique in the world, conducts primary-level classes for far-flung children via radio, and the most notable of its 26 bases across the Outback is in Alice, covering an area of 1.3 million sq km (500,000 sq miles). It is the world's

The famous *Ghan* train links Alice Springs with Adelaide

The Alice Springs School of the Air is a unique attraction

biggest classroom, and visitors here during school hours are able to view lessons being taught.

The Alice Springs Desert Park (Larapinta Drive; www.alicesprings desertpark.com.au; daily 7.30am–6pm; charge), situated just outside Alice at the base of the MacDonnell Ranges, is a must-see primer for anyone about to explore the desert. Its 35 hectares (86 acres) contain 320 arid-zone plant species and more than 400 desert-dwelling animals. The birds of prey nature theatre, where wild birds interact with park rangers, is unforgettable.

The Araluen Cultural Precinct (corner Larapinta Drive and Memorial Avenue; www.araluenartscentre. nt.gov.au; Mon–Fri 10am–4pm, Sat–Sun 11am–4pm; charge), on Larapinta Drive, comprises the Strehlow Research Centre, the Museum of Central Australia, the Central Australian Aviation Museum, the Araluen Arts Centre, the Central Craft studio and shop, and the Albert Namatjira

Gallery. The site is home to seven registered sacred sites and trees of significance that are important to the local indigenous Arrernte people. Visitors particularly interested in Aboriginal culture can take a guided Cultural Art Tour *(see p.166)*.

Around Alice

To the south is **Finke Gorge National Park** ❹ (www.nt.gov.au/nreta/parks/find/finkegorge.html), featuring the picturesque Palm Valley, with its distinctive red cabbage palms, and the Finke River, whose watercourse is one of the oldest in the world at 350 million years in some areas.

Due west of here is one of Central Australia's star attractions – spectacular Kings Canyon in **Watarrka National Park** ❺ (www.nt.gov.au/nreta/parks/

Northern Territory

Albert Namatjira

Albert (Elea) Namatjira (1902–59) was the most important Aboriginal artist of the early 20th century. Born and educated on the Hermannsburg Lutheran Mission near Alice Springs, he was a member of the Arrernte people and became well known for his watercolour paintings of the MacDonnell Ranges, reproductions of which were ubiquitous in suburban homes throughout Australia in the 1950s. His fame led to he and his wife Rubina being granted the right to vote, own land and build a house in 1957, five years before these basic human rights were granted to Indigenous Australians in Queensland and Western Australia and two years before they were applied in the other states and territories.

★ THE ROYAL FLYING DOCTOR SERVICE

Examine the Australian $20 note and on one side you'll see the depiction of a gentle-looking man wearing glasses – this is the Reverend John Flynn, founder of a service that epitomises true Aussie Outback spirit: the Royal Flying Doctor Service (RFDS). Operating 21 bases throughout the country and flying 53 aircraft, the RFDS attends to the medical needs of over 700 patients every day and provides around 100 of these with aeromedical evacuations from remote locations to medical centres.

John Flynn (1880–1951) lived in the Outback for most of his life, setting up hostels and bush hospitals for pastoralists, miners, road workers, railwaymen and other settlers. In the Outback of that time, just two doctors provided the only medical care for an area of almost 2 million sq km (772,204 sq miles).

In 1917, Flynn received a letter from Lieutenant Clifford Peel, a Victorian medical student with an interest in aviation. The young airman suggested the use of aviation to bring medical help to the Outback. Shot down in France, he died at just 19 years of age and never knew that his

A glimpse inside a Royal Flying Doctor Service aircraft

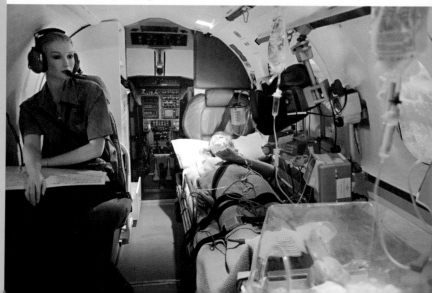

letter was to become a blueprint for the creation of the RFDS.

Flynn campaigned tirelessly for Peel's vision to be adopted, and in 1927 Qantas and the Aerial Medical Service signed an agreement to operate an aerial ambulance from Cloncurry, Queensland. The first plane – a De Havilland named *Victory* – took off on 17 May 1928, with a pilot and medical doctor on board.

Back in those days, not much territory was charted, so RFDS pilots were forced to navigate by river beds, fences, telegraph lines and other familiar landmarks. Despite these obstacles, in its inaugural year, the Aerial Medical Service (which changed its name to the Flying Doctor Service in 1942 and the Royal Flying Doctor Service in 1955) flew 50 flights to 26 destinations and treated 225 patients.

It is impossible to overestimate the importance of this service to isolated communities and cattle stations across the length and breadth of the Australian Outback. To gain an understanding of its history and role, visit the **Royal Flying Doctor Service Visitors' Centre** (tours every half hour Mon–Sat 9am–5pm, Sun 1–5pm; charge) in Alice Springs. There are also visitor centres in Mt Isa, Queensland (11 Barkley Highway; Mon–Fri 9.30am–4.30pm; donation), Broken Hill, NSW (Mon–Fri 9am–5pm, Sat–Sun 10am–3pm; charge) and John Flynn Place in Cloncurry (see p.138).

John Flynn's grave is 7km (4 miles) west of Alice Springs on Larapinta Drive.

At the Royal Flying Doctor Service Visitors' Centre

John Flynn established the Royal Flying Doctor Service in 1928

Spectacular Kings Canyon is some 350 million years old

find/watarrka.html). The 350-million-year-old canyon shelters a permanent rockpool, aptly named the Garden of Eden and visited during the magnificent four-hour Canyon Walk.

Alice to Katherine

This section of the Stuart Highway passes through the magnificent MacDonnell Ranges, parallel ridges running to the east and west of Alice Springs. The ranges feature spectacular gaps and gorges as well as many culturally significant Aboriginal sites. They often featured in the paintings of Aboriginal artist Albert Namatjira (*see box, p.153*).

Stretching west from Alice is the **West MacDonnell National Park** ❻ (www.nt.gov.au/nreta/parks/find/westmacdonnell.html), incorporating many of the gaps in the ranges. These include Simpson's Gap, accessible via an excellent cycle path from Alice; Standley Chasm, whose steep walls become alive with colour an hour either side of midday; Serpentine Gorge; the Ochre Pits, used by Aborigines for centuries; Ormiston Gorge and Pound, with some fine walking trails; Glen Helen Gorge, with a comfortable lodge nearby; and Redbank Gorge. A 223km (138-mile) walking track, the Larapinta Trail, constructed by local prisoners, connects many of the attractions of the MacDonnells.

Heading north from Alice for approximately 400km (249 miles), one comes to the tiny community of Barrow Creek. Nearby is **Karlu Karlu** ❼ (The Devil's Marbles Conservation Reserve; www.nt.gov.au/nreta/parks/find/devilsmarbles.html), a series of granite boulders that litter either side of the highway for several kilometres. The local Aboriginal people believe them to be the eggs of the rainbow serpent.

Tennant Creek (504km/313 miles from Alice) was the site of

Australia's last great gold rush in the 1930s, and the precious metal is still mined here. To the north, the tiny township of **Renner Springs** marks a geographical and climatic end to the long, dry journey through the Red Centre: this is the southern extremity of the monsoon-affected plains of the Top End.

The Daly Waters Pub (Stuart Street; www.dalywaterspub.com; daily 7am–late) about 400km (249 miles) further north is worth a pause for a drink and rest. Built in the 1930s as a staging post for Qantas crew and passengers on multi-hop international flights, it is full of related memorabilia.

Katherine, 270km (168 miles) up the Stuart Highway, has a well-developed infrastructure of shops, campsites, hotels and motels. To the east of the township, **Nitmiluk (Katherine Gorge) National Park ❽** (www.

nt.gov.au/nreta/parks/find/nitmiluk. html) is a 1,800-sq km (695-sq mile) park that has as its centrepiece a massive stretch of sandstone cliffs rising to more than 100m (330 ft) above the Katherine River, with 13 main canyons. The gorge is best explored by water. Tour boats (charge) operate two-hour cruises on the lower two canyons, and the third gorge is included in the half-day safari on offer. The more inquisitive traveller can explore the other 10 gorges upstream by hiring a canoe.

From Katherine the Victoria Highway strikes west towards the Kimberley region of Western Australia. Just before the WA border, there is a turn-off to **Keep River National Park ❾** (www.nt.gov.au/nreta/parks/find/keepriver.html), which features a series of fascinating banded sandstone towers that shelters a wide range of vegetation and animal life.

The Devil's Marbles

Best Bushwalks

The best way to explore the Northern Territory's many national parks and reserves is by taking a bushwalk. The best include:

- **Canyon Walk**, Watarrka National Park (see p.156)
- **Jatbula Trail**, Nitmiluk (Katherine Gorge) National Park (see above)
- **Larapinta Trail**, West MacDonnell National Park (see p.156)
- **Tabletop Track**, Litchfield National Park (see p.161)
- **Twin Falls Plateau Walk**, Kakadu National Park (see p.160)
- **Valley of the Winds Circuit**, Uluru-Kata Tjuta National Park (see p.161)

The Top End

This is the top 25 percent of the Territory, where monsoonal rains and tropical cyclones reign during the Wet season (Nov–Mar) and nights can be chilly in the Dry season (Apr–Oct). Both extremes bring compensations, though: the national parks and reserves teem with bird and animal life during the Wet, as it's called, and days are warm and mild during most of the Dry.

Kakadu

One of the brightest jewels in the whole array of Australian wilderness lies to the north of Katherine, at the World Heritage-listed **Kakadu National Park ⑩** (www.environment. gov.au/parks/kakadu; charge for a three-day pass). The park's prime accommodation and commercial centre is Jabiru, 250km (155 miles) southeast of Darwin. The richness of Kakadu defies description. Here, where the Arnhem Land escarpment meets the coastal floodplains, scenic splendour, ancient Aboriginal culture and paintings and an incredible array of flora and fauna merge in a brilliant, coherent whole.

The statistics give some indication of what this area has to offer. The park covers 19,804 sq km (7,200 sq miles) and is home to a quarter of all Australian freshwater fish, over 1,000 plant species, 300 types of birds, 75 species of reptiles, many mammals and innumerable insects. Its world-famous galleries of Aboriginal art – particularly at Nourlangie and Ubirr rocks – give a significant insight into early humankind more than 20,000 years ago.

Visitors can take a boat or four-wheel-drive tour, or a scenic fixed-wing or helicopter flight (see p.167). The boat tours are highly recommended, as they offer the finest natural wildlife viewing anywhere in Australia. Participants are likely to

Monsoonal rains and tropical cyclones rule the Top End during the Wet season

Taking the plunge in Kakadu National Park

see saltwater crocodiles, Jabiru storks, brolga cranes and a host of water birds, resident and migratory – but only during the Dry. During the Wet, when water is plentiful, the animals disperse across the region, and successful viewing is more haphazard.

The splendid **Bowali Visitor Centre** (daily 8am–5pm) has a permanent display on the park's features, including a 30-minute audiovisual presentation. The **Warradjan Aboriginal Cultural Centre** (daily 9am–5pm) provides detailed information about the local Bininj/Mungguy culture.

Kakadu's most famous features are the water holes nestling at the base of the escarpment. The most popular conjunction of swimming hole and waterfall is **Jim Jim Falls**. The deep, cool pool and the nearby sandy beach

Darwin

 Population: 125,000

 Local dialling code: 08

 Tourist office: Darwin Visitor Centre; 6 Bennett Street; tel: 08-8980 6000; www.tourismtopend.com.au

 Main police station (24hr): Mitchell Centre, corner Mitchell and Knuckey Streets; tel: 13 14 44

 Main post office: 48 Cavenaugh Street; tel: 131 318

 Hospital (24hr emergency department): Royal Darwin Hospital; Rocklands Drive, Tiwi; tel: 08-8922 8888; www.health.nt.gov.au/hospitals/royal_darwin_hospital

 Local newspaper: *Northern Territory News;* www.ntnews.com.au

 Time zone: Central Standard Time (GMT plus 9.5 hours)

 Airport: Darwin International Airport, Marrara; tel: 08-8920 1811; www.darwinairport.com.au

 Buses: Main bus operator: Greyhound Australia, tel: 1300 473 946, www.greyhound.com.au. Long-distance buses arrive at/leave from the Darwin Transit Centre (69 Mitchell Street)

 Taxis: Darwin Radio Taxis, tel: 13 10 08

Darwin is the cosmopolitan Territory capital

Visiting the Tiwi Islands

These two islands (Bathurst and Melville) 80km (50 miles) north of Darwin are famous for their indigenous art and devotion to the Australian Rules footy code. The islands can be visited on an organised day tour by boat or plane (see p.167). Those particularly interested in art should be sure not to miss Lamara Arts & Crafts at Milikapiti and Munupi Arts & Crafts at Pirlangimpi (both on Melville Island) and Tiwi Design at Nguiu on Bathurst Island.

are remarkably attractive and have the distinct benefit of being easy to visit, at least when the access road is open (June–Nov). Effort is well rewarded for those who decide to walk into nearby **Twin Falls**, where the two strands of water drop right onto the end of a palm-shaded beach. However, don't swim here – it's crocodile territory. Both Jim Jim and Twin Falls turn into seething maelstroms during wet-season flooding, at which time they are inaccessible to anyone without a helicopter.

Darwin

The Territory's capital, **Darwin** ⑪, was founded in 1869, after more than 40 years of failed settlements in the north – abandoned one after another because of malaria outbreaks, cyclones, Aboriginal attacks and supply failure due to the sheer distance from the other white settlements. It was named after Charles Darwin, one of whose shipmates on the *Beagle* discovered the bay in 1839.

The town remained a relaxed tropical outpost until February 1942, when some 243 people were killed and another 300 injured in a surprise Japanese bombing attack – grippingly evoked in Baz Lurhmann's 2008 film *Australia*. Darwin suffered repeated raids over the following 18 months so was forced to rebuild itself in the postwar period, growing relatively fast as a result of migration from within Australia and the region. Today's Darwin is a cosmopolitan mix of some 50 cultures including Aborigines, Vietnamese, Filipinos, Malays, New Guineans, Pacific Islanders, Japanese, Indonesians and European Australians. Perhaps the best way to appreciate this multiethnic mix is to visit the **Mindil Beach Sunset Market** ⓐ (www. mindil.com.au), held every Thursday and Sunday evening from April to October, with stalls selling foods from around the world and handmade craft including crocodile products, indigenous art and jewellery.

The city's built heritage is scant, the 1883 **Fannie Bay Gaol Museum** ⓑ (East Point Road; daily 10am–3pm; free) being one of the few 19th-century buildings to survive a devastating cyclone in 1974. The gaol stands in stark contrast to Darwin's sleek new cyclone-proof architecture, represented by the city's high-rise hotels, Darwin City Waterfront Development, Sky City Casino and Parliament House.

The **Museum and Art Gallery of the Northern Territory** Ⓒ (Conacher Street, Fannie Bay; Mon–Fri 9am–5pm; Sat–Sun 10am–5pm; free) has one of the world's best collections of Aboriginal art and cultural artefacts, as well as archaeological finds from the Pacific region.

For six months of the year Darwin Harbour becomes the playground of the area's boating populace. Many people swim here, even though huge saltwater crocodiles are regularly pulled from the water. It may be more relaxing to swim safely alongside

crocs in the 'Cage of Death' at **Crocosaurus Cove** (58 Mitchell Street; www.crocosauruscove.com; daily 9am–7pm; charge). Alternatively, head 15km (9 miles) from the centre of town to **Crocodylus Park** (815 McMillans Road, Berrimah; www.crocodyluspark.com; daily 9am–5pm; charge), where you can come face to face with these huge reptiles.

Litchfield National Park

A two-hour drive to the southwest of Darwin is **Litchfield National Park** ⑫ (www.nt.gov.au/nreta/parks/find/litchfield.html), 153 sq km (59 sq miles) of sandstone plateau with pockets of rainforest. It is one of the best areas in the Top End for bushwalking, but is even more popular for its waterfalls and pools, which provide excellent swimming.

161

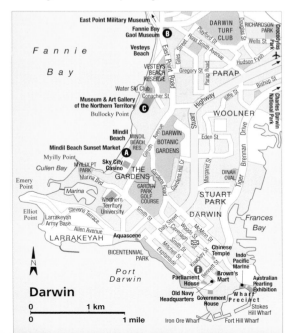

Out for a drive off the Darwin coast

ACCOMMODATION

Known for its luxury lodges and backpacker hostels, The Territory is relatively light on good mid-range options – and those that are on offer tend to fill up quickly. Keep in mind that hotel rates are significantly higher in the Dry season than in the Wet, particularly in the Top End.

The Red Centre

The only accommodation at Uluru (Ayers Rock) is at the overpriced Ayers Rock Resort (www.ayersrockresort.com.au) in the settlement of Yulara, 20km (12 miles) from Uluru and 53km (33 miles) from Kata Tjuta, or at the even-more-pricey Longitude 131 Camp, 9km (6 miles) from Uluru.

Longitude 131
Yulara
Tel: 02-8296 8010
www.longitude131.com.au
A line of individual tents forms the accommodation of this luxurious eco-resort. Guest numbers are restricted to 30 at a time. **$$$$$**

Outback Pioneer Hotel and Lodge
Yulara Drive, Yulara
Tel: 02-8296 8010
www.ayersrockresort.com.au
The cheapest Yulara option, offering dorm beds in the Lodge and simple rooms

with or without bathrooms in the hotel. **$$–$$$$**

Sails in the Desert Hotel
Yulara Drive, Yulara
Tel: 02-8296 8010
www.ayersrockresort.com.au
The premier hotel at Yulara, famous for its soaring white 'sails' which shelter outdoor areas from the intense desert sun. **$$$$$**

Alice Springs and Around

Annie's Place
4 Traeger Avenue
Tel: 08-8952 1545
www.anniesplace.com.au
Annie's double rooms and six- or eight-bed dorms all have bathrooms. This is Alice's rowdiest backpacker joint – only stay here if you want to party. **$–$$**

Chifley Alice Springs Resort
34 Stott Terrace
Tel: 08-8951 4545
www.alicespringsresort.com.au
Five minutes' walk to town, this resort offers comfortable rooms, a palm-fringed pool area and a seafood restaurant. **$$–$$$**

Desert Rose Inn
15 Railway Terrace
Tel: 08-8952 1411
www.desertroseinn.com.au
Choose between budget rooms with shower and handbasin or rooms with full en suite. There's a pool, communal kitchen and lounge, and free Wi-fi. **$$**

Sails in the Desert Hotel

Crowne Plaza Alice Springs
82 Barrett Drive
Tel: 08-8950 8000
www.ichotelsgroup.com
This low-rise luxury resort has spectacular views of the MacDonnell ranges and the reputation for being the town's best accommodation option. **$$$–$$$$**

Kings Canyon Resort
Luritja Road, Watarrka National Park
Tel: 03-9413 6288
www.kingscanyonresort.com.au
Six kilometres (4 miles) from the spectacular canyon, this huge facility provides campsites, rooms and plenty of eating options. **$–$$$**

Pioneer Youth Hostel
Corner of Parsons Street and Leichhardt Terrace
Tel: 08-8952 8855
www.yha.com.au
Guests can watch nightly films on the huge outdoor screen in this YHA hostel, which was built within the walls of a Heritage-classed outdoor cinema. **$–$$**

Alice to Katherine
Maud Creek Lodge
Gorge Road, Katherine
Tel: 08-8971 0877
www.maudecreeklodge.com.au
Managed by Aboriginal-owned company Nitmiluk Tours, this peaceful 80-hectare (198-acre) property 6km (4 miles) from Katherine Gorge offers comfortable lodge rooms and one self-contained cottage. **$$$**

The Top End
Botanic Gardens Apartments
17 Geranium Street, The Gardens, Darwin
Tel: 08-8946 0300
www.botanicgardens.com.au
High on a hill overlooking the Botanic Gardens and the Arafura Sea, this centrally located, peaceful complex offers motel rooms and self-contained apartments.  **$$$$**

Maud Creek Lodge

Darwin City B&B
4 Zealandia Crescent, Larrakeyah, Darwin
Tel: 08-8941 3636
www.darwinbnb.com.au
This private, quiet B&B is close to shops, tourist facilities, the Mindil Beach Market and the Botanic Gardens. Hosts Janette and Roger are knowledgeable long-term Territorians. **$$–$$$**

Gagudju Crocodile Holiday Inn
1 Flinders Street, Jabiru
Tel: 08-8979 9000
www.gagudju-dreaming.com/gagudju-crocodile-holiday-inn
Shaped like a giant crocodile, with the swimming pool as its stomach, this Aboriginal-owned operation offers the only deluxe accommodation in the Kakadu National Park. **$$$**

Gagudju Lodge Cooinda
Kakadu Highway, Jim Jim
Tel: 08-8979 0145
www.gagudjulodgecooinda.com.au
Situated on the Yellow Water Billabong in Kakadu National Park, this popular Aboriginal-owned place comprises campsites, dorm rooms and 48 private bungalows. **$–$$$**

Lakeview Park
27 Lakeside Drive, Jabiru
Tel: 08-8979 3144
www.lakeviewkakadu.com.au
Lakeview Park has self-contained tropical-style rooms and cabins set in beautiful gardens, as well as basic bush bungalows.
$$–$$$

Melaleuca on Mitchell
52 Lindsay Street, Darwin
Tel: 08-8941 7800
www.melaleucaonmitchell.com.au
Party central, with a rooftop leisure deck comprising two pools, waterfall spa, bar, big-screen TV, self-catering kitchen and pool table. Rooms and dorms are bland but serviceable. **$–$$**

Novotel Atrium Darwin
100 The Esplanade, Darwin
Tel: 08-8941 0755

Darwin City B&B

www.noveldarwin.com.au
Overlooking the harbour and a short walk from the city centre, the Novotel has an indoor tropical rainforest and spacious hotel rooms.
$$$–$$$$

RESTAURANTS

The Northern Territory isn't really a gourmet destination, but its cuisine is quite unique. Specialities include barramundi, buffalo, kangaroo, emu, crocodile and camel, often served in burger or steak form and seasoned with native berries and herbs. Outside the main cities of Darwin and Alice Springs, you'll find most of the good restaurants are located in resorts.

Restaurants Price Categories
Prices are for a two-course meal
$ = below A$20
$$ = A$20–45
$$$ = A$45–75
$$$$ = over A$75

The Red Centre
Kuniya
Sails in the Desert Hotel, Yulara
Tel: 08-8957 7888
The poshest eatery in town, with a sophisticated decor and menu inspired by local native ingredients. **$$$$**

Sounds of Silence
Yulara
www.ayersrockresort.com.au
Enjoy a BBQ dinner accompanied by Australian wines and beers under the Outback's magnificent starry sky,
accompanied by a commentary from a 'startalker' who will take you on a visual tour of the heavens. Includes transfers and drinks. **$$$$**

Alice Springs
Hanuman Restaurant
Crowne Plaza Hotel, 82 Barrett Drive
Tel: 08-8953 7188
www.hanuman.com.au
The sister restaurant to Hanuman's in Darwin serves similarly impressive Thai and Indian dishes. A fine-dining experience in a desert setting. **$$$**

Overlanders Steakhouse
72 Hartley Street
Tel: 08-8952 2159
www.overlanders.com.au
Carnivore heaven, with huge steaks of beef, kangaroo, crocodile and emu on offer. The signature dish is the 'Drover's Blowout', four true-blue Aussie courses including favourites such as damper, rump steak or barramundi fillet and pavlova. **$$$**

Red Ochre Grill
Todd Mall
Tel: 08-8952 9614
www.redochrealice.com.au
Outback meats, seafood and bush foods feature on the menu of this popular restaurant. **$$$**

The Top End
Buzz Café
48 Marina Boulevard, Cullen Bay, Darwin
Tel: 08-8941 1141
Overlooking the splendid turquoise waters of the Cullen Bay marina along a boardwalk of fine retaurants, this stylish bar/restaurant is the perfect venue for a long lunch. **$$**

Char Restaurant
Admiralty House, corner The Esplanade and Knuckey Street, Darwin
Tel: 08-8981 4544
www.charrestaurant.com.au
Located in the former navy HQ, Char serves high-quality steak in an outdoor setting among magnificent fig trees and frangipani. Superb inner-city location. **$$$**

Ducks Nuts Bar and Grill
76 Mitchell Street, Darwin
Tel: 08-8942 2122
www.ducksnuts.com.au
Is it a bar? Or an all-day alfresco restaurant? Perhaps it's a music venue? Or maybe it's best described as a café-patisserie? Whatever the answer, you're sure to find something to tempt your palate at this popular place. Meals are good value, with plentiful servings. **$$**

Hanuman
93 Mitchell Street, Darwin
Tel: 08-8941 3500
www.hanuman.com.au
Sitting on Hanuman's outdoor deck and savouring its highly spiced, superbly presented Indian and Thai dishes is a wonderful way to spend a balmy Darwin evening, particularly when the food, renowned for its consistent quality, is accompanied by choices from the excellent, if pricey, wine list. **$$$**

Pee Wee's at the Point
Alec Fong Lim Drive, East Point Reserve, Darwin
Tel: 08-8981 6868
www.peewees.com.au
Alfresco dining on the shores of Fannie Bay. Darwin's most up-market restaurant with prices and exotic menu to match. The place for that special occasion. Essential to book. **$$$**

The Roma Bar
9–11 Cavanagh Street, Darwin
Tel: 08-8981 6729
www.romabar.com.au
Aficionados claim that this long-standing favourite serves the best coffee in the city. Its breakfast menu is particularly delicious. **$**

Shenannigans
69 Mitchell Street, Darwin
Tel: 08-8981 2100
www.shenannigans.com.au
Another old-style, rambling pub with a crowded beer menu and fair-quality food in cheerful outdoor setting. The kind of middle-ranking pub that fills rapidly on Friday nights; music and dancing on Friday and Saturday. Always busy. **$**

Vietnam Saigon Star
Darwin Central, 60 Smith Street, Darwin
Tel: 08-8981 1420
Bargain prices and the tastiest Vietnamese cuisine in the Territory make this an attractive eating option. **$**

NIGHTLIFE AND ENTERTAINMENT

Entertainment in the Northern Territory is inextricably linked with drinking alcohol (often to excess). Darwin pubs are popular meeting places for the locals, with a varied nightlife ranging from rowdy live-band performances to the relative sophistication of imported casino entertainers. Although the city's hard-drinking, macho/sexist culture is on the wane, pubs are still the centre of social life. A good start is the Tourist & Entertainment Precinct, running the length of Mitchell Street. There are also a handful of acceptable options in Alice Springs and at least one watering hole in every town. Some pubs offer live music – usually of the country and western variety – but other than this, pool tables and slot machines are about the only entertainment options on offer.

TOURS

There are innumerable tours and organised activities on offer in the Territory's spectacular national parks and reserves. Check the Tourism NT website (http://en.travelnt.com) for details or contact the following companies.

Ananguwai Tours
Tel: 08-8950 3030
www.ananguwaaai.com.au
This Alice-based company is Aboriginal-owned and -operated. It offers camel tours in the Uluru-Kata Tjuta National Park as well as dot painting workshops and a cultural walking tour of Uluru led by an Anangu guide, on which you will see demonstrations of ancient bush skills and learn the art of spear throwing.

Araluen Arts Centre
Alice Springs
Tel: 08-8951 1121
www.nt.gov.au/nreta/arts/ascp/index.html
Tours conducted and organised by the Arrernte people teach participants about the connection between the Dreaming, contemporary Aboriginal art and the land of Mparntwe (Alice Springs).

Aussie Adventures
Shop 6, 52 Mitchell Street, Darwin
Tel: 08-8923 6523
www.aussieadventures.com.au
Conducts tours of Kakadu and Litchfield National Parks as well as a one-day Tiwi Island tour by charter flight.

Gagudju Dreaming
Tel: 08-8979 0145
www.gagudju-dreaming.com
This Kakadu outfit runs the park's renowned Yellow Water Cruises as well as four-wheel-drive off-road adventures to visit waterfalls, swimming holes and escarpments.

Kakadu Animal Tracks
Cooinda Lodge, Kakadu Highway, Cooinda
Tel: 08-8979 0145
www.animaltracks.com.au
These Aboriginal-guided full-day tours combine a wildlife safari with bush tucker–gathering and a campfire cook-up at sunset.

Ananguwai Tours are Aboriginal-run

Kakadu Tours
6 Jabiru Plaza, Jabiru
www.kakadutours.com.au
Flights, fishing tours, boat tours and
Aboriginal cultural tours in Kakadu
National Park.

Nitmiluk Tours
Tel: 08-8972 1253
www.nitmiluktours.com.au
An Aboriginal-owned and -operated tour
company based at Nitmuluk (Katherine
Gorge) National Park that organises
camping, canoeing and walking tours, as
well as helicopter flights, rock art tours and
bush tucker walks.

Tiwi Art
Tel: 08-8941 3593
www.tiwiart.com
Small tours (between four and eight people)
to the three main art centres on the Tiwi
islands in which participants can meet the
artists while they work.

Yulara Resort Tours
Tel: 02-8296 8010
www.ayersrockresort.com.au
The many tours on offer from the Ayers
Rock resort include scenic helicopter
flights, guided walks, camel tours,
motorcycle tours and Mt Connor four-
wheel-drive sightseeing expeditions.

FESTIVALS AND EVENTS

For details of Aboriginal festivals and events, *see p.56*. Other than these, most of
The Territory's shindigs are excuses for excessive drinking and silliness, and are
held in the Dry season.

Around July
Camel Cup
Alice Springs
Camel racing and a carnival at Blatherskite
Park.

August
Darwin Festival
www.darwinfestival.org.au
The Top End's premier arts festival profiles
the region in August through multicultural
and Indigenous performances.

Around August
Beer Can Regatta
Darwin
www.beercanregatta.org.au
A race on Mindil Beach in which all the boats
are constructed of used beer cans and the
entry fees go to charity.

Henley-on-Todd Regatta
Alice Springs
www.henleyontodd.com.au
Famous throughout the country, this regatta

The Camel Cup takes place around July

is run (literally) on the dry bed of the Todd
River, with all proceeds from entry fees going
to charity.

September
Alice Desert Festival
Alice Springs
www.alicedesertfestival.com.au
Circus performances, music, film, comedy
and lots more.

Victoria

Though the smallest of the mainland states, Victoria is home to 5.3 million people. Most of these live in Melbourne, so the countryside is characterised by wide, uncluttered horizons and pristine bush. The majority of tourist sights are found on or near the state's stunningly beautiful, often wild, coastline, and all are within a day's drive from the state capital.

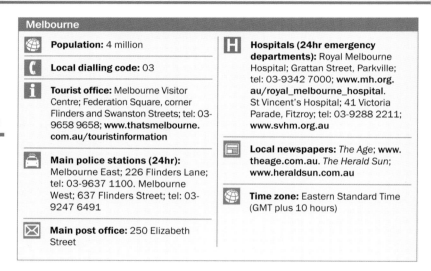

Melbourne

Population: 4 million

Local dialling code: 03

Tourist office: Melbourne Visitor Centre; Federation Square, corner Flinders and Swanston Streets; tel: 03-9658 9658; www.thatsmelbourne.com.au/touristinformation

Main police stations (24hr): Melbourne East; 226 Flinders Lane; tel: 03-9637 1100. Melbourne West; 637 Flinders Street; tel: 03-9247 6491

Main post office: 250 Elizabeth Street

Hospitals (24hr emergency departments): Royal Melbourne Hospital; Grattan Street, Parkville; tel: 03-9342 7000; www.mh.org.au/royal_melbourne_hospital. St Vincent's Hospital; 41 Victoria Parade, Fitzroy; tel: 03-9288 2211; www.svhm.org.au

Local newspapers: The Age; www.theage.com.au. The Herald Sun; www.heraldsun.com.au

Time zone: Eastern Standard Time (GMT plus 10 hours)

Victoria stuttered into life in 1834 with the first permanent European settlement at Portland. Pastoralists soon started crossing the Murray from the north and Bass Strait to the south and population increase was rapid, particularly in Melbourne. At the same time, Aboriginal numbers fell rapidly as introduced diseases and firearms took their toll.

In 1851 Victoria seceded from New South Wales. Within weeks gold was discovered, the new state's population boomed and decades of prosperity ensued. Many regional towns boast stately public buildings, mansions and hotels built with gold money, while the countryside is littered with gracious properties built by the 'squattocracy', landowners who made vast fortunes grazing livestock.

The state may be small, but it is jam-packed with attractions. The Great Ocean Road, the Goldfields and Wilson's Promontory are amongst the best known but there are also coastal resorts, wineries, the inland ports of the Murray and some wonderful mountain scenery to enjoy. The bushfires of February 2009 – Australia's worst in terms of lives lost – affected thousands of hectares to the north and east of Melbourne but their impact was minimal in the areas covered below.

Melbourne

Friendly and culturally diverse **Melbourne ❶** combines imposing Victorian architecture, exceptional eating and shopping, and an exuberant inclination for sporting and cultural events.

Central Business District (CBD)

Melbourne's CBD is arranged on a grid, which makes it easily walkable and navigable. Alternatively, you can hop on and off the City Circle tram

The imposing facade of
Flinders Street Railway Station

Federation Square is Melbourne's entertainment and culture centre

(www.metlinkmelbourne.com.au), a free service that operates in a loop round the edge of the CBD.

Built to commemorate the centenary of Australia's Federation in 2001, the entertainment and culture hub of **Federation Square ❹**, located on the banks of the Yarra at the southern gateway to the CBD, hosts major public events and is home to two high-profile cultural institutions: **The Australian Centre for the Moving Image** (ACMI; Fri–Wed 10am–6pm, Thur 10am–9pm; charge) and the **Ian Potter Centre NGV Australia** (www. ngv.vic.gov.au/ngvaustralia; Fri–Sun and Tue–Wed 10am–5pm, Thur 10am–9pm; permanent collection free, charge for special exhibitions).

Meeting friends 'under the clocks' at neighbouring **Flinders Street Railway Station ❸** is a long and proud Melburnian tradition. The distinctive banded-brick-and-render facade, copper dome and row of clocks of the station building attained iconic status almost immediately after being constructed in 1910. Diagonally opposite the station is **St Paul's Anglican Cathedral ❻**, built

The elegant Block Arcade

home to a swathe of cutting-edge art galleries, boutiques and cafés. Past Flinders Lane is Collins Street, the CBD's premier retail and commercial stretch. The impressive bulk of the **Melbourne Town Hall** **D** occupies the northeast corner of Collins and Swanston streets. On its ground floor, accessed directly from Swanston Street, is the tiny **City Gallery** (110 Swanston Street; Mon 10am–2pm, Tue–Fri 11am–6pm; Sat 10am–4pm; free), which hosts a changing programme of exhibitions about Melbourne's cultural, historical and artistic life.

between 1880 and 1891 on the site where, in March 1836, the first religious service in the new colony was held under a great gum tree.

Travelling north, Swanston Street is crossed by Flinders Lane, once the centre of the city's rag trade and now

Walking west down Collins Street for one block brings you to the opulent **Block Arcade** **E**, built between 1891 and 1893. The ornate Victorian facade of this building is impressive, but the wow factor really kicks in when the grand interior, with its ornate shopfronts, glass skylights, mosaic-tiled floor and octangular core, is viewed.

Further west along Collins Street is Market Street and two blocks downhill is one of Melbourne's major 19th-century public buildings, the handsome, classically proportioned **Old Customs House** , built between 1856 and 1876 near the city's then port. It now houses the **Immigration Museum** (www.museumvictoria.com.au/immigration museum; daily 10am–5pm; charge for adults, children free).

Back on Swanston Street, the next major cross street after the Town Hall is Bourke Street, home to the busy Myer and David Jones department stores. At its eastern end is **Parliament House** (corner Spring and Bourke streets; tel: 03-9651 8911; www.parliament.vic.gov. au; tours at 9.30am, 10.30am, 11.30am, 1.30pm, 2.30pm and 3.45 on weekdays when parliament is not sitting; free), which dates from 1856.

Opposite Parliament House, on the corner of Little Bourke Street, is the pretty-as-a-picture **Princess Theatre**, designed in the French Second Empire style and opened in 1886 with the Australian premiere of Gilbert & Sullivan's *The Mikado*. Local theatre lore insists that there is a resident ghost here.

Melbourne Transport

Airports: Melbourne Airport (tel: 03-9297 1401; **www.melbourneairport.com.au**) is 22km (14 miles) northwest of the city centre; transport to Melbourne: taxi (20–30 minutes; A$50). Skybus (tel: 03-9335 2811; **www.skybus.com.au**; every 10–15 minutes 4am–midnight, every hour midnight–4am; to Southern Cross Railway Station/hotels if pre-booked; adult A$16 one way, A$26 return). Avalon Airport (tel: 1800 282 566; **www.avalonairport.com.au**) is 55km (34 miles) southwest of the city centre; transport to Melbourne: taxi (50 minutes; A$130); Sita Coaches (tel: 03-9689 7999; **www.sitacoaches.com.au/avalon**; to Southern Cross Station/Franklin Street/hotels if pre-booked; adult A$20 one way, A$36 return)

Buses: Run by Metlink (tel: 131 638; **www.metlinkmelbourne.com.au**). Times: Mon–Fri 6am–9pm, Sat 8am–9pm, Sun 9am–9pm; NightRider buses: every 30 minutes Sat 1.30am–4.30am, Sun 1.30am–5.30am, from City Square in Swanston Street to the outer suburbs. Tickets: the reusable myki smart card (A$10 adults, A$7 under-16s, before topping up with cash), which offers discounted travel across buses, trams and trains, is available at **www.myki.com.au**, from the MetShop (corner of Swanston and Collins streets) and retailers displaying a myki sign. You can also purchase city saver, 2-hour or one-day tickets on board trams, from bus drivers and at railway stations

 Trains and trams: Run by Metlink; Sun–Thur 5am–midnight, Fri–Sat 5am–1am

 Taxis: Yellow, metered, deposit required 10pm–5am. 13 CABS; tel: 132 227. Silver Top: tel: 131 008; **www.silvertop.com.au**

 Parking: Road parking is metered; there are plenty of privately operated undercover car parks

Little Bourke Street is home to Melbourne's **Chinatown** . Cantonese-speaking Chinese immigrants arrived in great numbers during the 1850s, hopeful of making fortunes in the colony they described as 'New Gold Mountain'. After periods of backbreaking work on the goldfields, they came to this part of town for some R&R, eating, gambling and smoking opium with their fellow countrymen. Those keen to find out more about the history of the Chinese in Melbourne can pop into the **Chinese Museum** (22 Cohen Place; www.chinesemuseum.com.au; daily 10am–5pm; charge).

Back on Swanston Street, further north again, is the magnificent **State Library of Victoria** (328 Swanston Street; www.slv.vic.gov.au; Mon–Thur 10am–9pm, Fri–Sun 10am–6pm; free), built in the 19th century. Items from the library's permanent collection are on display in the Dome Galleries.

172

Melbourne's Magnificent Market

Visiting foodies should book a guided tasting tour of the historic **Queen Victoria Market** (corner Elizabeth and Victoria streets; tel: 03-9320 5822; www.qvm.com.au; Tue and Thur 6am–2pm, Fri 6am–5pm, Sat 6am–3pm, Sun 9am–4pm; charge for tour), where Melburnians have done their weekly produce shopping since 1878. Tours are held 10am–noon on Tuesdays, Thursdays, Fridays and Saturdays.

Northeast of the library is one of the city's major tourist attractions, the **Old Melbourne Gaol** (near corner of Russell and Victoria streets; www.oldmelbournegaol.com.au; daily 9.30am–5pm; charge). Fascinating and forbidding in equal measure, this bluestone gaol functioned from 1852 to 1929. Macabre exhibits include death masks of well-known criminals

Inside the State Library of Victoria

The striking interior of the Royal Exhibition Building

such as the infamous bushranger Ned Kelly (whose armour is on show at the nearby State Library).

Carlton and Parkville

Carlton was christened in 1852, when the *Government Gazette* advertised land for sale in 'Carlton Gardens' on the northern edge of the fledgling colonial settlement (now the CBD). In 1853 Melbourne University was established on its western border, in the suburb of Parkville, endowing the two suburbs with a bohemian flavour that they retain to this day.

Melbourne's **Royal Exhibition Building** (Carlton Gardens, Carlton; tel: 03-131 102; www.museum.vic. gov.au/reb; guided tours subject to availability; charge) was completed in 1880 and reflects the boundless energy,

optimism and wealth of goldrush-era Victoria. Immediately north of the huge exhibition pavilion is the **Melbourne Museum ❶** (Carlton Gardens, Carlton; www.museumvictoria.com.au/melbournemuseum; daily 10am–5pm; charge 🅼), a multimedia institution with eight galleries aimed at giving visitors an insight into Australia's natural environment, culture and history.

From the museum, the city's Italian quarter, **Lygon Street**, is a short walk northwest. A further two blocks away is the **University of Melbourne**, home to the impressive **Ian Potter Museum of Art** (corner Swanston and Elgin streets, Parkville; www.art-museum.unimelb.edu.au; Tue–Fri 10am–5pm, Sat–Sun noon–5pm, closed late Dec–mid-Jan; free).

Nearby Royal Park is the home of innumerable sporting fields, bike tracks and the **Melbourne Zoo** (Elliott Avenue, Parkville; www.zoo.org.au/melbourne; daily 9am–5pm; charge 🅼), one of the state's most popular tourist attractions. Opened in 1862, it has a renowned conservation research programme and over 300 species of animals, many native and all housed in different bioclimatic (habitat) zones.

King's Domain, South Yarra and Toorak

On the southern side of the Yarra River is the grand boulevard of St Kilda Road, home to the **NGV International ❹** (180 St Kilda Road;

🚶 YARRA RIVER WALK

Melbourne's indigenous Wurundjeri people know the Yarra as Birrarung, the River of Mist. This walk explores its city section.

Start this walk at Melbourne's sporting shrine – the **Melbourne Cricket Ground** (MCG; Brunton Avenue; tel: 03-9657 8879; www.mcg.org.au; guided tours daily on non-event days; charge 🚊). Known to Melburnians as 'The G', this massive structure hosts international cricket and Australian Rules football. It's also home to the **National Sports Museum** (tel: 03-9657 8879; www.nsm. org.au; daily 10am–5pm; charge 🚊).

From the MCG, cross the footbridge opposite Gate 1 of the stadium and you will arrive at **Melbourne & Olympic Parks** (www.mopt.com.au). Cross Batman Avenue in front of the Rod Laver Arena, home to the Australian Tennis Open, and enter **Birrarung Marr**, a 8.3-

hectare (20-acre) park featuring indigenous flora, river views and a playground.

Follow the river to **Federation Square** *(see p.169)*, stopping to check one or more of its museums. Riverland on the Lower Promenade offers tables overlooking the water and is a pleasant spot for a drink or light meal.

Cross to the opposite side of the river via Princes Bridge. On the western side of St Kilda Road is one of the city's major visual landmarks, the distinctive latticed spire of the **Arts Centre**, which houses concert halls and a performing arts collection. Next to the arts centre is the impressive **NGV International** *(see p.173)*.

From the Arts Centre, take any of the connected pathways or stairs down to **Southbank**, a wide paved promenade along the river. Its view of the city skyline is spiked with the spire of St Paul's Cathedral, the dome of Flinders Street Station and a profusion of office

Stop for a drink in Federation Square

A ferry makes its way along the Yarra

towers. Make sure you check out *The Travellers*, a sculptural installation by Lebanese artist Nadim Karam on the **Sandridge Footbridge**, a remnant of the city's first – now decommissioned – railway line, which ran from Port Melbourne to Flinders Street.

Staying on the south bank of the river, walk west and cross Queensbridge Street to arrive at **Crown Casino**. There's only a modicum of Vegas-style glitz and glamour here but the complex has an excellent cinema complex and a smorgasbord of five-star restaurants.

Cross busy Clarendon Street and you will arrive at the recently redeveloped **South Wharf** complex, home to the **Melbourne Exhibition and Convention Centre** and the National Trust-run **Melbourne Maritime Museum** (www.pollywoodside.com.au), which was refurbished in 2010 and is a showcase for the beautifully restored three-masted iron barque *Polly Woodside*, launched in Belfast in 1885. From South Wharf you could

cross the sculptural **Webb Footbridge**, designed to resemble the traps that the Wurundjeri people traditionally used to catch eels, to access the Docklands precinct. Alternatively, backtrack to Clarendon Street to catch a tram to the city centre or St Kilda.

Tips

- Distance: 5.5km (3½ miles)
- Time: Half a day
- To get to the MCG, walk from the city centre, or take the no. 48 or 75 tram travelling east along Flinders Street (alight at Stop 11, Clarendon Street).
- Ferries offer tours along the Yarra to the Docklands and over the bay to Williamstown. Embark at the Lower Promenade under Federation Square, next to Riverland Bar and Café.

Yarra River Walk

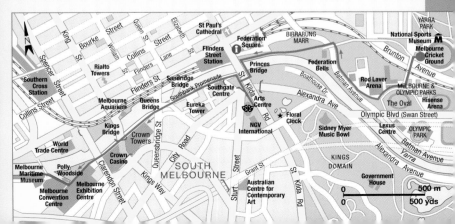

www.ngv.vic.gov.au; Wed–Mon 10am–5pm; permanent collection free, charge for some temporary exhibitions), which showcases decorative arts, Asian and Oceanic art, 18th- and 19th-century English painting and European Old Masters.

After the first bridge over the Yarra was constructed in 1845, a large tract of land on the eastern side of St Kilda road was set aside as the location for a botanical reserve, now the stunning **Royal Botanic Gardens** ❶ (Birdwood Avenue, South Yarra; www.rbg.vic.gov.au; daily 7.30am–sunset; free 🏛).

From the gardens you can see the landmark square tower of the Italianate **Government House** (tel: 03-8663 7260; guided tours Mon and Wed, booking essential at least one week in advance), the home of Victoria's governors since 1876.

Government House may be the largest building in Kings Domain, but it is well and truly overshadowed in the hearts and minds of Melburnians by the nearby **Shrine of Remembrance** (Birdwood Ave; www.shrine.org.au; daily 10am–5pm, guided tours 11am and 2pm; free),

The Royal Botanic Gardens

A sculptural frontage on a St Kilda hair salon

built to honour the 114,000 Australians who served the Empire in the Great War and to memorialise the 19,000 who died doing so.

A tram ride east (catch the no. 8 from Domain Road near the entrance to the Botanical Gardens and alight at Williams Road in Toorak) is **Como House** (Corner Williams Road and Lechlade Avenue; www.comohouse. com.au; Sept–Apr daily 10am–4pm, May–Aug Wed, Sat–Sun 10am–5pm; charge ), a graceful colonial mansion set in 2-hectare (5-acre) gardens and built in 1847.

St Kilda

This heavily populated bayside suburb is Melbourne's urban beach. There may not be surf to speak of, and few choose to swim here, but the sand is clean and the beachfront on weekends is rather like Los Angeles' Venice Beach: rollerbladers and cyclists speed past, models preen themselves in the sun, and bodybuilders work out on the grass.

It's busiest here on summer weekends, when people from every corner of the city descend on Fitzroy and Acland streets to enjoy their cafés, bars, restaurants and slightly seedy nocturnal street life. Those with children often stop at **Luna Park** (18 Lower Esplanade, St Kilda; www.lunapark.com.au; opening hours vary – check website for details; charge), built in 1912 and long famous as the home of the exhilarating Scenic Railway roller-coaster.

To experience the suburb's serious rather than sybaritic side, visit the **Jewish Museum of Australia** (26 Alma Road, St Kilda; www. jewishmuseum.com.au; Tue–Thur 10am–4pm, Sun 10am–5pm; charge). The multimedia exhibits at this community museum give visitors a crash course in Jewish history and culture as well as documenting the history of Jews in Australia.

★ SPORTING MADNESS

Images of bronzed Aussie athletes often adorn tourist brochures, but true Aussie sports aficionados are far more likely to be slightly overweight chaps sitting in the stands and watching a sporting match while scoffing a meat pie and downing a beer. That said, there's something enormously endearing about the general obsession with spectator sport in Melbourne — attend any of the city's major sporting events and you're bound to be bowled over by the crowd's infectious enthusiasm, fierce partisanship and general bonhomie.

The **Australian Football League** (AFL; www.afl.com.au) season starts in March each year and culminates in the finals series in September. Melbourne goes footy crazy during the finals — club colours are seen everywhere, pubs screen televised coverage of matches and finals BBQs dominate the social scene. Every office has its tipping competition and everyone has to 'barrack' for a team, irrespective of age or gender.

The Grand Final is played at the MCG *(see p.174)* on the last Saturday of the month before a crowd of 100,000.

On the first Tuesday in November, Melburnians don their smartest outfits and make their way to Flemington Racecourse to one of the world's great horse races, **The Melbourne Cup** (www.vrc. net.au/melbourne-cup-carnival). The glitterati spend the day in lavish corporate marquees, but most punters claim

Melbourne plays host to the Australian Formula One Grand Prix

The city goes crazy during the Australian Football League finals

a patch of lawn or grandstand seat and settle in to enjoy great horse racing and more than a few glasses of bubbly. Other popular events on the **Spring Racing Carnival** fixture are Oaks Day and Derby Day at Flemington (www.vrc.net.au), The Caulfield Cup at Caulfield Racecourse (www.melbourneracingclub.net.au) and the Cox Plate at Moonee Valley Racecourse (www.mvrc.net.au).

The **Australian Tennis Open** (www.australianopen.com) is a high-profile event on the International Grand Slam circuit. Held in the second half of January each year at Melbourne Park on the Yarra, it sees the world's best players slogging it out in often-sweltering conditions. The crowd is vociferous in its support of local contenders and visiting favourites.

When Victorians think of summer, two things come to mind: the beach and cricket (sometimes the two are conflated in the popular pastime of beach cricket). The international **Test Cricket** season kicks off with the famous Boxing Day Test at the MCG and continues through January and into February. For more information and to buy tickets, go to www.cricket.com.au.

Locals are divided when it comes to the **Australian Formula One Grand Prix** – fans are loud in their support and opponents are even louder in voicing their displeasure. Held in the usually tranquil surrounds of Albert Park Lake in March each year, the four-day event (www.grandprix.com.au) certainly causes a buzz around town, particularly on Carlton's Ferrari-obsessed Lygon Street.

The Australian Tennis Open is held in Melbourne every January

Around Melbourne

There are plenty of easy day excursions from Melbourne, the most popular of which are to the wine regions of the Yarra Valley and Mornington Peninsula, home to scenic landscapes and alluring wineries and restaurants.

The Dandenongs

About 50km (31 miles) east of Melbourne lie the **Dandenong Ranges ❷**. Here, the mountain bluffs are adorned with soaring mountain ash trees and lush fern gullies, while small towns in the area are home to weatherboard houses with impressive private gardens, a motley collection of arty-crafty shops and the odd café serving cream teas.

Attractions include the **William Ricketts Sanctuary** (Mt Dandenong Tourist Road, Mt Dandenong; www.parkweb.vic.gov.au; daily 10am–4.30pm; charge), where romantically idealised Aboriginal spirit figures have been carved from wood and placed in a forest setting, and **Puffing Billy** (Old Monbulk Rd, Belgrave; www.puffingbilly.com.au; trip times vary throughout the year and do not occur on total fire ban days; charge), a quaint narrow-gauge steam train that plies a 24km (15-mile) track from Belgrave to Gembrook.

Yarra Valley

Directly north of the Dandenongs, the gently rolling countryside of the **Yarra Valley ❸** is home to many notable wineries and cheese producers. Don't miss **Yering Station** (38 Melba Highway, Yarra Glen; www.yering.com; Mon–Fri 10am–5pm, Sat–Sun 10am–6pm), which produced Victoria's first vintage way back in 1845 and welcomes visitors to its cellar door, restaurant and hotel.

The quaint Puffing Billy steam train runs from Belgrave to Gembrook

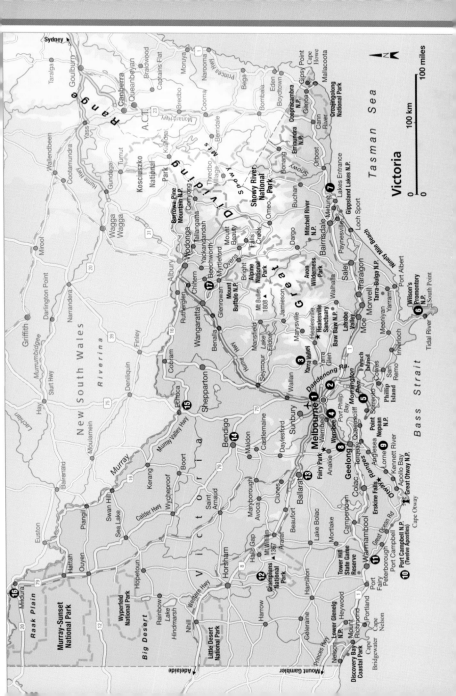

Another winery with spectacular views and an enticing eatery is **Domaine Chandon** (727 Maroondah Hwy, Coldstream; tel: 03-9738 9200; www.domainechandon.com.au; daily 10.30am–4.30pm), established by French champagne house Moët & Chandon in 1986. There are free 30-minute guided tours at 11am, 1pm and 3pm daily and a two-hour wine discovery class on Sundays at 11am (bookings essential; charge).

Set in an award-winning vineyard, the **TarraWarra Museum of Art** (311 Healesville–Yarra Glen Road; www.twma.com.au; Tue–Sun 11am–5pm; charge) is notable for its elegant purpose-designed building and for its uniformly impressive exhibitions of Australian contemporary art. There's also a stylish wine bar where you can enjoy tastings of TarraWarra's vintages (try the Chardonnay and Pinot Noir) or sit down for a meal.

The pretty town of Healesville, nestled in the foothills of the Great Dividing Range, was settled during the gold rush. On its southeastern edge is the **Healesville Sanctuary** (www.zoo.org.au/healesville; daily 9am–5pm; charge 🅜), a bushland reserve that's home to more than 200 species of Australian birds, mammals and reptiles.

Werribee Park

Only a 30-minute drive west of central Melbourne, **Werribee Park** ❹ (K Road, Werribee; www.werribeepark.com.au; Nov–Apr daily 10am–5pm, May–Oct Mon–Fri 10am–4pm, Sat–Sun 10am–5pm; charge 🅜) was built for pastoralist Thomas Chirnside, who had begun acquiring land in this area in the 1850s. Its 60-room mansion dates from 1873–8 and an interesting audio-tour gives a glimpse of what life must have been like in the mansion's heyday. A walk around the mansion's extensive formal gardens is a highlight, particularly as they are dotted with visually arresting contemporary sculptures.

Mornington Peninsula and Gippsland

The **Mornington Peninsula** ❺ stretches down the southeastern side of Port Phillip Bay. From Melbourne it's accessed via the Nepean Highway (Highway 3), which follows the bay past a procession of suburbs and towns, all with beaches, some with bathing huts and many with magnificent holiday homes perched on cliff tops overlooking the bay. On the

Knocking back a vintage at the TarraWarra wine bar

Phillip Island

eastern side of the peninsula are Western Port Bay and the rich farming and mining region of Gippsland.

Sorrento, towards the tip of the peninsula, is the oldest and most attractive settlement on the Mornington Peninsula and has both ocean and bayside beaches. A car ferry (www.searoad.com.au) makes the short trip across the mouth of the bay to Queenscliff on the Bellarine Peninsula, and is often accompanied on its way by a school of dolphins.

The spectacular **Point Nepean National Park** (Point Nepean Rd, Portsea; www.parkweb.vic.gov.au; daily 9am–5pm; charge) occupies the peninsula's tip, and inland there are numerous vineyards and gourmet restaurants, particularly in the area around the town of Red Hill.

On the eastern side of the peninsula sits **French Island**, once home to a prison farm but now the site of a peaceful national park where visitors can bushwalk, bike ride and spot

members of the island's large koala colony. Ferries to the island leave from Stony Point, or from the town of Cowes on **Phillip Island**, the home of the famous **Penguin Parade** (www. penguins.org.au; charge 🅜).

East of Phillip Island is **Wilson's Promontory ❻**, the southernmost tip of the Australian mainland. This huge granite peninsula, known to all Victorians as 'The Prom', is the site of

---

Camping at the Prom

An estimated 100,000 people visit the **Wilson's Promontory National Park** (www.parkweb.vic.gov.au) each year and access is managed carefully, meaning that even the hotspots of Tidal River, Squeaky Beach and Picnic Bay rarely feel crowded. Just don't expect to find a camping spot, cabin or wilderness retreat in peak season without booking up to a year in advance. To do so, telephone 03-131 963 (from Australia) or 61 3 8627 4700 (international).

the most popular national park in Victoria. It offers 130km (81 miles) of coastline, more than 80km (50 miles) of walking tracks, long sandy beaches, forested mountain slopes, and heaths and marshes packed with bird, animal and plant life.

East of the Prom, in East Gippsland, is **Bairnsdale**, a sheep, dairy and timber centre. From here, the Princes Highway westwards runs all the way to Sydney, but the only time it touches the coast in Victoria is at **Lakes Entrance ❼**, situated at the narrow man-made inlet to the Gippsland Lakes, a long string of interconnected lagoons stretching west along the inner shore of the Bass Strait for some 80km (50 miles).

Away from the coast, in Gippsland's industrial heartland, is the Latrobe Valley, which sits upon the world's largest deposit of brown coal. Mining has always been important in this part of the state, as the tiny mountain community of Walhalla – home to what was once Victoria's richest gold mine – evocatively attests. Visitors can tour **Long Tunnel Extended Gold Mine** (tours weekdays 1.30pm and weekends at noon, 1.30pm and 3pm; charge 🅼) and take a ride on the historic **Goldfields Railway** (www.walhallarail.com; Wed, Sat–Sun 11am and 1pm; charge 🅼).

Western Districts

The plains west of Melbourne are where many of the colony's early settlers made their fortunes. The volcanic soil here is rich and the plains are characterised by wide horizons and studded with mansions built to show off fortunes made 'on a sheep's back' (ie, with wool). The coastline sports trophy homes of a later era – holiday homes built by Melbourne's middle classes in the years after World War II and accessed via the world-famous Great Ocean Road, built between 1919 and 1932 by 3,000 ex-servicemen ('Diggers') who had returned to Australia from overseas duty in World War I.

Sculptures on the Geelong waterfront

Geelong

Though best known as the gateway to the Great Ocean Road, **Geelong**  has a long history and a picturesque location on Corio Bay that mean it's worth a visit in its own right. Sights include the **Geelong Gallery** (Little Malop Street; www.geelonggallery.org.au; Mon–Fri 10am–5pm, Sat–Sun 1–5pm; free), which has a well-respected permanent collection that includes highlights such as Frederick McCubbin's moving 1890 work *A Bush Burial*.

The Great Ocean Road

Torquay, touted as the 'birthplace of the global surf industry', is where the Great Ocean Road starts. Famous for its surf beaches, this rapidly growing town is where the Rip Curl Pro Surf & Music Festival is held each Easter. There are safe swimming beaches for families at Cosy Corner and Fisherman's Beach, and Torquay and Jan Juc beaches offer perfect conditions for novice surfers. Also here is the world's largest surfing museum, **Surfworld** (Surf City Plaza, Beach Road; www.surfworld.com.au; daily 9am–5pm; charge ).

From Torquay, the Great Ocean Road passes **Anglesea**, known for its wide front beach, sheer cliffs and coastal heathland. It's a hive of activity during summer, when thousands of families from Melbourne pack their boogie boards and bathers and make the pilgrimage here for their annual beach holiday.

Aireys Inlet, home to the landmark Split Point Lighthouse, is

Surfworld is the world's largest surfing museum

another busy summer destination, but the town of **Lorne** ❾, which is set between the sparkling waters of Loutit Bay and the forests of the Otway Ranges, is a year-round favourite. The beach here is perfect for families, with gentle waves lapping a wide stretch of golden sand, and the main street is crammed with cafés, a cinema and shops. From Lorne you can enjoy bush walks in the nearby Angahook-Lorne State Park, the most popular being to dramatic **Erskine Falls**, a series of waterfalls cascading into a beautiful gully filled with native tree ferns.

The most stunning section of the Great Ocean Road, with sheer cliffs and majestic ocean views on one side and the Otway Ranges and Angahook-Lorne State Park on the other, stretches between Lorne and Apollo

Port Campbell National Park is best known for its world-famous Twelve Apostles

Bay. Six kilometres (4 miles) west of Apollo Bay is the **Great Otway National Park**, 103,000 hectares (255,000 acres) of ancient rainforest, heathlands and woodlands. The park is home to the oldest surviving lighthouse in Australia, the 1848

Swimming Between the Flags

The beaches along the Great Ocean Road are as dangerous as they are beautiful. Rips and undertows abound, and visitors unfamiliar with local conditions should always swim between the red-and-yellow flags at beaches patrolled by trained surf lifesavers. These include Torquay, Cosy Corner, Jan Juc, Anglesea, Point Roadknight, Fairhaven, Lorne, Wye River, Kennett River, Apollo Bay and Port Campbell. The patrol period runs from late November to mid-April.

Cape Otway Lightstation (Great Ocean Road, Cape Otway; www.lightstation.com; daily 9am–5pm, Shipwreck Discovery tours at 10am and 2pm; charge 🅜).

Though it features on postcards and tourist brochures galore, no photographic image can do true justice to the utterly magnificent **Port Campbell National Park** ❿ (www.parkweb.vic.gov.au). This stretch of coastline from Princetown to Peterborough is best known for the world-famous **Twelve Apostles**, giant rock stacks left isolated from the mainland by the erosive power of the ocean. A visitor centre (daily 9am–5pm) provides information about the geology and history of the area, and a tunnel underneath the Great Ocean Road leads to the viewing platforms.

Beyond Peterborough and the dramatic Bay of Islands lies **Warrnambool** ⓫. People flock here in winter to see the southern right whales off Logans Beach. Around the lighthouse is the **Flagstaff Hill Maritime Village**, a re-created 19th-century port with its chandlers, shipwrights and sailmakers (Merri Street; www.flagstaffhill.com; daily 9am–5pm; charge 📋). The spectacular *Shipwrecked* sound-and-laser show runs nightly at dusk.

The Grampians
Inland, the wool town of Hamilton is a gateway to the **Grampians National Park** ⓬, with its distinctive ranges rising abruptly to dominate the surrounding plains. The base here is the tiny town of Halls Gap with its impressive **Brambuk Cultural Centre** (www.brambuk. com.au; daily 9am–5pm; free 📋), a purpose-built, architect-designed building profiling local Aboriginal culture and history.

The Goldfields
Central Victoria was built on gold – huge nuggets of it. The towns here date from the 1851–1860s gold rush and almost inevitably possess main streets full of grand public buildings and opulent private mansions.

Ballarat
A drive 113km (70 miles) west of Melbourne will take you well over a century back in time to the town of **Ballarat** ⓭, rich with the spoils and atmosphere of Australia's gold-rush era. The precious metal was

discovered here in 1851, and thousands of miners trekked to the fields.

Almost from the outset the government collected a licence fee from the miners – many of whom couldn't afford to pay. In the Eureka Uprising miners protesting against the licence fee were besieged in a stockade by colonial troops, and 35 people – mostly diggers – lost their lives. The battle is re-created nightly at the exciting **Blood on the Southern Cross** sound-and-light show (hours vary; charge 📋) staged at **Sovereign Hill** (Bradshaw Street; www.sovereign hill.com.au; daily 10am–5pm; charge 📋), an open-air museum re-creating the sights, sounds and smells of the gold rush. Tourists can try their hand with a digger's pan and take a tour of an underground mine.

Experience the gold rush at the Sovereign Hill open-air museum

When peace eventually returned to the goldfields after the uprising, Ballarat went back to the business of making a fortune. The town's many grand buildings, including the impressive **Art Gallery of Ballarat** (40 Lydiard Street North; www.balgal. com; daily 9am–5pm, guided tours 2pm; free), date from this time.

Gold Towns

Other gold towns are found to the north of Ballarat. **Clunes**, the scene of the first gold strike on 1 July 1851, has an ornate town hall, and elegant banks and bluestone churches. **Daylesford**, a picturesque town on Wombat Hill, is known (along with its neighbour Hepburn Springs) as the spa centre of Australia. In **Castlemaine**, the market building and other fine edifices date from an era of promise never quite fulfilled. From its handsome railway station, a short ride on one of the steam trains of the **Victorian Goldfields Railway** (www.vgr.

com.au; most Suns and Weds except on total fire ban days; charge ) will take you to **Maldon**, the National Trust's first 'notable town in Australia'. Its gold-rush era streetscapes are terrific, as much for their tranquillity as their remarkable state of preservation.

Another treat for nostalgia fans is the town of **Bendigo** ⓮, situated 150km (93 miles) northwest of Melbourne. In the 1850s, Bendigo Creek, running through the centre of town, was besieged with miners from every corner of the world who came to pan for gold. The **Central Deborah Gold Mine** (76 Violet Street; www. central-deborah.com; daily 9am–5pm; charge ), the last commercial mine to operate in Bendigo, is now a museum of 19th-century mining technology; a visit includes a one-hour underground mine tour. From the mine you can take a 'Talking Tram', an antique vehicle that follows an 8km (5-mile) historic itinerary. The last stop is the **Joss House Temple** (Finn

A peaceful lake at Castlemaine

Beechworth is Victoria's best-preserved gold town

Street; Wed, Sat–Sun 11am–4pm; charge), built in the 1860s by the many Chinese miners who came here to make their fortunes.

Like Ballarat, Bendigo has an **Art Gallery** (42 View Street; www.bendigoartgallery.com.au; daily 10am–5pm, guided tours 2pm; free) housing an impressive collection of Australian art.

Northern Victoria

The mighty Murray is the longest river in Australia, and functions as the border with NSW. Victorians living in the northern half of the state have long treated it as a holiday destination and houseboats and paddle steamers aplenty still ply its waters. When not on the river, holiday-makers can be found on the slopes of the state's impressive ski resorts in the Victorian Alps or 'High Country.'

Echuca ⓯, 88km (55 miles) north of Bendigo, was an important port on the Murray River and a walk along its magnificent **Old Port Precinct** (52 Murray Esplanade, www.portofechuca.org.au; daily 9am–4.30pm; charge ⓜ) is now a major drawcard for tourists.

The Murray Valley Highway loosely tracks the river as it heads northwest and rejoins it at modest **Swan Hill** in the Mallee (a flat and dry district named after the mallee eucalypt). From here, it's another 196km (122 miles) to the city of **Mildura ⓰**, isolated in the northwestern corner of the state. Surrounded by fruit-laden orchards and lush vineyards, in recent years Mildura has developed a reputation as a gastronomic mecca, largely due to the presence of affable restaurateur Stefano di Pieri, who runs the restaurant at The Grand Hotel and a swathe of other town eateries.

In the High Country to the northeast of the state is Victoria's best-preserved gold town, **Beechworth ⓱**.

The Ned Kelly statue at Glenrowan, where the bushranger was captured in 1880

No fewer than 32 of its buildings have been classified by the National Trust, including the 1863 **Burke Museum** (www.beechworth.com/burkemus; daily 10am–5pm; charge), part of the historic precinct on Loch Street. This museum exhibits myriad relics and memorabilia of the gold-rush era – when 3 million ounces of gold were garnered in just 14 years – along with other pioneer objects, and there is even a life-sized re-creation of a section of Beechworth's former main street. During its heyday the town had 61 hotels and a theatre which hosted international acts.

From Beechworth, it's possible to follow the scenic Great Alpine Road past the quaint town of **Bright**, where oaks, maples and other hardwoods promote a serenity which belies its violent gold-rush days, including the notorious 1857 Buckland riots when white prospectors brutally ousted Chinese miners from their claims.

From here the Great Alpine Road continues up to the popular ski resorts of **Falls Creek** (1,500m/4,920ft) and **Mt Hotham** (1,750m/5,740ft) and on to Gippsland.

Alternatively, **Mansfield**, an important grazing and timber centre and the gateway to **Mount Buller** (1,808m/5,932ft), Victoria's largest ski resort, is southwest of Beechworth in the direction of Melbourne. It lies just 3km (2 miles) from 130 sq-km (50 sq-mile) **Lake Eildon**, a paradise for water-skiers and fishermen.

Kelly Country

The Hume Highway between Sydney and Melbourne goes through 'Kelly Country', the stamping ground of legendary bushranger and Aussie folk hero, Ned Kelly. Ned's gang was caught in a shoot-out with police at the Glenrowan Inn in 1880 – he was captured and brought to trial in Melbourne, where he was sentenced to be hanged to death in the old Melbourne Gaol (see p.172); the rest of the gang died in the shoot-out. These days, the town of Glenrowan makes the most of its Kelly connection at **Ned Kelly's Last Stand** (Tourist Centre, 41 Gladstone Street; www.glenrowantouristcentre. com.au; daily 9.30am–4.30pm; charge M), with computerised mannequins judderingly re-enacting the siege.

ACCOMMODATION

Melbourne offers the full gamut of accommodation types, but is particularly blessed when it comes to apartment and boutique hotels. In regional Victoria, there are a number of top-notch options that have superb restaurants.

Melbourne

Alto Hotel on Bourke Street
636 Bourke Street
Tel: 03-8608 5500
www.altohotel.com.au
Close to Southern Cross Railway Station and the Docklands, Alto Hotel markets itself as being environmentally friendly. **$$$**

Art Series [The Olsen]
637–641 Chapel Street, South Yarra
Tel: 03-9040 1222
www.artserieshotels.com.au
Full of work by highly regarded artist John Olsen, this newly opened boutique hotel joins its sister establishments The Cullen (in Prahran) and The Blackman (in St Kilda) in being Melbourne's hippest hotels. **$$$**

Base Backpackers Melbourne
17 Carlisle Street, St Kilda
Tel: 03-8598 6200
www.stayatbase.com/base-backpackers-melbourne-hostel
This sleek operation markets itself as Australia's hippest hostel. Dorms have bunk beds, air conditioning and private en suites. **$**

Greenhouse Backpackers Melbourne
228 Flinders Lane
Tel: 1800-249 207
http://greenhouse.melbourne-hostels.com.au
This no-nonsense backpacker joint near Flinders Street Railway Station offers the cheapest singles accommodation in the central city. **$–$$**

Hilton Melbourne South Wharf
2 Convention Centre Place
Tel: 03-9027 2000

http://hiltonmelbourne.com.au
This recently opened business hotel on the Yarra features comfortable rooms, a spa and a good restaurant. **$$$$**

Hotel Lindrum
26 Flinders Street
Tel: 03-9668 1111
www.hotellindrum.com.au
Near Federation Square, this boutique hotel has 59 rooms and suites that are as stylish as they are spacious. **$$$–$$$$$**

The Lyall
14 Murphy Street, South Yarra
Tel: 03-9868 8222
www.thelyall.com
A location on a leafy residential street and the feel and decor of a private club gives this boutique option the edge. **$$$$**

Medina Grand Melbourne
189 Queen Street
Tel: 03-9934 0000
www.medina.com.au

Hotel Lindrum

The Medina chain operates a number of comfortable apartment hotels around town. This one has a great location, as well as a rooftop lap pool and a gym. **$$$**

The Nunnery
116 Nicholson Street
Tel: 03-9419 8637
www.nunnery.com.au
Offering three tiers of accommodation (hostel, guesthouse and townhouse), The Nunnery is deservedly popular. Its city-edge location faces the Carlton Gardens. **$–$$**

The Prince
2 Acland Street, St Kilda
Tel: 03-9536 1111
www.theprince.com.au
Rooms here feature de-luxe linen, distinctive artwork and soothing colour schemes. Facilities include the highly regarded Aurora Spa and Circa Restaurant. **$$$–$$$$**

Punt Hill Little Bourke
11–17 Cohen Place
Tel: 03-9631 1111
www.littlebourke.punthill.com.au
This attractive modern building in Melbourne's Chinatown offers comfortable apartments with kitchenettes and laundry facilities. **$$$**

Stamford Plaza
111 Little Collins Street;
Tel: 03-9659 1000
www.stamford.com.au
A five-star suite hotel in a charming location at the top end of town. Amenities include an indoor/outdoor pool, restaurant, bar and two gyms. **$$$–$$$$**

Around Melbourne
Amaroo Caravan Park and Hostel
67 Church Street, Cowes
Tel: 03-5952 2548
www.amaroopark.com
In Phillip Island's main town, this friendly place offers cabins, rooms, dorm beds and campsites. **$**

The Nunnery

Sofitel Werribee Park Mansion Hotel & Spa
K Road, Werribee
Tel: 03-9731 4000
Luxurious accommodation set in the splendid surrounds of historic Werribee Park (see p.182). There's a spa, on-site winery and excellent restaurant. **$$$–$$$$**

Western Districts
Grampians YHA Eco-Hostel
Corner Grampians Road and Buckler Street, Halls Gap
Tel: 03-5356 4544
www.yha.com.au
An attractive, eco-friendly and well-equipped hostel offering dorm beds and a welcoming atmosphere. **$$–$$$**

Qdos
Allendale Road, Lorne
Tel: 03-5289 1989
www.qdosarts.com
Tranquil architect-designed treehouse accommodation in a bush compound with adjoining restaurant and art gallery. **$$$**

The Goldfields
Craig's Royal Hotel
10 Lydiard Street South, Ballarat
Tel: 03-5331 1377
www.craigsroyal.com
Dating from 1853, this elegant hostelry has 41 attractively decorated rooms, including swish Royal Suites. **$$$–$$$$$**

Lake House
King Street, Daylesford
Tel: 03-5348 3329
www.lakehouse.com.au
Located in 'Spa Country', this luxurious
retreat on the shore of Lake Daylesford
offers well-appointed rooms and one of
Victoria's finest restaurants. **$$$$$**

Northern Victoria
Grand Hotel
Seventh Street, Mildura
Tel: 03-5023 0511
www.milduragrandhotel.com.au
Mildura's most famous accommodation
option boasts multiple room types, a pool
and an award-winning restaurant. **$$–$$$$$**

RESTAURANTS

Melbourne has one of the most
impressive and diverse food scenes
in the world – catering for every
budget and palate. In country areas,
seasonally driven local produce
characterises the best establishments.

Restaurants Price Categories
Prices are for a two-course meal

$ = below A$20
$$ = A$20–45
$$$ = A$45–75
$$$$ = over A$75

Melbourne
Abla's
109 Elgin Street, Carlton
Tel: 03-9347 0006
www.ablas.com.au
Abla Amad's delectable home-style Lebanese
food has devotees throughout the city. **$$**

Añada
197 Gertrude Street, Fitzroy
Tel: 03-9415 6101
www.anada.com.au
On Melbourne's most happening strip,
Añada has an atmosphere, menu and decor
that immediately recall Spain. **$$**

Balzari
130 Lygon Street, Carlton
Tel: 03-9639 9383
www.balzari.com.au
A haven of style and good Italian food
wedged among the tatty tourist restaurants
of Lygon Street. **$$**

Becco
11–25 Crossley Street
Tel: 03-9663 3000
www.becco.com.au
This buzzy Italian place is tucked down a lane
at the eastern end of Bourke Street. **$$$**

Café di Stasio
31 Fitzroy Street, St Kilda
Tel: 03-9525 3999
Owner Ronnie di Stasio faithfully adheres
to unfussy, perfectly executed Italian cui-
sine. The well-priced set lunch menu of two
courses and a glass of wine is a Melbourne
institution. **$$$**

City Wine Shop
159 Spring Street
Tel: 03-9654 6657
www.citywineshop.net.au
Home to communal tables, an impressive
wine list and consistently excellent, well-
priced food. **$$**

Cumulus Inc
45 Flinders Lane
Tel: 03-9650 1445
www.cumulusinc.com.au
This fashionable place lives up to its hype.
You can wander in for a leisurely breakfast,
join the local gallery set for lunch or queue
for a dinner table. **$$**

Gigibaba
102 Smith Street, Collingwood
Tel: 03-9486 0345
Ismail Tosun's modern takes on Turkish

Listings

classics have the city's foodie fraternity frantically queuing for tables. **$$**

Gingerboy
27–29 Crossley Street
Tel: 03-9662 4200
www.gingerboy.com.au
Southeast Asian hawker food gets a designer makeover here. Regulars inevitably kick off their evening with a cocktail in the glam upstairs bar. **$$**

Grossi Florentino Cellar Bar
80 Bourke Street
Tel: 03-9662 1811
http://grossiflorentino.com
A classic enoteca serving casual but delicious meals, excellent coffee and a good selection of wines by the glass. **$**

Il Bàcaro
168 Little Collins Street
Tel: 03-9654 6778
www.ilbacaro.com.au
The hallmarks here are sleek and sexy Italian decor, flirtatious Italian staff and skilfully cooked modern versions of classic Italian dishes. **$$$**

Jacques Reymond
78 Williams Road, Windsor
Tel: 03-9525 2178
www.jacquesreymond.com.au
Vue de Monde may be more fashionable, but local epicures prefer the restrained elegance and sophisticated execution of Jacques Reymond's food, which he's been serving from this suburban mansion for decades. **$$$$**

MoVida

Ladro
224 Gertrude Street, Fitzroy
Tel: 03-9415 7575
Melbourne's best pizza is on offer at this bustling and noisy place. The arty chic clientele matches the decor. **$**

Longrain
44 Little Bourke Street
Tel: 03-9671 3151
www.longrain.com
Longrain's communal tables are inevitably full of glamorous young things snacking on fragrant and spicy Thai dishes. **$$**

Mama Ganoush
56 Chapel Street, Windsor
Tel: 03-9521 4141
www.mamaganoush.com
A visit to this chic restaurant at the southern end of Chapel Street is the local equivalent of a trip to the exotic souqs of Egypt and the Levant – with heady spices, bright colours and tasty treats on offer. **$$**

MoVida
1 Hosier Lane
Tel: 03-9663 3038
www.movida.com.au
One of the city's favourite eateries, MoVida is famed for its tapas, which utilise a mix of top-quality local produce and the best Iberian imports. **$$**

Oriental Tea House
455 Chapel Street, South Yarra
Tel: 03-9826 0168
www.orientalteahouse.com.au
Giving a South Yarra twist to the traditional Chinese teahouse, this stylish emporium tempts with fragrant teas and tasty yum cha morsels. **$$**

Pizza e Birra
60a Fitzroy Street
Tel: 03-9537 3465
The chef hails from Campania, so the pizzas served up here are of the medium-crust variety and are a perfect match for the ice-cold beer provided on tap. **$**

The Press Club
72 Flinders Street
Tel: 03-9677 9677
www.thepressclub.com.au
In the former newspaper offices of the
Herald & Weekly Times (hence the name),
this sleek restaurant/bar serves Modern
Greek cuisine. **$$$$**

Rumi
132 Lygon Street, East Brunswick
Tel: 03-9388 8255
Rumi's low prices, consistently marvellous
Lebanese-Persian food and always-charm-
ing staff can't be faulted. **$$**

Stokehouse
30 Jacka Boulevard
Tel: 03-9525 5555
www.stokehouse.com.au
The downstairs bar serves café fare, and
the upstairs restaurant, which has a superb
view of the bay, offers a sophisticated Mod
Med menu. **$$–$$$$**

Vue de Monde
430 Little Collins Street
Tel: 03-9691 3888
www.vuedemonde.com.au
Regularly nominated as one of Australia's
two best restaurants, Shannon Bennett's
Vue de Monde is for diners who don't mind
paying top dollar for extraordinary food. The
adjoining **Bistro Vue** (tel: 03-9691 3838;
$$) pleases both the palate and the budget.
$$$$

Melbourne Excursions
Bella Vedere
874 Maroondah Hwy, Coldstream,
Yarra Valley
Tel: 03-5962 6161
www.badgersbrook.com.au
Inspiration for the menu at this restaurant at
Badger's Brook Estate comes courtesy of its
huge vegetable and herb garden. **$$–$$$**

Salix
Willow Creek Vineyard, 166 Balnarring
Road, Merricks North

Stokehouse

Tel: 03-5989 7640
www.willow-creek.com.au
Excellent food, organic local ingredients,
extraordinary views and local wines make
Salix well worth a trip from Melbourne. **$$$**

Western Districts
A La Grècque
60 Great Ocean Road, Aireys Inlet
Tel: 03-5289 6922
www.alagrecque.com.au
Stylish surrounds and an unpretentious and
delicious Mediterranean-flavoured menu
are on offer at this hugely popular taverna.
$$–$$$

Royal Mail Hotel
Corner Glenelg Highway and Parker
Street, Dunkeld
Tel: 03-5577 2241
www.royalmail.com.au
Generally regarded as the best restaurant
in the Grampians, with innovative tasting
menus and an acclaimed wine list. **$$$$**

The Goldfields
The Bridge
49 Bridge Street, Bendigo
Tel: 03-5443 7811
www.thebridgebendigo.com.au
This beautifully renovated landmark building
houses Bendigo's most popular gastro-pub.
$$$

L'Espresso
417 Sturt Street, Ballarat

Tel: 03-5333 1789
Always full of locals enjoying exceptional coffee, tasty food and a welcoming vibe. **$**

Northern Victoria
Oscar W's
101 Murray Esplanade, Port of Echuca, Echuca
Tel: 03-5482 5133
www.oscarws.com.au
Magnificent views of the paddle steamers chugging along the Murray below are matched by top-notch food and wine. **$$$**

Simone's
98 Gavan Street, Bright
Tel: 03-5755 2266
www.simonesrestaurant.com.au
Patrizia Simone applies her Italian expertise to seasonal local produce to stunning effect at this highly regarded restaurant. **$$$**

NIGHTLIFE AND ENTERTAINMENT

Melbourne's bar scene is famous throughout Australia. Stylish drinking dens are located in obscure lanes throughout the city, and suburbs such as Fitzroy and St Kilda are full of edgy bars, pubs and clubs, many of which host live music.

Melbourne
Bennetts Lane
25 Bennetts Lane
Tel: 03-9663 2856
www.bennettslane.com
The city's top jazz club, hosting local luminaries and occasional high-profile international acts.

The Gin Palace
190 Little Collins Street
Tel: 03-9654 0533
www.ginpalace.com.au
The seductive strains of lounge music and the sound of cocktail shakers getting a workout greet you at this Melbourne institution.

Melbourne Supper Club
161 Spring Street
Tel: 03-9654 6300
Deep sofas and discreet alcoves entice Melburnians of every age, as does the Siglo outdoor terrace with its great views of Parliament House.

Rocking out at The Toff in Town

The Toff in Town
2nd Floor, 252 Swanston Street, Melbourne
Tel: 03-9639 8770
www.thetoffintown.com
Upstairs from another popular bar, Cookie (www.cookie.net.au), TTIT hosts cabaret shows and has private booths for intimate drinking sessions.

St Kilda
The Esplanade Hotel
11 Upper Esplanade, St Kilda
Tel: 03-9534 0211
www.espy.com.au
The Espy is one of Melbourne's quintessential music venues, hosting live bands every night. The nearby Prince Bandroom (29 Fitzroy Street, tel: 03-9536 1168, www.princebandroom.com.au) offers more of the same.

TOURS

For details of tours about Indigenous culture, see *p.54*. For tours and activities in the state's national parks, check the Parks Victoria website (www.parkweb.vic.gov.au).

Balloon Sunrise
Tel: 1800 468 247
www.hotairballooning.com.au
Take a balloon ride over Melbourne or the Yarra Valley; or try **Global Ballooning** (www. globalballooning.com.au).

Go West Tours
10/167 Beavers Road, Northcote, Melbourne
Tel: 03-8508 9008
www.gowest.com.au
Day tours to Phillip Island or the Great Ocean Road run by a small eco-friendly operator.

Moonraker Charters
Sorrento Car Ferry Terminal,
Mornington Peninsula
Tel: 03-5984 4211

www.moonrakercharters.com.au
Swim with the dolphins and seals in Port Phillip Bay, or take a cruise to spot them. **Polperro Dolphin Swims** (www.polperro. com.au) offers similar tours.

12 Apostles Helicopters
9400 Great Ocean Road, Port Campbell
Tel: 03-5598 8283
www.12ah.com
See the famous rock formations from the air.

Yarra Valley Winery Tours
299 Maroondah Highway, Healesville
Tel: 03-5962 3870
www.yarravalleywinerytours.com.au
Daily bus tours from Melbourne in which you visit wineries and enjoy a delicious lunch.

Listings

FESTIVALS AND EVENTS

For details of Melbourne's world-famous sporting events, *see p.178.*

January/February
Midsumma
www.midsumma.org.au
Gay and lesbian cultural festival.

March/April
Melbourne Food & Wine Festival
www.melbournefoodandwine.com.au
Tastings, master classes and the 'world's longest lunch'.

Melbourne International Comedy Festival
www.comedyfestival.com.au
One of the world's biggest comedy festivals.

Melbourne International Flower & Garden Show
www.melbflowershow.com.au
The best of Australian gardening in the Royal Exhibition Building and Carlton Gardens.

May
Next Wave Festival
http://2010.nextwave.org.au
A celebration of the alternative arts scene.

August/September
Melbourne Writers' Festival
www.mwf.com.au
A celebration of books and writing.

October
Melbourne International Arts Festival
www.melbournefestival.com.au
The best theatre, music, dance and opera.

November
Queenscliff Music Festival
www.qmf.net.au
Blues and folk in this heritage town on the Bellarine Peninsula at the end of November.

South Australia

This state, with its multinational culture, is renowned for food, wine and festivals. South Australia is blessed with a Mediterranean coastal climate and its sights are many and varied, from the rugged grandeur of the Flinders Ranges and sand dunes of the north, to the green banks of the Murray River and untamed surf of the Great Australian Bight.

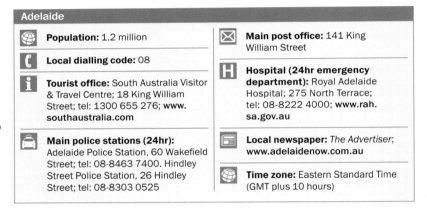

Adelaide

Population: 1.2 million

Local dialling code: 08

Tourist office: South Australia Visitor & Travel Centre; 18 King William Street; tel: 1300 655 276; www. southaustralia.com

Main police stations (24hr): Adelaide Police Station, 60 Wakefield Street; tel: 08-8463 7400. Hindley Street Police Station, 26 Hindley Street; tel: 08-8303 0525

Main post office: 141 King William Street

Hospital (24hr emergency department): Royal Adelaide Hospital; 275 North Terrace; tel: 08-8222 4000; www.rah. sa.gov.au

Local newspaper: *The Advertiser*; www.adelaidenow.com.au

Time zone: Eastern Standard Time (GMT plus 10 hours)

South Australia is a self-reliant state, with all its needs found within its borders: coal from the open-cut mines of Leigh Creek, gas from under the northeastern desert, grain and cattle from across hundreds of kilometres of land, fish from the Southern Ocean, and renowned wines from scenic vineyards.

The history of South Australia is distinctive. There were no convicts, as the colony was founded as a planned community run by wealthy idealists. The 'free settlers only' tag is a source of local pride, and sobriety and morality were the keystones of the master plan. This gave rise to a reputation for stuffy Puritanism, but fortunately the influence of the state's 'wowsers' (killjoys) has long faded.

Spread across 1 million sq km (390,000 sq miles), the state occupies one-eighth of the entire continent of Australia. Because most of the state is unendurable desert, however, the inhabitants number around only onethirteenth of the country's total population and more than three-quarters of South Australians live in the graceful capital, Adelaide.

Adelaide and Suburbs

With a population of over 1 million, **Adelaide ❶** is a sophisticated capital where culture and good living are key elements of the local scene. The sunny, dry climate beams on the city's many parks and gardens, as well as its elegant squares and broad boulevards. Known as the 'Festival City', the city hosts a significant art gallery and the world's largest collection of Aboriginal artefacts in the South Australian Museum.

North Terrace

The stateliest of Adelaide's streets is **North Terrace**, which delineates the northern edge of the business district and is lined with trees and distinguished buildings – mansions and museums, churches and memorials.

Between North Terrace and the landscaped bank of the river is the **Adelaide Festival Centre** Ⓐ (www.adelaide festivalcentre.com.au), which calls to mind Sydney's Opera House but with

Adelaide Festival Centre has a theatre for every occasion

Take in the elegant state capital from the comfort of a pedal boat

angular planes in place of billowing curves. The complex has a theatre for every occasion. You can eat outdoors in the Festival Centre's bistro overlooking the river, or enjoy a picnic on the lawn of the surrounding **Elder Park**.

From Elder Park you can take a river cruise on the *Popeye* **passenger launch** up the river to the **Adelaide Zoo** Ⓑ (www.zoossa.com. au/adelaide-zoo; daily 9.30am–5pm; charge Ⓜ), where the big attraction is the giant pandas. You can also pet the

South Australia

The Chocolate Factory

Haigh's has been producing delicious chocolates since 1915, making it the oldest family-run chocolate manufacturer in Australia. The **Haigh's Chocolate Visitors Centre** (154 Greenhill Road, Parkside; tel: 08-8372 7077; www. haighschocolates.com.au; Mon–Fri 8.30am–5.30pm, Sat 9am–5pm; free Ⓜ) runs factory tours (at 11am, 1pm and 2pm) covering the history of the company and providing behind-the-scenes insights into the alchemy that turns the humble cocoa bean into devastatingly good chocolate. Phone bookings are essential.

kangaroos and admire an outstanding collection of Australian birds.

Just behind the Festival Centre, the **South Australian Parliament House** ❸ (www.parliament.sa.gov.au; guided tours non-sitting days Mon–Fri 10am and 2pm; free) is dignified by 10 Corinthian columns and so much expensive stonework it is nicknamed the 'marble palace'. Just across the road is **Government House**, the official residence of the Governor of South Australia. Behind the State Library is the **Migration Museum** ❹ (www.history.sa.gov.au; Mon–Fri 10am–5pm, Sat–Sun 1pm–5pm; free 🅜), which tells the stories of migrants to South Australia.

Elsewhere along North Terrace, the **University of Adelaide** is at the heart of a cluster of cultural institutions. The excellent **South Australian Museum** ❺ (www.samuseum.sa.gov.au; daily 10am–5pm; free 🅜) houses a monumental collection of Aboriginal artefacts, biodiversity galleries and an excellent gallery dedicated to the Pacific Islands. The **Art Gallery of South Australia** ❻ (www.artgallery.sa.gov.au; daily 10am–5pm; free 🅜), which officially opened in 1881, covers many centuries of the world's art, ranging from ancient Chinese ceramics to contemporary Australian prints, drawings, paintings and sculptures. The gallery is also home to an extensive collection of Aboriginal art.

To the north of Ayers House lie the **Botanic Gardens** ❼ (www.environment.sa.gov.au; Mon–Fri 7am–sunset, Sat–Sun 9am–sunset; free), 20 hectares (50 acres) of lawns, trees, shrubs and lakes. Exceptional botanical buildings include the old Palm House, brought here from Germany

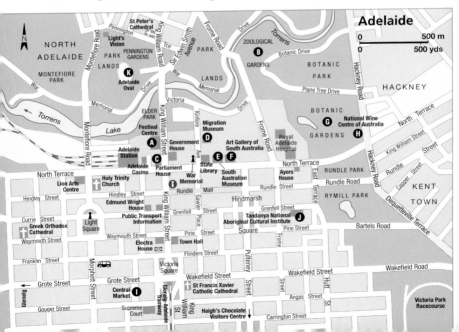

Central Market is an epicurean's delight

in 1871, and the extraordinary Bicentennial Conservatory of 1988.

Adjacent to the Botanic Gardens, at the corner of Botanic and Hackney roads, the **National Wine Centre of Australia** ❽ (www.wineaustralia.com.au; daily 10am–5pm; free) is the place to visit if you want to get to grips with what's involved in wine production and how better to appreciate different wines. Test what you've learnt with a wine tasting in the on-site café.

Rundle Mall

Parallel with North Terrace is **Rundle Mall**, an all-weather pedestrian mall and the heart of Adelaide's shopping area. Adelaide's **Central Market** ❶ (Gouger Street; www.adelaidecentral market.com.au; Tue 7am–5.30pm, Thur 9am–5.30pm, Fri 7am–9pm, Sat 7am–3pm; free) is a 140-year-old produce market with all the hustle and bustle you'd expect considering the fantastic selection of foodie delights on offer. The market encompasses Adelaide's Chinatown, which spills out into Gouger Street, one of the city's main restaurant strips.

On Grenfell Street, the **Tandanya National Aboriginal Cultural Institute** ❿ (www.tandanya.com.au; daily

Adelaide Transport

 Airport: Adelaide Airport (tel: 08-8309 9211; **www.aal.com.au**) is 6km (4 miles) west of the city centre. Transport to Adelaide: taxi (15–20 minutes; A$20); Skylink shuttle bus (tel: 1300 383 783; **www.skylinkadelaide.com**; 1–2 hourly between 6.30am and 9.45pm; adult A$8.50 one way, A$14 return)

 Trains, buses and trams: Run by Adelaide Metro (tel: 1800 182 160; **www.adelaidemetro.com.au**). Single tickets, multi-trip tickets and all-day tickets can be purchased at the Adelaide Metro InfoCentre (corner of King William and Curry streets), on board, at staffed train stations and at newsagents. Services vary but in general public transport runs from 6am to midnight

 Taxis: Adelaide Independent Taxis; tel: 132 211. Yellow Cabs; tel: 132 227

 Parking: Road parking is metered; there are plenty of privately operated undercover car parks

North of the city centre, **Light's Vision** is not a sound-and-light show, as its name might suggest. It's a monument to the foresight of Lt-Col William Light, who was sent out from Britain in 1836 to find the ideal site for a model city and devise the entire plan for its development. Atop a pedestal on Montefiore Hill, his statue peers over the parklands, pointing at the city of Adelaide, which he created.

10am–5pm; charge ) is an outstanding Aboriginal cultural centre hosting art galleries, a workshop and performing arts. The shop stocks a range of authentic Aboriginal arts and crafts.

North Adelaide

This upmarket suburb was established as an exclusive enclave for the transplanted English gentry, who shipped out grand pianos and chandeliers to decorate the salons of the grand colonial houses they built here. On the northern side of the River Torrens is historic **Adelaide Oval** Ⓚ, the most beautiful cricket ground in the country, which is well worth a visit during the summer cricket season. At the northern end of the Oval stands the neo-Gothic St Peter's Cathedral.

Glenelg

The last surviving tramcars still clatter between the edge of Victoria Square and the seashore at suburban **Glenelg**. This lively beach resort was the original landing place of the colonists who founded South Australia. A full-size replica of their vessel, a converted freighter named **HMS** *Buffalo*, moored nearby, is now a restaurant. In the historic Glenelg Town Hall, the **Bay Discovery Centre** (www.holdfast. sa.gov.au; daily 10am–5pm; free) is an interpretive museum dedicated to the social history and culture of the area.

Wine Regions

Cosmopolitan though it can be, Adelaide never loses that country-town feeling. You can drive across the city in half an hour, and you can be in beautiful countryside in no time.

Adelaide Hills

South and east of the city, the **Adelaide Hills**, the last manifestation of the Flinders Ranges, provide a backdrop of forests, orchards and vineyards. There are lovely drives, walks and views, and plenty of picnic spots. You can also

The full-size replica HMS *Buffalo* in Glenelg is now a restaurant

Barossa Valley

South Australia

see wildlife at close range at the **Warrawong Wildlife Sanctuary** (www.warrawong.com; daily 9am–7pm; free ), home to South Australia's only mainland platypus population.

The **Petaluma Winery** (Mount Barker Road, Bridgewater; www.petaluma.com.au; cellar door daily 10am–5pm) is set in the heritage-listed, restored stone-floor Bridgewater Mill. Tasting highlights include Riesling, Chardonnay and a lovely botrytis Semillon. You can also dine at the **Bridgewater Mill** restaurant *(see p.213)*.

The **Penfolds Magill Estate** (78 Penfold Road, Magill; tel 08-8301 5569; www.penfolds.com; cellar door daily Mon–Fri 10am–5pm) is the original home of the company responsible for Australia's iconic wine, Grange *(see p.31)*. Its restaurant *(see p.214)* is one of the best in the state and it is possible to take a tasting tour (daily 11am and 3pm; charge) of the historic estate – bookings are recommended.

Hahndorf, a hill village 30km (19 miles) southeast of Adelaide, has changed little since it was settled in 1839 by German refugees. It is the oldest surviving German settlement in Australia, and the **Hahndorf Academy** (www.hahndorfacademy.org.au; 10am–5pm; free ) features a German migration museum, exhibition centre and restored heritage buildings.

Barossa Valley

Australia's best-known wine-producing region, the **Barossa Valley** ❷ is 50km (30 miles) northeast of Adelaide, perfect for an easy all-day excursion. There are well over 50 cellar doors to choose from, with a few of the best including **Grant Burge Wines** (Barossa Valley Way, Tanunda; daily 10am–5pm; www.grantburgewines.com.au), **Penfold's Winery** (Tanunda Road, Nuriootpa; www.penfolds.com; daily 10am–5pm) and **Peter Lehmann Wines** (Para Road, Tanunda; www.peterlehmann wines.com.au; Mon–Fri 10am–5pm).

While in the area, a visit to **Maggie Beer's Farm Shop** (Pheasant Farm Road, Nuriootpa; www.maggiebeer.

com.au; daily 10.30am–5pm) is a must. Maggie is one of Australia's leading celebrity cooks and a Barossa icon – at her farm shop you can catch a daily cooking demonstration at 2pm or pick up some picnic supplies. Nearby, in Angaston, the popular **Barossa Farmers' Market** (corner Stockwell and Nuriootpa Roads; www.barossafarmers market.com; Sat 7.30–11.30am) is a great place to stock up on the freshest Barossa fruit and vegetables and sit down to a fry-up breakfast.

Clare Valley

Although the Barossa is the best-known wine-producing area in Australia, it is only one of five major wine regions within easy driving distance of Adelaide. Clare is the centre of the wine area of the **Clare Valley** ❸ and Watervale region, about 130km (80 miles) north of Adelaide, with more than 20 wineries and 40 cellar doors in a 25km (15-mile) strip. The region is famed for its Rieslings but you will also find fine Shiraz and Cabernet Sauvignon drops.

The region's wine-making industry was launched by Jesuit priests fleeing persecution in Silesia, who settled in the Clare Valley in 1848 and began

Mount Lofty is the highest of the Adelaide Hills

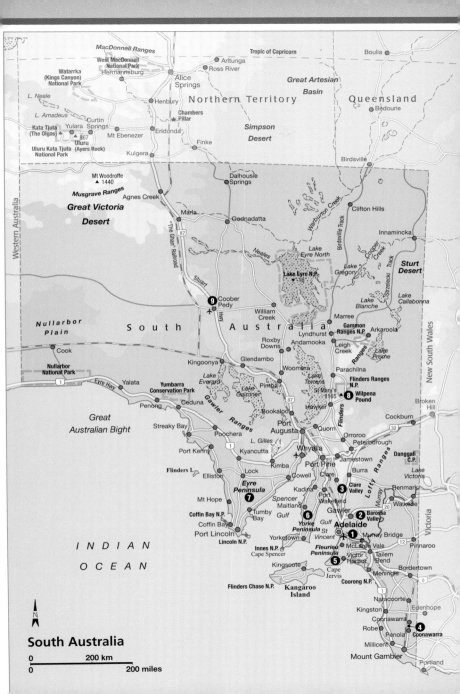

South Australia

0   200 km

0   200 miles

⭐ FESTIVAL FEVER

South Australia may sit towards the bottom of the Australian scale when it comes to population, GDP and other dry statistics, but it punches well and truly above its weight when it comes to hosting cultural festivals. The 'Festival State', as it is known, prides itself on its arts, food and wine shindigs, and the streets of Adelaide are thronged with locals and visitors from interstate and overseas between February and April, the main festival season.

Sydney, Melbourne and Perth all have their arts festivals, but none compares in size, prestige or sheer excitement to the **Adelaide Festival** (www.adelaide festival.com.au), which is held in March annually and trades on the city's natural advantages. Few places in the world have such an extraordinary range of performance spaces, from the gleaming white Festival Centre to the outdoor amphitheatres and intimate lofts. The weather is nigh perfect, with dry, hot days and clear, star-studded nights, and you can walk between every venue within about 15 minutes.

During the Arts Festival, Adelaide hosts the associated **Writers' Week**, an event that lures the literary heavies from around the globe. Sessions are free to all, with readings by famous authors and book launches held in the Pioneer Women's Memorial Gardens on King William Street, across from the Festival Centre.

Writers' Week is a highlight of Adelaide's cultural calendar

The **Adelaide Fringe** (www.adelaide fringe.com.au), which runs for approximately three weeks every February and March, is second in size only to Edinburgh. Thousands of arts acts arrive from all over Australia, Europe and North America to perform during the Fringe. The focus tends to be around the bars and restaurants of Rundle Street East, where the festivities continue until dawn at the Fringe Club, but buskers and performers spread throughout the city.

The huge World Music Festival known as **WOMADelaide** (www.womadelaide. com.au) is held in the city's Botanic Park every March, while **Tasting Australia** (www.tasting-australia.com.au) sees food and wine media and celebrity chefs from around the world cooking and talking up a storm in late April/early May every even-numbered year.

The **Adelaide Festival of Ideas** (www. adelaidefestival.com.au) is a more recent addition to the state's cornucopia of celebrations, and takes place every odd year in varying months. It attracts leading writers and thinkers from around the world, including ex-prime ministers, journalists, political commentators and university professors.

Between May and October most wine-producing areas hold food, wine and music festivals, the most notable being the **Barossa Vintage Festival** (www.barossavintagefestival.com.au) every April in odd-numbered years, the **Clare Valley Gourmet Weekend** (www.clarevalleygourmet.com.au) in May and the McLaren Vale's **Sea and Vines Festival** (www.mclarenvale.info/ seaandvines) in June.

WOMADelaide takes over the Botanic Park every March

making sacramental wines at **Sevenhill Cellars** (College Road; www.sevenhill.com.au; Mon–Fri 9am–5pm). **Annie's Lane** (www.annieslane.com.au) incorporates a cellar door (located in a century-old cellar), wine-making museum and art gallery and is also worth a visit.

The **Riesling Trail** (www.southaustralia.com) is a 35km (22-mile) trail linking the townships of Auburn, Leasingham, Watervale, Penwortham, Sevenhill, Clare and White Hut. The route has plenty of cellar doors, cafés and restaurants. You can stroll or take a bike to ride along one of the trail loops.

Coonawarra

In the southeast of the state, between Adelaide and Melbourne, the vineyards of the **Coonawarra ❹** area are justly famed for their reds. Vineyards at Keppoch and Padthaway are becoming equally well known. **Padthaway Estate** (Riddoch Highway, Padthaway; www.padthawayestate.com; daily 10am–4pm) combines vineyards, a winery and the homestead, a Victorian-era mansion offering boutique accommodation, set in an oasis of green English-style gardens. **Wynn's Coonawarra Estate** (Memorial Drive; www.wynns.com.au; daily 10am–5pm) was founded by Scottish pioneer John Riddoch in 1861, and is the region's oldest winery. The winery produces lovely Shiraz, Cabernet Sauvignon and Chardonnay wines.

While in the area, take some time to visit the **Mary McKillop Penola Centre** (corner Portland Street and Petticoat Lane; www.mackilloppenola.org.au; daily 10am–4pm; charge), a museum and interpretive centre dedicated to Australia's first saint.

The Fleurieu, Yorke and Eyre Peninsulas

The deeply indented coastline of South Australia has made a set of natural divisions, each with its own appeal.

Fleurieu Peninsula

Just south of Adelaide, the **Fleurieu Peninsula ❺** is an easy-to-reach vacationland of surfing beaches, vineyards and history. The peninsula's first industry was whaling, centred on **Victor Harbor**. It's now the area's biggest town, and a popular year-round resort. Nearby, **Granite Island** (connected to the mainland by a causeway with a horse-drawn tram) is an adventure park and winter whale-watching spot.

Further inland, scores of vineyards basking in the sunshine of the Southern Vales are the reason for the peninsula's fame. They've been making great wine since 1838. The best-known area of wine production is **McLaren Vale**,

A tram links Granite Island with the mainland

The ruggedly beautiful Eyre Peninsula

served by Willunga with its heritage buildings, gourmet cafés and galleries.

Cape Jervis, at the end of the peninsula, is the stepping-off point for Kangaroo Island (*see box, right*).

Yorke and Eyre Peninsulas

A loop of picturesque towns, the **Yorke Peninsula** ❻ takes in the east-coast port of **Ardrossan** and **Edithburgh**, with its splendid cliff-top views and famous old pub, the Troubridge Hotel. The magical drive south to **Yorketown** offers great coastal views of offshore reefs, popular with local scuba divers.

It was from places such as **Port Victoria** and **Wallaroo**, on Yorke Peninsula's west coast, that great windjammers departed to race back to Britain and Europe with their cargoes of grain. Farming and fishing still play important parts in the peninsula's modest economy, but mineral wealth contributed a colourful chapter to the area's history. The discovery of copper at **Kadina** and **Moonta** led to the mass migration of Cornish miners and their families from southwest England.

The **Eyre Peninsula** ❼ reaches as far west as **Ceduna**, where the vast expanse of the Nullarbor Plain begins. It's more than 1,200km (745 miles) from Ceduna westward to the next town of any significance (Norseman, WA). The highway follows the dunes and cliffs lining the Great Australian Bight.

South Australia

Kangaroo Island

South Australia's favourite playground, **Kangaroo Island** is Australia's third-largest island – you could spend a week here finding the best places for swimming, fishing and sightseeing.

From the gentle sandy beaches of the **Dudley Peninsula** to the pounding surf on **Cape du Couedic**, the island has a wide range of terrains. The island's main towns are **Kingscote**, **American River** and **Penneshaw**, and exploring the scenery and observing wildlife are the main activities here. Nightly processions of little penguins can be seen on the beaches around Kingscote and Penneshaw, and you can walk among one of Australia's largest colonies of sea lions at Seal Bay.

Flinders Ranges and the Outback

For scenic splendour, South Australia's Outback competes well with the remote areas of the other Australian states, nowhere more impressively than in the Flinders Ranges, 450km (280 miles) due north of Adelaide.

An outstanding phenomenon found in the spectacular **Flinders Ranges National Park** (www.environment.sa.gov.au/parks/sanpr/flindersranges; charge) is a huge natural basin called **Wilpena Pound ❽**. Rimmed by sheer cliffs, the saucer is around 20km (12 miles) long and 8km (5 miles) wide. Wilpena Pound is not only spectacular for its scenery and geology; it also wins admiring squawks from birdwatchers.

The flat floor of the Pound is perfectly designed for bush walks (suggested routes are signposted) – but not in summer, when it's altogether too hot for unnecessary exertion. In any season it's essential to carry drinking water.

Coober Pedy

The opal-mining town of **Coober Pedy ❾** must rate as one of the most bizarre tourist attractions in the world. When you say 'desert' this is what it means: in the summer the daytime temperature can reach 50°C (122°F), yet nearly 4,000 people make their home in this far corner of the Outback.

The name Coober Pedy comes from an Aboriginal phrase meaning 'white fellow's hole in the ground', for the settlers have survived here by burrowing hobbit-like into the side of a low hill. The temperatures within are constant and comfortable, regardless of the excesses outside. Among the dugouts are homes, a Roman Catholic chapel, several motels and B&Bs, a café, restaurant and shops.

Opal mining at Coober Pedy

ACCOMMODATION

Adelaide has been spaciously planned, so if you need to be within walking distance of the Festival Centre, South Australian Art Gallery and lively East End neighbourhood, make sure to stay in the Central Business District. North Adelaide has a wealth of historic B&Bs with views of the Adelaide Hills. Attractive Glenelg offers restful ocean views and a good choice of accommodation.

Adelaide and Suburbs

Adelaide Backpackers Inn
112 Carrington Street
Tel: 08-8223 6635
www.adelaidebackpackersinn.net.au
This small and well set-up backpacker hotel with dorms and double rooms has free internet access. **$$**

Adelaide Central YHA
135 Waymouth Street
Tel: 08-8414 3010
www.yha.com.au
A modern and very comfortable YHA hostel with top-notch facilities, the Adelaide Central has family rooms and doubles/twins with private bathrooms available. **$$**

Adelaide Meridien Hotel & Apartments
21–37 Melbourne Street, North Adelaide
Tel: 08-8267 3033
www.adelaidemeridien.com.au
Offering well-located accommodation close to cafés, boutiques and parklands, the Meridien has a range of tastefully refurbished rooms and apartments. **$$$**

Clarion Hotel Soho
264 Flinders Street
Tel: 08-8412 5611
www.clarionhotelsoho.com.au
Sleek and stylish without being too minimal, the Clarion offers a gorgeous range of suites and studios. **$$$$**

Glenelg Beach Hostel & Bar
1–7 Moseley Street, Glenelg
Tel: 08-8376 0007
www.glenelgbeachhostel.com.au
Close to the beach, and located in a lovely heritage-listed building, this hostel offers comfortable dorms, singles, doubles and family rooms. **$$**

Majestic Roof Garden Hotel
55 Frome Street
Tel: 08-8100 4400
www.majestichotels.com.au
Close to the heart of the city, the Majestic has a friendly atmosphere and offers spacious, comfortable and well-appointed rooms. **$$$$**

Medina Grand Adelaide Treasury
2 Flinders Street
Tel: 08-8112 0000
www.medina.com.au
Serviced apartments and studios are located in the centre of town on Victoria Square, in the grand heritage-listed treasury building. **$$$**

Princes Lodge
73 Lefevre Terrace, North Adelaide
Tel: 08-8267 5566
www.princeslodge.com.au
This Edwardian mansion may have seen better days, but it's a friendly place in a good location within walking distance of the city. **$$**

Stamford Grand Hotel
Moseley Square, Glenelg
Tel: 08-8376 1222
www.stamford.com.au
With beautiful views of the ocean or the Adelaide Hills, this award-winning high-rise

Stamford Grand Hotel

resort offers extra-large rooms and touches of Victorian-era grandeur. **$$$$**

Stamford Plaza Adelaide
150 North Terrace
Tel: 08-8461 1111
www.stamford.com.au
In the centre of town, Adelaide's original five-star hotel has been refurbished and includes a delightful terrace garden. **$$$**

Wine Regions
Collingrove Homestead
Eden Valley Road, Angaston
Tel: 08-8564 2061
www.collingrovehomestead.com.au
A National Trust–listed homestead in the Barossa Ranges, Collingrove has extensive English-style gardens. **$**

Langmeil Cottages
89 Langmeil Road, Tanunda
Tel: 08-8563 2987
www.langmeilcottages.com
Take in beautiful views from self-contained units, and enjoy the use of bicycles, barbecue and swimming pool. **$$**

Mount Lofty House
74 Mount Lofty Summit Road, Crafers
Tel: 08-8339 6777
www.mtloftyhouse.com.au
In the Adelaide Hills, this elegant boutique hotel has views of the Piccadilly Valley. **$$$**

Padthaway Estate Homestead
Riddoch Highway, Padthaway
Tel: 08-8765 5555
www.padthawayestate.com
Choose from six rooms and several cosy lounges at this magnificent 19th-century mansion amid vineyards. **$$$**

Thorngrove Country Manor
2 Glenside Lane, Stirling
Tel: 08-8339 6748
www.slh.com
This Gothic fantasy complete with turrets and gables offers sophisticated five-star luxury. There's a fine restaurant on site. **$$$$**

Fleurieu Peninsula
Willunga House B&B
1 St Peter's Terrace, Willunga
Tel: 08-8556 2467
www.willungahouse.com.au
Heritage-listed and fully restored, this Georgian house has five beautifully appointed rooms. The excellent breakfast includes home-grown organic produce. **$$$**

Outback
Arkaroola Wilderness Sanctuary
Arkaroola, Northern Flinders Ranges via Port Augusta
Tel: 08-8648 4848
www.arkaroola.com.au
Set in a rugged Outback landscape, the accommodation options here range from campsites to cabins and lodges. **$$$**

Desert Cave Hotel
Hutchison Street, Coober Pedy
Tel: 08-8672 5688
www.desertcave.com.au
For something different, stay in this deluxe underground hotel in Australia's most famous opal-mining Outback community. **$$$**

The Underground Motel
Catacomb Road, Coober Pedy
Tel: 08-8672 5324
www.theundergroundmotel.com.au
This friendly, comfortable motel has a guest kitchen for self-catered breakfasts. **$$**

RESTAURANTS

South Australia is home to a thriving food and wine scene, and is particularly well known for its vineyard restaurants. These are dotted throughout the Adelaide Hills, Coonawarra district and Barossa and Clare valleys.

Adelaide and Suburbs

Amalfi Pizzeria Ristorante
29 Frome Street
Tel: 08-8223 1948
Amalfi serves authentic Italian specials to its loyal supper crowd. The good-natured staff add to the appeal. **$$**

Auge
22 Grote Street
Tel: 08-8410 9332
www.auge.com.au
Auge is known for its award-winning modern Italian cuisine and smart decor. Espresso and juices are available all day from the impressive bar. **$$$**

Chianti Classico
160 Hutt Street, Glenelg
Tel: 08-8232 7955
www.chianticlassico.com.au
A popular, family-orientated restaurant offering pasta and other classic Italian dishes. **$$$**

Good Life Pizza
170 Hutt Street, Glenelg
Tel: 08-8223 2618
www.goodlifepizza.com
Great pizzas are made here using local free-range and organic ingredients. **$$**

The Manse
142 Tynte Street, North Adelaide
Tel: 08-8267 4636
www.themanserestaurant.com.au
A sophisticated menu and even-more sophisticated setting make this the number one choice for a special night out in Adelaide. **$$$**

The Pot Food & Wine
Shop 2, 160 King William Road, Hyde Park
Tel: 08-8373 2044
www.thepotfoodandwine.com.au
This intimate place has all of the charm and some of the menu items that make Parisian bistros so alluring. The wine list is fabulous. **$$–$$$**

Red Ochre Grill
War Memorial Drive
Tel: 08-8211 8555
www.redochre.com.au
Specialising in bush tucker/native Australian produce, this is the place to sample wallaby shanks or emu pâté. The waterfront location on Torrens Lake boasts city views. **$$$**

Stanley's Fish Café
76 Gouger Street
Tel: 08-8410 0909
King George whiting, garfish and tommy ruffs are some of the tastiest catches to look out for on the menu at Stanley's. **$$$**

Wine Regions

Bridgewater Mill
Mount Barker Road, Bridgewater
Tel: 08-8339 9200
www.bridgewatermill.com.au
Dine alfresco in the historic setting of this Adelaide Hills winery. The mill also houses the cellar door and tastings for Petaluma wines. **$$$**

The Lane Vineyard
Ravenswood Lane, Hahndorf
Tel: 08-8388 1250
www.thelane.com.au
The vineyard views, bistro-style dining and fine selection of wines make this restaurant a perfect locale for a long, lazy lunch. **$$$**

Red Ochre Grill

Penfolds Magill Estate
78 Penfold Road, Magill
Tel: 08-8301 5551
www.penfolds.com
Overlooking five hectares of Shiraz vines, this up-market restaurant only 15 minutes' drive from Adelaide is a glorious spot for lunch (Fri only) or dinner (Tue–Sat). The sophisticated menu is complemented by a wine list that is as impressive as one would expect from this industry-leading company. **$$$–$$$$**

Pipers of Penola
58 Riddoch St, Penola
Tel: 08-8737 3999
www.pipersofpenola.com.au
Pipers offers an elegant fine-dining experience. The classic Mod Oz menu is complemented by the restaurant's polished wood and clean white lines. **$$$**

Windy Point Restaurant
Windy Point Lookout, Belair Road, Belair
Tel: 08-8278 8255
www.windypoint.com.au
Just above the lookout area at Windy Point, this restaurant has fantastic panoramic views over the city, a seasonal menu and a wine list sourced mainly from South Australia. **$$$**

Fleurieu Peninsula
Fino
8 Hill Street, Willunga
08-8556 4488
www.fino.net.au
Fino's award-winning menu features dishes with a rustic Mediterranean twist. **$$$**

NIGHTLIFE AND ENTERTAINMENT
Adelaide is a mix and match of grungy pubs, hip bars and clubs. Much of the action takes place around Rundle Street, Hindley Street and seaside Glenelg.

Apothecary 1878
118 Hindley Street
Tel: 08-8212 9099
www.theapothecary1878.com.au
Antique pharmacy cabinets, marble tables and chaise longues adorn the heritage-listed Apothecary bar and restaurant, which has a fabulous wine list.

The Exeter Hotel
264 Rundle Street
Tel: 08-82232623
The Exeter is a fine gastro-pub, offering a mix of great atmosphere, good food and live music.

Glenelg Pier Hotel
18 Holdfast Promenade, Glenelg
08-8350 3188
www.glenelgpier.com.au
At this multipurpose venue the panoramic beach views are more than matched by a mix of bars, cafés, restaurants and live music.

Universal Wine Bar
285 Rundle Street
Tel: 08-8232 5000
www.universalwinebar.com.au
Slick and stylish, the Universal has an impressive wine list and ever-changing menu.

TOURS

From wine to Indigenous culture, there's no shortage of tours in South Australia.

Adelaide Sightseeing
85 Franklin Street
Tel: 1300-769 762
www.adelaidesightseeing.com.au
Offers a variety of excellent tours in and
around Adelaide and South Australia.

Arabunna Tours
Tel: 08-8675 8351
www.arabunnatours.com
Aboriginal-owned Arabunna offers tours on
Indigenous culture, tradition and sacred sites.

Balloon Adventure
Tel: 08-8389 3195
www.balloonadventures.com.au
Soak up the famous wine region of the
Barossa Valley from above.

Wine Lovers Tours
Tel: 08-8270 5500
www.wineloverstours.com.au
Specialises in a range of wine tours of the
Adelaide region, including the Barossa
Valley, Adelaide Hills and McLaren Vale.

FESTIVALS AND EVENTS

Adelaide is renowned as the festival city. *See p.206* for more information.

January
Tour Down Under
www.tourdownunder.com.au
The first race in cycling's yearly pro-tour calendar attracts big names and big crowds.

February/March
Adelaide Fringe
www.adelaidefringe.com.au
This world-renowned international arts festival showcases independent artists.

Adelaide Festival of Arts
www.adelaidefestival.com.au
Held in March every even-numbered year,
the festival covers all aspects of the arts.

WOMADelaide
www.womadelaide.com.au
This world music festival in March attracts
diverse performers from around the world.

April/May
Barossa Vintage Festival
www.barossavintagefestival.com.au
The Barossa Valley stages a week-long festival in April during odd-numbered years.

Clare Valley Gourmet Weekend
www.clarevalleygourmet.com.au
A celebration of local tipples is held in May.

Tasting Australia
www.tasting-australia.com.au
This food and wine festival is held in late
April/early May every even-numbered year.

June
Adelaide Cabaret Festival
www.adelaidecabaretfestival.com.au
Cabaret acts head up this two-week festival.

Sea and Vines Festival
www.mclarenvale.info/seaandvines
The McLaren Vale celebrates its produce.

November
Feast Festival
www.feast.org.au
A three-week gay and lesbian festival.

December
Bay Sports Festival
www.baysportsfestival.com.au
Held at the Glenelg foreshore, 26–31 Dec.

Western Australia

Western Australia is enormous, covering more than 2.5 million sq km (960,000 sq miles). Most of the state's vast expanse is desert or otherwise difficult terrain, but you'll also find lush forests, rugged canyons and far-flung gold-mining towns. The bulk of the population of 2 million has gravitated to the Mediterranean climate found around the beautiful capital city of Perth.

Perth

Population: 1.7 million

Local dialling code: 08

Tourist office: Western Australia Visitor Centre; Forrest Place, corner Wellington Street; tel: 08-9483 1111

Main police station (24hr): Ground Floor, Curtin House, 60 Beaufort Street; tel: 08-9223 3716

Main post office: 3 Forrest Place; tel: 08-9237 5460

Hospital: Royal Perth Hospital; 197 Wellington Street; tel: 08-9224 2244

Local newspaper: *The West Australian*; http://au.news.yahoo.com/thewest

Time zone: Eastern Standard Time (GMT plus 10 hours)

The first European to set eyes on a Western Australian beach was Dirk Hartog, a Dutch navigator making his way from the Cape of Good Hope to Java in 1616. More than 200 years after Hartog's discovery, the British finally got around to colonising the region. The site chosen, on the Swan River, became the city of Perth.

Western Australia's Outback produces great wealth, and even the forbidding deserts are bursting with minerals. It was gold that brought the state's first bonanza during the 1880s and 1890s, followed by nickel, bauxite and iron. Considerably more appealing are the above-ground riches: hardwood forests, orchards, vineyards, springtime wild-flowers and innumerable beaches along a magnificent coastline that stretches for 6,400km (4,000 miles).

Perth and Around

Brimming with vigour and energy, **Perth** ❶ takes full advantage of its setting on the serpentine Swan River. The dominant view is over Perth Water, where the Swan River widens into a broad bay about 1km (¾ mile) across. A little further downstream, fringing the river mouth, is a string of surfing beaches.

Central Business District (CBD)

Glittering high-rise office buildings scrape the clear blue skies of Perth.

The city's historic attractions, art galleries, stylish shopping and entertainment opportunities are complemented by myriad outdoor activities including great sailing, swimming, surfing and fishing. Further afield, the port of Fremantle combines heritage and history with plenty of relaxed café, dining and nightlife action.

On the edge of the business district, set high on an escarpment, **Kings Park & Botanic Garden** A (Kings Park Road; www.bgpa.wa.gov.au ) is a wonderful introduction for visitors to the city. There are over 400 hectares (990 acres) of natural woodland and wild-flowers, manicured lawns and picnic sites, bike tracks and trails. The Botanic Garden is home to a selection

Government House was built in the 1860s by convict labour

of over 2,000 indigenous plants. From the garden you have wonderful views of the city and Swan River as it meanders towards the sea.

Dominating the jetty on Riverside Drive are the sail-shaped copper wings of the tower containing the **Swan Bells** B (www.ringmybells. com.au; daily 10am–4pm; charge). The 82.5m (270ft) spire houses the 14th-century bells of the church of St-Martin-in-the-Fields, London – a Bicentennial present from Queen Elizabeth II. A top-floor observation deck gives views of the Perth skyline.

Tucked into the back of Stirling Gardens is the **Old Court House** (1837), Perth's first brick building, which has a modest facade of Doric columns. On the whole, however, buildings predating the state's 1890s gold rush are rare. **Government House** C (also in Stirling Gardens) stands as a true reflection of the beginning of the state. Constructed in the 1860s by convict labour, it placed a regal stamp of authority on the new settlement. Some say the emerging Australian 'larrikin' characteristic shows through in the upstairs

Looking over Perth's CBD, with its glittering high-rises

Western Australia

windows, which are in the shape of a broad arrow – the motif on the uniforms of the convict builders.

Perth's architecture of the 1890s gold rush includes **His Majesty's Theatre** ('The Maj') at the west end of Hay Street. To discover more about the gold rush and its pivotal role in the city's development, visit the 1899 **Perth Mint** ❶ at the eastern end of Hay Street (www.perth mint.com.au; Mon–Fri 9am–5pm, Sat–Sun 9am–1pm; charge 🏛), one of the world's oldest operating mints. Try picking up a block of gold worth A$250,000, minting your own medallion, or watch gold being smelted.

Two sections of town with contrasting histories are **London Court** and **East Murray Street Precinct**. London Court dates back to 1937 and is a monument to mock-Tudor kitsch; its

curiosities include a clock tower at each end: one a replica of London's Big Ben, the other of the Gros Horloge in Rouen, France. East Murray Street, by contrast, is the genuine Colonial item. It appears on the original town plans of 1838 and is now lined by early 20th-century buildings and old public offices.

On the northern side of the railway station, across the lovely **Horseshoe Bridge**, lies the **Perth Cultural Centre** ❺ (between Roe, Beaufort, Francis and William streets, Northbridge; www.perthculturalcentre. com.au), comprising the Western Australian Museum, Art Gallery of WA, State Library and Perth Institute of Contemporary Arts.

The **Western Australian Museum** (www.museum.wa.gov.au; daily 9.30am–5pm; free 🏛) is located in the

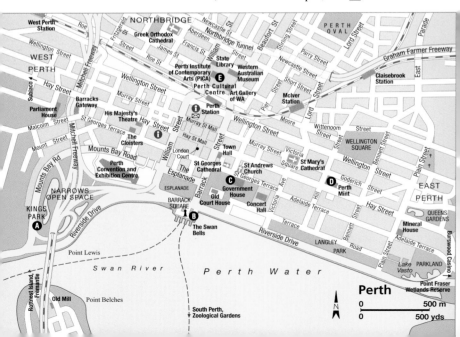

Old Gaol, constructed by convicts in 1856. The museum offers more than penal relics – it traces the history of the state from the formation of the Australian continent 120 million years ago to the present day. There is also an extensive collection of Aboriginal rock paintings, headdresses and weapons.

The **Art Gallery of Western Australia** (www.artgallery.wa.gov.au; daily 10am–5pm; free) houses a remarkable collection of Indigenous art as well as Western Australian, Australian and European collections.

The **Perth Institute of Contemporary Arts** (www.pica.org.au; Tue–Sun 11am–6pm; free) runs a lively programme of exhibitions, installations and events focusing on all areas of contemporary and experimental art.

Also north of the city centre is the **Northbridge** district, which is full

Art Gallery of Western Australia

of lively ethnic restaurants, pubs and nightclubs, especially around James and Lake streets.

Another fruitful neighbourhood for restaurants and bars is **Subiaco**, a fashionable suburb on the western side of town, directly accessed by the Perth–Fremantle railway. Come here for brunch on Friday or Saturday and visit

Perth Transport

 Airport: Perth Airport (tel: 08-9478 8888; **www.perthairport.net.au**) is 12km (7 miles) northeast of the city centre. Transport to Perth: taxi (20–30 minutes; A$50); Perth Airport Shuttle (tel: 1300 666 806; **www.perthairportconnect.com.au**; every 50 minutes, 6am–11.30pm; to CBD/hotels if pre-booked; adult A$15 one way, A$25 return)

 Trains and buses: Run by Transperth (tel: 136 213; **www.transperth.wa.gov.au**). Tickets: the reusable SmartRider card (A$10 for adults, A$5 for under-16s), which offers discounted travel, is available from Transperth InfoCentres and SmartRider Retail Sales Outlets. The Transperth bus and train DayRider pass is valid for unlimited travel after 9am weekdays and all day on weekends. Zone one, two and three single-trip tickets are also available. A Free Transit Zone (FTZ) for buses and trains operates within the Perth city boundaries. Look for the FTZ logo at bus stops. Trains and buses run from around 6am–11.30pm, with reduced services on weekends and public holidays

 Ferries: Run by Transperth. A ferry service connects Barrack Street Jetty in the city to Mends Street Jetty in South Perth. Ferries run every 20–30 minutes Mon–Fri 6.50am–7.24pm

 Taxis: Swan Taxis; tel: 131 330. Black & White; tel: 131 008

P **Parking:** Road parking is metered; there are plenty of privately operated undercover car parks

Contemporary sculptures on the beach at Fremantle

its busy weekend markets, perhaps after a walk in nearby Kings Park.

Fremantle and Beaches

The port city of **Fremantle ❷** combines a cosmopolitan Mediterranean ambience with a lovely Victorian-era quaintness.

In pride of place on Victoria Quay is the **Western Australian Maritime Museum** (www.museum.wa.gov.au; daily 9.30am–5pm; charge 🅜), which highlights the state's maritime heritage. The **Shipwreck Galleries** (daily 9.30am–5pm; free 🅜) are housed separately in the convict-built Commissariat on Cliff Street. They offer the chance to see some notable wrecks including the wooden hull of the *Batavia*, the flagship of the Dutch East India Company, which went aground in 1629 and was salvaged and restored in the late 20th century.

Fremantle Prison (1 The Terrace; www.fremantleprison.com.au; daily 10am–5pm; charge 🅜), a maximum security prison until 1991, offers a variety of tours including a spooky 'torchlight tour'.

One of the chief pleasures of Fremantle is to soak up the laid-back atmosphere and admire the gold-rush architecture. There's no shortage of restaurants, coffee shops and interesting specialist stores. On Fridays and weekends, scout the splendidly restored **Fremantle Markets** (corner South Terrace and Henderson Street; www.fremantlemarkets.com.au; free 🅜) for interesting crafts and souvenirs.

From Fremantle, a string of sandy beaches stretches north to **Hillarys Boat Harbour**, 50km (30 miles) along the coast. Development, though continuous, is almost without exception low-rise and low-key, set well back from the shore. Each of the beaches has its fans. For surfing, head for **Scarborough** or **Trigg**; for a lively après-beach scene, choose

Cottesloe, where the Indiana Tea Rooms offer good food, cocktails and fabulous sunset views.

For family-friendly attractions, head for the **Aquarium of Western Australia** (Hillarys Boat Harbour, 91 Southside Drive, Hillarys; www.aqwa.com.au; daily 10am–5pm; charge ). The aquarium re-creates the state's five coastal environments, the highlight being the walk-through 'shipwreck coast', where sharks, loggerhead turtles and stingrays glide smoothly overhead.

Swan Valley

If you have limited time during your stay in Perth, and can manage only one out-of-town trip, make it the **Swan Valley** ❸. A major wine-producing area, it offers vineyard tours and elegant towns such as **Guildford**, one of the earliest settlements in Western Australia and only 30 minutes by train or road from the city. The Swan Valley food and wine trail (www.swanvalley.com.au), a 32km (20-mile) loop, links some of the best vineyards and microbreweries. Also along the route is the **Caversham Wildlife Park** (www.cavershamwildlife.com.au), a good kangaroo-spotting location for visitors too short of time to 'go bush'. Caversham forms part of **Whiteman Park** (www.whitemanpark.com.au), packed with family attractions, including an excellent **Motor Museum** (daily 10am–4pm; charge).

221

Western Australia

Rottnest Island

Fremantle, Hillarys Boat Harbour and Barrack Street Jetty in Perth are springboards for Rottnest Island, an idyllic getaway just 19km (13 miles) offshore. First settled as a natural prison for West Australian Aborigines, 'Rotto', as it is known locally, is now a favourite holiday spot for Perth families. Private motor vehicles aren't allowed on the island, making it a superb place for cycling. Visitors spend their time boating, golfing, playing tennis, lazing on a quiet beach or trying to spot a quokka, the island's cute wallaby-like marsupials. In summer, divers come here to explore the world's southernmost coral reef. The island's pub, the Quokka Arms, has live music on summer evenings.

Fremantle Prison was a maximum-security facility until 1991

Southern Coast and the Goldfields

Head south of Perth for the region's top wineries, organic food producers and dense karri and jarrah forests. West of Perth, the frontier-style towns of the Goldfields have had their natural landscapes denuded by huge working mines ('super pits') and couldn't be more different.

Southern Coast

Immediately south of Fremantle, the landscape is fairly industrial apart from **Rockingham**, a springboard for **Penguin Island Conservation Park** (www.dec.wa.gov.au), named for its colony of over 1,000 penguins. Nearby **Mandurah** is a delightful town on the Peel Estuary and an easy day trip from Perth.

Further down the coast is the dairy town of **Harvey**, dating back to 1890. Nearby **Yalgorup National Park** (www.dec.wa.gov.au), reached by the old coast road, is a sanctuary for water birds and wildlife. Even more of an attraction is its colony of living, rare rock-like creatures known as thrombolites, the earliest-known life form on earth.

Bunbury ❹, a pleasant vacation town in the southwest, 180km (110 miles) from Perth, is a busy port that owes its existence to Lt Henry St Pierre Bunbury, who travelled overland to the coast from Pinjarra in 1836. One of the main reasons to stop off here is to visit the **Dolphin Discovery Centre** (Koombana Beach; www.dolphindiscovery.com. au; Oct–May 8am–4pm, June–Sept 9am–2pm; charge 🅼). About 100 bottlenose dolphins live in the bay and they're regular visitors to the shallows. Dolphin swim or watching tours are available.

It was logging of the nearby forests that brought prosperity to the region; jarrah and blackbutt hardwoods abound in the area, and can be seen in much of the early

Yalgorup National Park's fascinating thrombolites

The Margaret River region boasts vineyards galore

The **Margaret River** region, between Cape Naturaliste and Cape Leeuwin, is honeycombed with limestone caves, some of which are open to the public. Near Yallingup, **Ngilgi Caves** (daily 9.30am–3.30pm; charge; 👥) form a fantastic underground world of elaborately carved limestone.

The township of **Margaret River** ❺ is the perfect spot from which to tour the region's noted vineyards. This area is also famed as one of the nation's best surfing locations. The closest beaches are at Prevelly, a 10-minute drive from town. Visiting spectacular caves such as Mammoth, Lake and Jewel, and browsing in arts and crafts shops are alternatives to wine sampling.

Cape Leeuwin marks the southwest extremity of Australia and the junction of the Indian and Southern oceans. This point is written into

Western Australia

architecture. Bunbury sits at the northern end of **Geographe Bay**, a large sheltered waterway that has **Cape Naturaliste** as its northern spur. From here a cape-to-cape hiking trail leads south to Cape Leeuwin, 135km (84 miles) away.

On the southern coast of the bay, the resort town of **Busselton** has a fine setting on the Vasse River. The 2km (1¼-mile) **Busseltown Jetty** (www.busseltonjetty.com.au), the longest in the southern hemisphere, has an interpretive centre and **Underwater Observatory** (daily Dec–Apr 8am–5pm, May–Sept 10am–4pm, Oct–Nov 9am–5pm; charge 👥) that takes visitors 8m (26ft) below sea level for amazing views of fish and coral.

Margaret River Wines

The Margaret River wine-growing region is renowned for its wonderfully rich Cabernets, Merlots and intensely flavoured Chardonnays. Here are a few places to charge your glass over lunch:

Clairault Wines (3277 Caves Road, Wilyabrup; www.clairaultwines.com.au)

Cullen Wines (Caves Road, Wilyabrup; www.cullenwines.com.au)

Vasse Felix (corner Caves and Harmans roads, South Cowaramup; www.vassefelix.com.au)

Xanadu Estate (Boodjidup Road, Margaret River; www.xanaduwines.com).

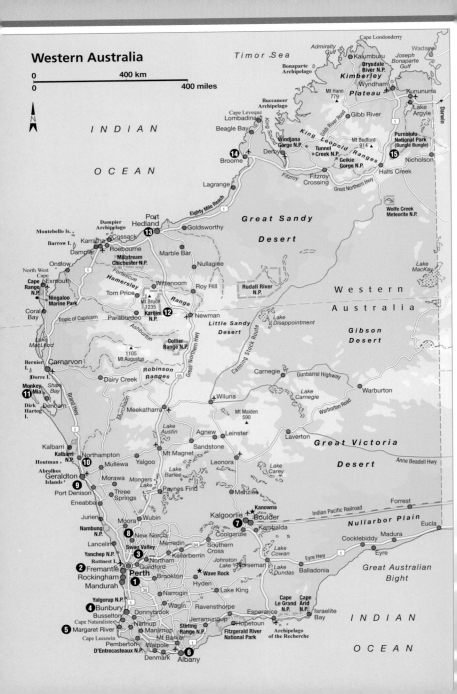

the marine lore of many navies and marked the start of Matthew Flinders' odyssey when he set out to circumnavigate and chart the Australian coastline in 1790.

Travelling east along the coast road towards Denmark and Albany, stop at Walpole where the **Tree Top Walk** (daily 9am–4.15pm, Christmas school holidays 8am–5.15pm; charge ) offers stunning views of the ancient Tingle Forest from a lofty ramp looping over the **Valley of the Giants**. Further east is the **Stirling Range National Park** (www.dec.wa.gov.au; charge), its conical hills and jagged peaks rising to 1,000m (3,300 ft), presenting challenging walks. A seasonal centre for wild flowers, including native orchids, it receives Western Australia's only snowfalls.

To the south, **Albany ❻** is one of Australia's most picturesque towns, with a wonderful bayside location and well-preserved 19th-century streetscapes. Tourists flock here from July to November to spot whales – an ironic attraction for a town that until 1978 was the last operating whaling station in the southern hemisphere. **Albany Whale World** (www.whale world.org; daily 9am–5pm; charge) in Frenchman's Bay tells the story.

Perhaps the most spectacular park in the region is the **Fitzgerald River National Park** (www.dec.wa.gov. au; charge), northeast of Albany, an impressive stretch of coastal landscape with dramatic views of the Southern Ocean. The easternmost town of **Esperance** leads to **Cape Le Grand** and **Cape Arid National Parks** (www.dec.wa.gov.au; charge) with superb beaches and an abundance of birdlife.

The Goldfields

Kalgoorlie–Boulder ❼ was a riotous gold-rush town in the 1890s, and the Wild West atmosphere remains.

225

Western Australia

The Super Pit at Kalgoorlie

The streets, laid out in a grid, are wide enough for stagecoaches or camel trains to make a U-turn. As the prospectors came in from the surrounding desert with their new-found wealth, Kalgoorlie – and its neighbouring twin town of Boulder – became a rip-roaring supplier of wine, women and song.

You can gauge how prosperous the town was by the elegance of the Victorian buildings, most notably the three-storey **Western Australia Museum, Kalgoorlie–Boulder** (17 Hannan Street; www.museum.wa.gov.au; daily 9.30am–4.30pm; free). This institution is stacked with exhibits detailing the life and work of those early prospectors.

The **Super Pit Lookout** (www.superpit.com.au; daily 7am–9pm; free) just off the Goldfields Highway is a great place to grasp the sheer scale of a working mine in operation. It's best to come at night when the pit is lit up by high-voltage lights.

Five kilometres (3 miles) north of Kalgoorlie, along the Goldfields Highway on the site of a disused mine, is the **Mining Hall of Fame** (www.mininghall.com; daily 9am–4.30pm; charge 🅜), which high-lights Australia's mining industry. There are gold-panning demonstrations, and underground tours are conducted by former miners.

Northern Highways

The Perth to Darwin route is Australia's longest capital-to-capital haul, and its most desolate. The Great Northern Highway cuts inland and is the quickest route to Port Hedland. The scenic coastal highway is populated with small towns, great beaches, national parks and the rugged shipwreck coast.

A major attraction of taking the Great Northern Highway inland route rather than the coastal Brand Highway is **New Norcia ❽**, 130km (80 miles) from Perth. The settlement

The monastery at New Norcia

A stunning array of wildlife can be found in Yanchep National Park

Yanchep National Park (www.dec. wa.gov.au; charge) features wetlands, woodlands, bushwalks, caves and an Aboriginal heritage trail. The next stop is **Lancelin**, protected by two large islands and surrounded by towering sand dunes. Gusty winds off the Indian Ocean make it ideal for windsurfing and surfing.

Continuing north along the Brand Highway, the **Central Greenough Historical Settlement** (daily 9am–5pm; charge) is a collection of 19th-century colonial buildings that has been restored by the National Trust.

Geraldton

Geraldton ❾, with a population of about 20,000, is the administrative centre for West Australia's mid-coast region. It has a near-perfect climate and fine sandy beaches that stretch north and south of Champion Bay. This stretch of coast

was established by Benedictine monks in 1846 as an Aboriginal mission. The monastery is still operating, although many of the town's more impressive buildings are closed to the public. The **New Norcia Museum & Art Gallery** (http://newnorcia. wa.edu.au; 9.30am–4.30pm; charge ) provides fascinating insights into pioneer life. Guided tours of the settlement are available, or visitors can take a self-guided 2km (1½-mile) walk linking the major sites, including the Abbey Church.

Following the coastal **Brand Highway**, the tiny town of **Gingin** is one of the state's oldest towns and worth a visit for its historical attractions. Continuing along the coast,

Western Australia

City of Sand

Nambung National Park (www.dec. wa.gov.au; charge), 29km (18 miles) south of the coastal town of Cervantes, shouldn't be missed. The **Pinnacles Desert** within the park is a bizarre sight: a world of limestone spires – varying from the size of a truck to smaller than a finger – all rising from smooth sand dunes. When Dutch explorers first saw the Pinnacles from their vessels, they thought they had found the ruins of a long-deserted city. A circular track leads around the limestone spire formations.

saw many shipwrecks when early Dutch mariners heading for the East Indies were swept too far south. The **Abrolhos Islands**, 64km (40 miles) offshore, have claimed many ships over the years, including the Dutch East Indiaman *Batavia*, which ran aground in 1629. Many relics rescued from the deep are on view in the **Western Australian Museum** (www.museum.wa.gov.au; Thur–Tue 10am–4pm; free 🅜) in Geraldton and at Fremantle's Shipwreck Gallery, where the hull of the *Batavia* is on display.

A century ago, **Northampton ⑩**, north of Geraldton, was an important mining town. Now classified by the National Trust, its historical attractions include the **Chiverton House Museum** (Hampton Road; Fri–Mon 10am–noon and 2–4pm; charge 🅜), **Church of St Mary** and the ruins of **Gwalla Church**.

Kalbarri National Park
Comprising 186,000 hectares (460,000 acres), **Kalbarri National Park** (www.dec.wa.gov.au; charge) features a combination of stunning river gorges and towering sea cliffs. The park is set around the lower reaches of the Murchison River.

Further along the coast, Shark Bay is the site of **Monkey Mia ⑪**, one of Australia's most delightful tourist attractions. In the small bay near Denham township, wild dolphins come to shore to be fed and mingle with visitors. Shark Bay was declared a World Heritage area in 1991.

Tropical North and Pilbara
The **Tropical North**, with its magnificent coral reefs, wealth of marine life and national parks, stands in stark contrast to the **Pilbara** region, which is the focal point of the state's manifold mineral wealth.

You can get up close to both pelicans and dolphins at Monkey Mia

Karijini National Park

Lovely **Coral Bay** is a small seaside town protected from the Indian Ocean by **Ningaloo Reef**, a perfect spot to snorkel with coral gardens close to the shore. This remarkable marine park (www.dec.wa.gov.au) stretches 260km (160 miles) from Amherst Point around North West Cape into the Exmouth Gulf and is Western Australia's largest coral reef, with 250 species of coral and more than 500 types of fish. Coral outcrops can be reached just 20m (65ft) from the beach, though they extend 7km (4 miles) into the ocean. Dolphins, dugongs, manta rays, giant cod and sharks abound. Whale sharks visit the reef from March to June.

The northwest was first explored by the English pirate and explorer William Dampier in 1688 and 1699. The **Dampier Archipelago** includes Barrow Island, the centre for the North West Shelf oil and gas fields. Far from being an environmentally threatened area, it is classified as a wildlife sanctuary and has some unusual animal, bird and plant life.

Magnificent **Karijini National Park** ⑫ (www.dec.wa.gov.au; charge), with spectacular gorges and bluffs, can be reached from Tom Price. The **Karijini visitor centre** (Banyjima Drive; daily 9am–4pm, times vary seasonally) is well worth a visit. Designed to withstand bushfires, the centre is shaped like a goanna (an animal sacred to the local Banyjima Aboriginal people) and contains information on the natural and cultural history of the area.

The seaside town of **Port Hedland** ⑬ copes with more tonnage than any other port in Australia, and is almost exclusively geared to handle the iron ore from the huge open-cut

Sunset over Cable Beach

and strip mining centres of the Pilbara. The **Dalgety House Museum** (corner Wedge and Anderson streets; Mon–Fri 10am–2pm; charge 🏛) has displays, artefacts and recordings charting the impact of early settlement on the region and its indigenous people.

The Kimberley

The Kimberley region is Western Australia's final frontier. About half the size of Texas, it has only 26,000 inhabitants and encompasses ½-million-hectare (1¼-million-acre) cattle ranches. The landscapes here are awe-inspiring, even by Antipodean standards: the blood-red desert is sliced by lush, forest-filled gorges where freshwater crocodiles and stingrays swim. The isolation has left the Kimberley region the most Aboriginal part of Australia, protecting immense tracts of tribal land.

Broome

Coming from the south, along the vast monotony of the road between **Port Hedland** and **Broome** ⓮, the highway describes a gentle arc along a stretch of coastline known aptly as the Eighty Mile Reach.

The seaport of **Broome** has a romantic past, once supplying 80 percent of the world's mother-of-pearl (*see p.232*). You will find evidence of past glories in Chinatown, in the old Japanese boarding houses, and in the gambling and other pleasure palaces – all reminders of the port's early 20th-century heyday.

One of Broome's main attractions today is **Cable Beach**, a fantastic 22km (14-mile) stretch of golden sands. At **Gantheaume Point**, low tide exposes dinosaur footprints about 130 million years old.

Broome Bird Observatory (Crab Creek Road; www.

broomebirdobservatory.com; free ),
on the shores of Roebuck Bay east of
Broome, is an ornithologist's dream
come true. A vast number of our
feathered friends stop here, with over
150,000 shore birds visiting each year.
Several tours are available.

The Kimberley Highlights

Until a few decades ago, the Kimberley was the domain of intrepid
explorers. It has since been opened
up, with tour operators using four-
wheel-drive vehicles, boats, helicopters and small aircraft to reach the
region's far-flung attractions.

Visitors come here to admire
**Purnululu (Bungle Bungle)
National Park** ⓯ (www.dec.wa.gov.
au; charge), whose orange-and-black
beehive-striped mounds are one of
the most astonishing natural features
in the world; the sandstone and
volcanic country of **Prince Regent**

Nature Reserve; the stunning 14km
(9-mile) gorge of the **Geikie Gorge
National Park** (www.dec.wa.gov.
au), with limestone cliffs up to 30m
(100ft) high; the tidal 'waterfalls' near
Derby; and the eerie **Wolfe Creek
Meteorite National Park** (www.
dec.wa.gov.au), home to the second
largest meteorite crater in the world,
formed 300,000 years ago.

231

Western Australia

The astonishing striped mounds of the Bungle Bungle Range

★ BROOME'S PEARLING PAST

The small town of Broome, in the Kimberley region of northern Western Australia, offers one of the country's most prestigious tourist souvenirs – the lustrous Broome pearl. The heritage of this desirable bauble and its associated industries is celebrated in the tours, cruises and local pearl-meat dishes unique to this remote coastal settlement.

Western Australia's pearling history began in the late 1870s with the discovery of the *Pinctada maxima* oyster, the largest pearl shell species found anywhere in the world. The discovery led to the establishment of the town of Broome in 1883, and a mother-of-pearl industry became lucrative almost immediately. Within 25 years, the ocean here provided around three-quarters of the world's stocks of this popular product, which was mainly used to make buttons. Initially, the oysters were collected from the sea bed by Aboriginal skin-divers, forced labourers who dived naked into the shallows along almost 160km (100 miles) of beach. As the oyster shells became scarcer in these waters, the skindivers were replaced by suited divers in weighted boots and copper helmets.

By the 1900s the pearling industry was at its zenith and Broome entered its golden age. Almost 1,500 Asian workers (mostly Japanese divers) were based in Broome, given exemption from the White Australian Policy

The pearling trade is still alive and well in Broome

introduced in 1901. More than 900 of these pearl divers are buried in Broome's Japanese Cemetery, many having died from the dangers posed by decompression sickness, beriberi and cyclones.

This golden age came to an end when the pearling industry crashed during World War I and continued to decline during the 1920s and 1930s. World War II brought the end of pearl-shell collecting and Broome became a virtual ghost town. While attempts were made to rebuild the industry post-war, the introduction of the plastic button appeared to be the final nail in the pearl industry's coffin. However, the wheels of a cultured pearl industry were already in motion and the collection of shells was to give way to the harvesting of pearls. The first cultured pearl was created in 1960 and Broome was given a second life, as luggers were still required to collect the pearl shells needed for seeding.

Today, Broome's pearling industry contributes hundreds of millions of dollars to the Western Australian economy, providing employment for more than 2,000 people. Visitors can gain an insight into the modern industry at **Willie Creek Pearl Farm** (www.williecreekpearls.com.au) or get a hint of the romance and excitement of the industry's past by taking a guided tour of the town's pearling heritage with **Pearl Luggers** (www.pearlluggers.com.au) or a cruise on a traditional gaff-rigged topsail schooner with **Willie Pearl Lugger Cruises** (www.williecruises.com.au).

Broome pearls are among Australia's most prestigious souvenirs

Many pearl divers are buried in Broome's Japanese Cemetery

ACCOMMODATION

Perth has a range of accommodation options to suit all budgets. Most are near the river or beach.

Perth and Around

Aarons Hotel
70 Pier Street
Tel: 08-9325 2133
www.aaronshotel.com.au
Located on the free bus route around Perth, Aarons has modern and comfortable rooms, a bright bar and grill, and friendly service. **$$$**

Bailey's Parkside Hotel-Motel
150 Bennett Street
Tel: 08-9220 9555
www.baileysmotel.com.au
This homely hotel opposite Kings Park, within walking distance of the city centre, has comfortable units with air conditioning, a swimming pool and barbecue. **$$$**

Criterion Hotel Perth
560 Hay Street
Tel: 08-9325 5155
www.criterion-hotel-perth.com.au
Basic and reasonably priced, this hotel is in a beautifully restored Art Deco building in the main shopping area. **$$$**

Durham Lodge
165 Shepperton Road, Victoria Park
Tel: 08-9361 8000
www.durhamlodge.com
A comfortable B&B south of the river, only a

The Melbourne

short drive to the centre of town, the choice of suites has spa bath or shower, air conditioning, TV, phone, bar and fridge. **$$$**

Duxton
1 St George's Terrace
Tel: 08-9261 8000
www.duxtonhotels.com
This beautifully renovated hotel in a heritage building, formerly Perth's old tax office, is close to the Concert Hall, Swan River and shops. **$$$$**

Kings Perth Hotel
517 Hay Street
Tel: 08-9325 6555
www.kingshotel.com.au
Good-value accommodation is offered close to the Hay Street Mall and Swan River. **$$$**

The Melbourne
942 Hay Street
Tel: 08-9320 3333
www.melbournehotel.com.au
The 1897 heritage-listed Melbourne has been transformed into a tastefully decorated boutique hotel. Some rooms open onto the ornate first-floor lattice balcony. **$$$**

Oneworld Backpackers
162 Aberdeen Street
Tel: 08-9228 8206
www.oneworldbackpackers.com.au
Bright and breezy accommodation with excellent facilities is offered by this eco-friendly backpackers. **$**

Seasons of Perth
37 Pier Street
Tel: 08-9325 7655
www.seasonsofperth.com.au
This boutique hotel features a large swimming pool in a spectacular courtyard and is ideally located close to the best shopping and the Swan River. **$$$**

Sheraton Perth
207 Adelaide Terrace
Tel: 08-9224 7777
www.sheraton.com/perth
Deluxe and centrally located, the Sheraton's rooms have breathtaking views of the Swan River or the city skyline. **$$$$**

The Witch's Hat Backpackers
148 Palmerston Street
Tel: 08-9228 4228
www.witchshat.com
This once grand Victorian residence is now a friendly hostel close to the centre of town with a choice of dorms, doubles and twins. **$**

Fremantle and Beaches
Atrium Hotel
65 Ormsby Terrace, Mandurah
Tel: 08-9535 6633
www.atriumhotel.com.au
Within walking distance of the beach, the Atrium has comfortable studio rooms and apartments. There's a heated indoor pool and spa, and the bar is only a splash away. **$$$**

Esplanade Hotel
Corner Marine Terrace and Essex Street, Fremantle
Tel: 08-9432 4000
www.esplanadehotelfremantle.com.au
An elegant goldrush-era building with well-appointed rooms, most with private balconies. There's also a pool, fitness centre, bar and restaurant. **$$$$**

Ocean Beach Hotel
Corner Eric Street and Marine Parade, Cottesloe Beach
Tel: 08-9384 2555
www.obh.com.au

The Witch's Hat Backpackers

Overlooking the Indian Ocean, this refurbished hotel is a popular Cottesloe attraction with a seafront restaurant, café and bars. **$$$**

Pier 21 Apartment Hotel
7–9 John Street, North Fremantle
Tel: 08-9336 2555
www.pier21.com.au
On the banks of the Swan River, fully serviced one- and two-bed air-conditioned apartments with kitchen have the use of indoor and outdoor pools overlooking the river marina. **$$$**

Port Mill B&B
3/17 Essex Street, Fremantle
Tel: 08-9443 3832
www.babs.com.au/portmil
In a charming old limestone mill circa 1863, tranquilly decorated colonial-style rooms overlook a courtyard with views of Fremantle. **$$$**

Rendezvous Observation City Hotel
The Esplanade, Scarborough Beach
Tel: 08-9245 1000
www.rendezvoushotels.com
A rare high-rise building on the coast, this luxury hotel has wide-ranging facilities including several restaurants and bars, nightclub, pool, spa, tennis courts and gym. **$$$**

Southern Coast
Basildene Manor
Wallcliffe Road, Margaret River
Tel: 08-9757 3140
This gorgeous historic home set among landscaped gardens has a choice of opulent

rooms and suites, some with garden and lakeside views. **$$$$**

Cape Lodge
Caves Road, Yallingup
Tel: 08-9755 6311
www.capelodge.com.au
A stunningly beautiful and tranquil country retreat between Yallingup and the Margaret River, the Cape Lodge mansion sits within gardens and overlooks a private lake. **$$$$$**

Chandlers Smiths Beach Villas
Smiths Beach Road, Yallingup
Tel: 08-9755 2062
www.chandlerssmithsbeach.com.au
On a hillside surrounded by national park, the 15 comfortable villas here have beach and ocean views. **$$$**

The Grange on Farrelly
18 Farrelly Street, Margaret River
Tel: 08-9757 3177
www.grangeonfarrelly.com.au
A small, stylish motel set in gardens, a short stroll to the main street, restaurants and shops. All rooms have en suite, air conditioning, TV and tea/coffee facilities. **$$$**

Merribrook Retreat
Armstrong Road
Tel: 08-9755 5599
www.merribrook.com.au
Small and relaxed, this luxury resort comprises nine private chalets. Treatments such as aromatherapy massage and reflexology are complemented by superb food. **$$$$**

The Goldfields
Rydges Kalgoorlie
21 Davidson Street, Kalgoorlie
Tel: 08-9080 0800
www.rydges.com
Comfortable rooms and suites close to the centre of town, with facilities including a much-welcomed outdoor pool. **$$$**

Northern Highways
New Norcia Hotel
Great Northern Highway, New Norcia

New Norcia Hotel

Tel: 08-9654 8034
www.newnorcia.wa.edu.au
The grandness of this Benedictine-built 1927 building isn't reflected in the hotel's basic facilities, which are in keeping with the monastic feel of the place. Pamper yourself with a glass of Abbey ale. **$$**

Ocean Centre Hotel
Corner Foreshore Drive and Cathedral Avenue, Geraldton
Tel: 08-9921 7777
www.oceancentrehotel.com.au
Right on the beach, the simple and tastefully decorated suites and rooms have great oceanfront views. **$$$**

Tropical North and Pilbara
Novotel Ningaloo Resort
Madaffari Drive, Exmouth
Tel: 08.9949 0000
www.novotelningaloo.com.au
The spacious apartments and bungalows have a beachfront location, cool minimal decoration and a beachy feel. There's also an outdoor pool and fine restaurant. **$$$$**

The Kimberley
Cable Beach Club Resort
Cable Beach Road, Broome
Tel: 08-9192 0400
www.cablebeachclub.com
On beautiful Cable Beach, the deluxe bungalows are designed in the style of pearlingmasters' houses, with wide verandahs and latticed screens. There are lush tropical gardens, waterfalls and swimming pools.
$$$$–$$$$$

RESTAURANTS

Western Australia's abundance of local produce and imaginative stable of chefs ensure you'll dine well in Perth, the Margaret River and other regional centres.

Perth

Fraser's Restaurant
Fraser Avenue, Kings Park
Tel: 08-9481 7100
www.frasersrestaurant.com.au
Dizzying city views, award-winning Mod Oz flavours and top-notch local produce ensure the enduring popularity of this fine-dining favourite. **$$$$**

Jackson's
483 Beaufort Street, Highgate
Tel: 08-9328 1177
www.jacksonsrestaurant.com.au
One of Perth's top dining experiences; expect interesting combinations such as apple risotto with grilled chorizo and scallops. **$$$$**

Lamont's
11 Brown Street
Tel: 08-9202 1566
www.lamonts.com.au
Kate Lamont is one of Perth's best-loved foodies, and her riverside East Perth property has become a local institution. She showcases the best in local produce. **$$$**

Matilda Bay Restaurant
3 Hackett Drive, Crawley
Tel: 08-9423 5000
www.matbay.com.au
On the banks of the Swan River at Matilda Bay, this place is popular for beautiful views and fine seafood and beef dishes. **$$$$**

Star Anise
225 Onslow Road, Shenton Park
Tel: 08-9381 9811
www.staraniserestaurant.com.au
Exceptional local produce and a wonderful Asian-influenced degustation menu make this an experience not to be missed. **$$$$**

Fremantle and Beaches

Indiana Tea House
99 Marine Parade, Cottesloe
Tel: 08-9385 5005
www.indiana.com.au
This majestic building sits perched above the sands at Cottesloe Beach. The style is colonial; food ranges from pasta to sushi. **$$**

Maya
75–77 Market Street, Fremantle
Tel: 08-93352796
www.mayarestaurant.com.au
A fabulous Indian restaurant with subtle flavours and an interesting range of dishes. **$$$**

Southern Coast and the Goldfields

Bay Organics
63 Duchess Street, Busselton
Tel: 08-9751 1315
Bay Organics is a little cottage café selling delicious healthy food. The owners grow all the vegetables and herbs organically, and there is also a small grocery store inside. **$**

The Goose
Geographe Bay Road, Busselton
Tel: 08-9754 7700
www.thegoose.com.au
Overlooking the ocean, right next to the Busselton Jetty, The Goose is a light and airy restaurant with a regularly changing menu and gorgeous views whatever the weather. **$$**

Lamont's Margaret River
Gunyulgup Valley Drive, Yallingup
Tel: 08-9755 2434
www.lamonts.com.au
The elegant food is matched by the wonderful setting – perched over a lake in the middle of the bush. **$$$**

Listings

Maleeya's Thai Café
1376 Porongurup Road, Porongurup
Tel: 08-9853 1123
www.maleeya.com.au
One of the best dining options in the south-west. The food is fresh and fantastic, and many of the organic vegetables and herbs are grown in the gardens. **$$**

Nornalup Teahouse Restaurant
South Coast Highway, Nornalup
Tel: 08-9840 1422
www.nornalupteahouse.com.au
This beautifully converted cottage has an idyllic setting and fine food utilising south-coast produce. **$$$**

Other Side of the Moon
Bunker Bay Road, Bunker Bay
Tel: 08-9756 9100
Located in the up-market Bunker Bay resort, with views over olive trees and the pool to the ocean, the food is Modern Australian and uses the best and freshest local produce. **$$$**

Vasse Felix
Corner Caves and Harman's South roads, Yallingup
Tel: 08-9756 5050
www.vassefelix.com.au
Vasse Felix is a top winery, and this is a top restaurant serving high-quality modern Australian food. The timber and stone building is a great place to sit and relax while you look out over the vineyards. **$$$$**

The Goose

Vat 2
2 Jetty Road, Bunbury
Tel: 08-9791 8833
www.vat2.com.au
Near the water in the Marlston Hill development, Vat 2 caters for those looking for a light snack (chicken salad with prosciutto, for example) or a more substantial meal (grilled meats and pastas). **$$**

Wild Duck
112 York Street, Albany
Tel: 08-9842 2554
www.wildduckrestaurant.com
Chef Andrew Holmes melds European/ modern Australian style and flavours to create a very special fine-dining experience. **$$$**

NIGHTLIFE AND ENTERTAINMENT

An eclectic mix of wine bars, classic pubs and entertainment venues can be found throughout Perth and its beach suburbs.

Perth
Bar One
250 St George's Terrace, Perth
Tel: 08-9481-8400
www.bar1.com.au
Modern, European-style bar serving fine Italian food and coffee.

Brass Monkey
Corner James and William streets, Northbridge
Tel: 08-9227 9596
www.thebrassmonkey.com.au
Have a drink on the upstairs verandah at this historic pub and watch the street life.

Must Wine Bar
519 Beaufort Street, Highgate
Tel: 08-9328 8255
www.must.com.au
Offers a large selection of excellent wines
and beers and seriously tempting French
bistro-style cuisine.

Universal Bar
221 William Street, Northbridge.
Tel: 08-9227 6771

www.universalbar.com.au
Catch some live jazz and blues at one of
Perth's favourite bars.

Fremantle and Beaches
Little Creatures
40 Mews Road, Fremantle
Tel: 08-9430 5555
www.littlecreatures.com.au
At this working brewery, try great beers while
watching boats in Fisherman's Harbour.

TOURS

Day tours of Western Australia's attractions cover coral reefs, national parks and
the famous wine-touring region.

Kings Ningaloo Reef Tours
Tel: 08-99491764
www.kingsningalooreeftours.com.au
Offers diving tours of Ningaloo Reef, whale
watching and whale shark tours.

Margaret River Tours
Tel: 0419 917 166
www.margaretrivertours.com

A range of half-day and full-day wine-and-dine
and scenic tours of the Margaret River region.

Rockingham Wild Encounters
Tel: 08-9591 1333
www.rockinghamwildencounters.com.au
Includes eco-friendly dolphin-watching tours
and visits to Penguin Island Marine Reserve
from Rockingham.

FESTIVALS AND EVENTS

It might only have a small programme of festivals, but Western Australia still has a
few high-profile events that attract visitors from interstate.

February
Perth International Arts Festival
www.perthfestival.com.au
Month-long festival of all aspects of the arts.

July
Good Food & Wine Show
www.goodfoodshow.com.au
Held during the first week of July, the show
features celebrity chefs, cooking classes
and cheese and wine tasting.

September
Kings Park Festival

www.bgpa.wa.gov.au
Celebration of spring with botanic garden
walks, exhibitions, music and spectacular
displays of Western Australian wild-flowers.

October
Perth Pride
www.pridewa.asn.au
Gay and lesbian cultural event.

November
Fremantle Festival
www.fremantlefestivals.com
Community arts and cultural festival.

Tasmania

Those who think of Tasmania as the last stop before the South Pole are right: Antarctic expeditions actually set sail from Hobart. But this is a staging post you will hate to leave, as 'Tassie' calls itself the Holiday Isle for good reason – there is plenty here to catch the visitors' interest, from a temperate climate to cool forests, rugged mountains, highland lakes, lush pasture and fruitful orchards.

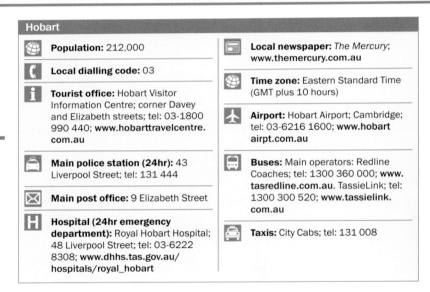

Hobart

Population: 212,000

Local dialling code: 03

Tourist office: Hobart Visitor Information Centre; corner Davey and Elizabeth streets; tel: 03-1800 990 440; www.hobarttravelcentre.com.au

Main police station (24hr): 43 Liverpool Street; tel: 131 444

Main post office: 9 Elizabeth Street

Hospital (24hr emergency department): Royal Hobart Hospital; 48 Liverpool Street; tel: 03-6222 8308; www.dhhs.tas.gov.au/hospitals/royal_hobart

Local newspaper: The Mercury; www.themercury.com.au

Time zone: Eastern Standard Time (GMT plus 10 hours)

Airport: Hobart Airport; Cambridge; tel: 03-6216 1600; www.hobart airpt.com.au

Buses: Main operators: Redline Coaches; tel: 1300 360 000; www.tasredline.com.au. TassieLink; tel: 1300 300 520; www.tassielink.com.au

Taxis: City Cabs; tel: 131 008

Dutch navigator Abel Tasman was the first European explorer to arrive here, way back in 1642. He named the island after his sponsor, Anton van Diemen, governor of the Dutch East Indies, but the Dutch never saw a future for Van Diemen's Land and Britain eventually claimed it.

Because of the cruel conditions inflicted on the British convicts who were sent here in its early decades as a penal colony, Van Diemen's Land acquired a sinister reputation. The transportation of convicts was abolished in 1852, and some three years later the name was changed to Tasmania in memory of its discoverer and to improve the island's image. These days, its image could hardly be improved upon – visitors will encounter pristine wilderness, magnificent beaches, Georgian architecture and some of the best food and wine in Australia.

Hobart

The small city of **Hobart** ❶ nestles between the waters of the Derwent and the brooding bulk of Mount Wellington. These features have stymied the urban sprawl that affects the mainland cities, and a spell in the economic doldrums in the 1960s and 1970s meant much of the old colonial architecture was luckily spared from development.

City Centre

Hobart's waterfront is a magnet. There are the classic views across to Mount Wellington and plenty of remnants of the thriving 19th-century port. **Salamanca Place** is the site of a pulsating Saturday-morning market and is full of attractive stone warehouses. These house a lively arts

Hobart harbour

centre as well as a selection of touristy shops, bars and cafés. Behind them is **Salamanca Square**, a modern development that successfully latches on to the original buildings.

East along Salamanca Place are Kelly's Steps, which lead to the eyrie of **Battery Point** ❹. The battery in question was a set of coastal artillery guns installed in 1818. The area is worth an hour or two of exploration on foot to absorb the narrow streets, mansions and cottages, churches and taverns. One of the colonial mansions is now the **Narryna Heritage Museum** ❺ (103 Hampden Road, Battery Point; www.narryna.com.au; Mon–Fri 10.30am–5pm, Sat–Sun 2–5pm, closed Mon in winter; charge).

Westwards along Salamanca Place is the administrative centre of the state, dominated by the Victorian bulk of **Parliament House** ❻ (tel: 03-6233 2288; www.parliament.tas. gov.au; tours when houses not sitting, Mon–Fri 10am and 2pm; free).

A block further back, Macquarie Street has the Georgian-style St David's Cathedral, the Treasury Building, the grand General Post Office,

Tasmania

Salamanca Place hosts a bustling Saturday-morning market

the Town Hall, the Art Deco Mercury Newspaper Building and the **Tasmanian Museum and Art Gallery** (40 Macquarie Street; www.tmag.tas. gov.au; daily 10am–5pm, free guided tours Wed–Sun 2.30pm; free ). The **Maritime Museum of Tasmania** (Carnegie Building, corner Davey and Argyle streets; www.maritimetas.org; daily 9am–5pm; charge) is nearby.

Another block back from the water, the main downtown shopping area centres on Elizabeth Street Mall. To the north is the 1837 **Theatre Royal** (29 Campbell Street; www.theatreroyal. com.au; tours Mon, Wed and Fri 11am subject to venue requirements; charge). A few blocks up, on the corner of Brisbane and Campbell streets, is the **Penitentiary Chapel Historic Site** (www.penitentiarychapel.com; guided tours Sun–Fri 10am, 11.30am, 1pm,

2.30pm, Sat 1pm and 2.30pm, ghost tour most days 8.30pm; charge), the remains of the original Hobart Gaol.

The Queens Domain

Northeast of the city centre, Queens Domain has traditionally been a place of recreation, remembrance and – for the occupant of **Government House** – residence. The **Cenotaph** is flanked by a couple of interesting modern glass and stone pyramids that incorporate audio tributes to those lost in combat. The **Royal Tasmanian Botanical Gardens** (www.rtbg.tas.gov.au) were established in 1828 and remain true to the early vision of the founders, collecting every conceivable variety of flora.

North Hobart

North Hobart is home to a plethora of cosmopolitan bars, restaurants

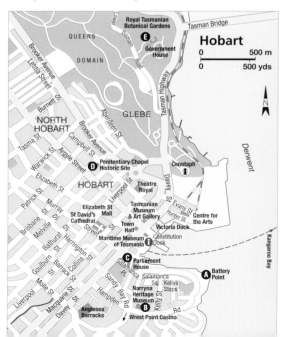

Penitentiary Chapel Historic Site

The tranquil Royal Tasmanian Botanical Gardens

Cadbury Road; www.cadbury.com.au; Sept–May Mon–Fri 8am–4pm, June–Aug Mon–Fri 9am–3pm).

South Hobart

A 90-minute tour of the **Cascade Brewery** (140 Cascade Road, South Hobart; tel: 03-6224 1117; www.carltonbrewhouse.com.au; tours daily, times vary, bookings essential; charge) gives participants the opportunity to investigate the sampling room. The brewery is also the starting point for **Louisa's Walk** (tel: 03-6230 8233; http://livehistoryhobart.com.au; daily 2pm, bookings essential; charge), a promenade through the Cascades Female Factory in which professional actors enact a gripping chapter in convict history.

Around Hobart

Once you've exhausted the sights of Hobart, there are lots of places to explore in easy day trips from the city.

and entertainment venues. Further north still, **Runnymede** (61 Bay Road, New Town; www.nationaltrusttas.org.au/properties-runnymede; Mon–Fri 10am–4.30pm, Sat–Sun noon–4.30pm; charge) in New Town is an early 1830s whaling family's home maintained by the National Trust. It's well worth a stop on the way to **Moorilla Estate** (655 Main Road, Berriedale; www.moorilla.com.au; daily 9am–4pm; free). This winery not only claims one of Tasmania's leading restaurants (*see p.255*) but also houses a purpose-built Museum of Antiquities gathered from around the globe. In 2011, it will open the much-anticipated Museum of Old and New Art (MONA).

In the suburb of Claremont, chocoholics flock to the **Cadbury Chocolate Factory Visitor Centre** (100

The Tasmanian Tiger

Visitors to the Tasmanian Museum and Art Gallery (*see p.242*) should be sure to see its collection relating to the Tasmanian tiger (thylacine). This striped, dog-like marsupial is believed to have been hunted to extinction by the 1930s, but some people swear they have seen thylacines in the wild. Rewards of over A$1 million have been offered over the years to anyone who could prove the existence of a living specimen, so far without any takers.

Richmond

The colonial gem of **Richmond** ❷, 27km (17 miles) northeast of Hobart, sits in the Coal River Valley and is known for its convict-constructed stone bridge. Most of Richmond was built between 1824 and 1840, and its consistency in style endows it with a charm that is only slightly tarnished by the presence of twee B&Bs, cafés and souvenir shops. The well-preserved **Richmond Gaol** (37 Bathurst Street; daily 9am–5pm; charge), built for this staging post on the Hobart to Port Arthur to Richmond road, is worth a visit, and other buildings of note include churches, the Richmond Arms Hotel and a post office.

Tasman Peninsula

The peninsula is best known as the location of the **Port Arthur Historic Sites** ❸ (Arthur Highway; daily 8.30am–dusk; tour bookings tel: 1800 659 101; www.portarthur.org.au; charge 🅜), a 90-minute drive from Hobart. This historic penal colony sits in a jaw-droppingly gorgeous setting: an amphitheatre of rolling green meadow leading down to the tranquil blue waters of Mason Cove, dotted with picturesque sandstone ruins glowing golden yellow in the watery sunlight. Founded in 1830 as Australia's ultimate prison settlement, it housed the most troublesome and intractable convicts – those who had committed second offences after being transported to Australia. Chain gangs, toiling under the lash, built the impressive stone buildings. The settlement's fascinating, if macabre, story is detailed at the visitor centre, as well as in the compelling museum in what used to be the penal colony's lunatic asylum. The admission cost includes a walking tour and a short harbour cruise. The famous Port Arthur Ghost Tour is run nightly at dusk – bookings are essential.

Bruny Island

Wildlife-rich **Bruny Island** ❹, accessed by ferry from the mainland town of Kettering, is really two islands joined by a narrow isthmus ('The Neck'), so locals refer to North Bruny and South Bruny. Either way, it's a lengthy 63km (39 miles) from top to bottom and a popular weekend destination for Hobartians. There are walking tracks and swimming coves in the **South Bruny National Park** (www.parks.tas.gov.au; park pass needed) and boat tours (www.brunycharters.com.au) from Adventure Bay.

Port Arthur Historic Sites

East Coast and Freycinet Peninsula

The Tasman Highway (A3) runs up the island's magnificent and unspoilt east coast, which is home to five national parks, three conservation areas and one state reserve.

Triabunna, approximately 80km (50 miles) from Hobart, is where ferries (www.mariaislandferry.com.au) depart for **Maria Island National Park ❺** (www.parks.tas.gov.au; park pass required). Originally a penal settlement, the island is now a haven for wildlife and walkers. No traffic is permitted unless you take a bicycle and the only accommodation options are campsites at French's farm and Encampment Cove or bunk beds in the unpowered old penitentiary at Darlington. Among the natural wonders are Fossil Cliffs and the Painted Cliffs.

'The Neck', Bruny Island's narrow isthmus

North of Triabunna is Swansea, a low-key resort with lovely views across Great Oyster Bay to the pink granite peaks of the Hazards on the **Freycinet Peninsula**, often described as one of the most beautiful places in the world. First stop for most visitors is Coles Bay, the service and accommodation centre that happens to have some rather

Tasmania

0   50 km
0   50 miles

fabulous beaches. However, the main attraction is **Freycinet National Park**  (www.parks.tas.gov.au) and its headline act, **Wineglass Bay**. Freycinet's mix of mountains, forest, beaches and achingly blue sea, not to mention the abundant wildlife (particularly birds), is impossible to beat. Walks of varying length and difficulty abound, the most popular of which is the fairly steep Wineglass Bay Lookout Walk up to the saddle between two of the Hazards: Mount Amos and Mount Mayson.

The Douglas-Apsley, Ben Lomond and Mt William national parks are all further north, as is the **Bay of Fires Conservation Area** (www.parks.tas. gov.au), which consists of 30km (19 miles) of some of the finest beach in the world stretching between Binalong Bay and Eddystone point, much of it inaccessible by road.

Launceston and the North Coast

The Midland Highway runs from Hobart north through a string of picturesque colonial towns *(see p.248)* to Launceston. From there, it and the A2 continue along the northern coast of the island, populated by towns buffeted by the 'Roaring Forties' winds that blow off the Southern Ocean.

Launceston

Tasmania's second city, **Launceston** ❼, has undergone a revival in recent years. Of particular note has been the development of the old railway workshops at Inveresk, especially the site run as the second campus of the **Queen Victoria Museum & Art Gallery** (daily 10am–5pm; www.qvmag.tas.gov.au; free).

Much pleasure comes from simply walking around the undulating streets

Tasmania

Admiring the view across Wineglass Bay

Well-preserved Cameron Street in central Launceston

of the city centre to admire the handsome Victorian architecture. Cameron Street, with its red-brick terraces replete with filigree ironwork, leads off Civic Square, which gathers up the grandiose Town Hall, the Library and Macquarie House, a stone warehouse from 1830.

Other highlights around the city include the original Royal Park site of the Queen Victoria Museum & Art Gallery, closed while it undergoes a major restoration scheduled to finish in 2011, and **Boag's Brewery** (39 William Street; www.boags.com.au; tours Mon–Fri; charge), where enthusiasts can sample a beer or two.

The remarkable **Cataract Gorge** (www.launcestoncataractgorge.com. au) is within easy walking distance of the centre. The gorge has walking paths along its steep walls – the southern one tough, the northern one easy – from Kings Bridge to the First Basin, where there are gardens and a rotunda on one side, and grassy banks and an open-air swimming pool on the other. A chair-lift (charge) and suspension bridge (free) link the two sides.

Tasmania

Launceston

 Population: 106,000

 Local dialling code: 03

 Tourist office: Launceston Visitor Information Centre; corner St John and Cimitiere streets; tel: 03-6336 3133; www.visitlauncestontamar.com.au

 Main police station (24hr): 89 Cimitiere Street; tel: 131 444

 Main post office: 111 St John Street

 Hospital (24hr emergency department): Launceston General Hospital; 287–91 Charles Street; tel: 03-6348 7111; www.dhhs.tas.gov. au/hospitals/launceston_general

 Airport: Launceston Airport; 201 Evandale Road, Western Junction; tel: 03-6391 6222; www. launcestonairport.com.au

 Ferries: Spirit of Tasmania Ferry Terminal; The Esplanade, Devonport; tel: 1800 634 906; www. spiritoftasmania.com.au

 Buses: Main operators: Redline Coaches; tel: 1300 360 000; www. tasredline.com.au. TassieLink; tel: 1300 300 520; www.tassielink. com.au

 Taxis: Taxi Combined Services; tel: 132 227; www.taxicombined. com.au

🚗 HERITAGE HIGHWAY TOUR

This drive along the Midland Highway (aka 'The Heritage Highway' or Highway 1) takes you through picturesque colonial towns aplenty.

This drive between Launceston and Hobart can start from either city – we've chosen to outline the route heading south from Launceston. The highway officially begins at the unremarkable town of Perth, south of Launceston Airport. Four kilometres (2½ miles) along the highway is a signed turn-off to the Georgian-era village of **Evandale**, established in 1820 and dotted with graceful buildings including the imposing 1839 St Andrew's Uniting Church on High Street, one of the oldest existing country churches in Australia. If

Evandale is home to annual penny farthing races

you're keen for a refreshment break, consider claiming a courtyard table at the **Ingleside Colonial Bakery** in Russell Street, housed in the former municipal chambers dating from 1867. Alternatively, the nearby **Prince of Wales Hotel** has been a cosy spot for a drink since 1836.

Eleven kilometres (7 miles) south of Evandale along the C416 is the grandest colonial house in Tasmania, **Clarendon** (www.nationaltrusttas.org.au; daily 10am–4pm; charge). Built in 1838 for pastoralist James Cox and now maintained by the National Trust, this imposing property with its classical columns, servants' wing and extensive gardens is well worth a visit.

Continue on the C416 and you will shortly rejoin the Heritage Highway. After 15km (9 miles) you'll come to **Campbell Town**, known for its convict-built Red Bridge (c.1836) and Foxhunter's Return pub, described by the National Trust as the 'finest and

Tips
• Distance: 190km (118 miles)
• Time: A full day
• If you decide to extend your tour and stay overnight in one of the colonial towns, make sure you book your accommodation in advance, particularly if you are travelling on a weekend.
• Official speed limits vary along the route – check for signs and when in doubt stick to 90kph (56mph), which is the default speed limit for sealed roads in Tasmania.

most substantial building of the late colonial period in Australia'.

Ten kilometres (6 miles) along the highway is a turn-off to the picturesque town of **Ross**, where you can learn about the grazing history of the Midlands (and purchase top-quality woollen products) at the **Tasmanian Wool Centre** (www.taswoolcentre. com.au; daily 9am–5pm) on Church Street. The centre also functions as a tourist information office. The nearby **Man O'Ross Hotel** (35 Church Street; tel: 03-6381 5445; www.manoross.

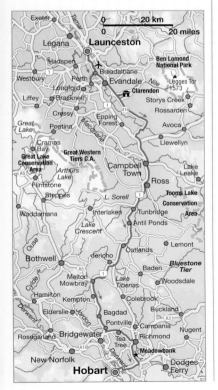

A trail of bricks remembering convicts extends from Campbell Town's Red Bridge

com.au) dates from 1835 and is known for its alluring beer garden, decent pub meals and comfortable accommodation.

Leaving Ross via its graceful stone bridge, rejoin the highway and drive approximately 36km (22 miles) to the small town of **Oatlands**, where you'll discover colonial sandstone buildings and the wind-driven **Callington Mill**, built in 1837 and recently refurbished. The mill grinds organic spelt and wheat, which is used by the artisanal **Companion Bakery** (106 High Street; tel: 03-6254 0088; Wed–Sun 9am–5pm).

Leaving Oatlands, continue to Pontville, 55km (34 miles) along the highway. Just after town, take the C321 to Tea Tree and then the C322 to picturesque **Richmond** *(see p.244)*. Outside town, on the road to Hobart, you'll find **Meadowbank Estate** (tel: 03-6248 4484; www.meadowbankwines.com. au), where you can admire the views of the Coal River Valley, visit the cellar door or dine in the highly regarded restaurant *(see p.255)*.

From Meadowbank, it's only a 10-minute drive to Hobart Airport and 20 minutes across the Tasman Bridge to the centre of town.

Cataract Gorge

A mere 8km (5 miles) south of the city is Franklin Village, best known for the National Trust property **Franklin House** (413–419 Hobart Road; Mon–Sat 9am–4pm, Sun noon–4pm; www.nationaltrusttas. org.au/properties-franklinhouse; charge), built by convicts in 1838 for businessman and former fellow convict, Britton Jones.

Tasmanian Wood Design

Tasmania is known for its talented craftspeople, particularly those who work in wood. Contemporary furniture and other pieces made from various species of Tasmanian timber can be purchased at the **Design Centre of Tasmania** (corner Tamar and Brisbane streets, Launceston; www.designcentre.com.au; Mon–Fri 9.30am–5.30pm, Sat–Sun 10am–2pm). The centre also stages exhibits from its museum collection of contemporary Tasmanian wood design.

The Tamar Valley

This area is best known for its vineyards. Look out for signposts (blue grapes on yellow) marking the Tamar Valley Wine Route. Wine buffs may want to travel northeast approximately 60km (37 miles) to the Piper's River region, home to one of the island's best-known wineries, **Piper's Brook** (1216 Pipers Brook Road; www.kreglingerwineestates.com; daily 10am–5pm).

George Town ❽, located on the mouth of the Tamar River, is the third-oldest white settlement in Australia (after Sydney and Hobart). You can purchase a George Town Historical Attractions Pass from the Visitor Information Centre (www. georgetown.tas.gov.au) on Main Road that gives entry to **The Watch House Museum** (Macquarie Street; Sept–May Mon–Fri 10am–4pm, Sat–Sun noon–2pm, June–Aug Mon–Fri 10am–3pm, Sat–Sun noon–2pm; donation), home to a community history room and female factory display; the atmospheric **Pilot Station/ Maritime Museum** (Low Head Road, Low Head; daily 9am–5pm; entrance fee); and the **Bass & Flinders Centre** (Elizabeth Street; www.bassand-flinders.org.au), with its replica of the *Norfolk*, the boat in which the two explorers circumnavigated the island in 1798.

The Northwest

Devonport ❾ is the home port for the Spirit of Tasmania ferries that traverse Bass Strait. The centre need not detain you, but there is a good **Maritime Museum** (Oct–Mar Tue–Sun 10am–4.30pm, Apr–Sept

Tue–Sun 10am–4pm; www.dmhs. org.au; charge) on Gloucester Avenue near the foreshore. The interesting **Tiagarra Aboriginal Culture Centre and Museum** (Mon–Sat 10am–5pm; charge) is perched on Mersey Bluff.

Near the northwest tip of the island, **Stanley** is dominated by The Nut, a huge plug of volcanic rock at the end of a spit. The Van Diemen's Land Company was crucial to the early history of this town, and the old company store, now a gallery and boutique hotel (*see p.254*), can be found near the wharf, while the cliff-top situated, Regency-style **Highfield House** (www.historic-highfield.com. au; Sept–May daily 10am–4pm, June–Aug by appointment; entrance fee) was company HQ.

West Coast

The landscape here has never been tamed by humans, and well deserves its tag of 'unspoilt wilderness'. Much of it is now protected as the Tasmanian Wilderness World Heritage Area (*see box, p.252*).

Strahan ❿ (pronounced Strawn), west of Lake St Clair, began life as a timber town and the railway port for an inland copper mine. These days, most visitors to the town take a cruise along the Gordon River past the Southwest National Park, stopping to visit the infamous penal establishment of Sarah Island en route; the two major operators are **World Heritage Cruises** (www.worldheritage-cruises.com.au; daily 9am; charge ▥) and **Gordon River Cruises** (www. gordonrivercruises.com.au; daily 8.30am; charge ▥).

The stunning Tasmanian Wilderness

Other activities include a pan-tomime-style performance called **The Ship That Never Was** (Strahan Visitor Centre; 5.30pm, plus Dec–Jan 8.30pm; charge 🅜), which tells a story from Sarah Island's history; and the **West Coast Wilderness Railway** (www.puretasmania.com.au; departs daily 10.15am, returning by bus at 3.45pm; charge 🅜), a 35km (22-mile) journey through native forests, past old timber towns and over wild rivers.

The road north of Strahan passes the Henty Dunes, which stretch for many kilometres behind Ocean Beach, and then turns inland to more mining towns. Zeehan is the most significant, having boomed in the 1900s on the back of silver. Its **West Coast Pioneers' Museum** (114 Main Street; www.west-coastheritage.com.au; daily 9am–5pm; charge 🅜) has extensive displays on mining, minerals and local history.

Strahan harbour with one of the Gordon River excursion boats

ACCOMMODATION

Tasmania is known for comfortable B&Bs, wilderness lodges and a growing number of stylish boutique hotels.

Hobart

Central City Backpackers
138 Collins Street
Tel: 03-6224 2404
www.centralbackpackers.com.au
Sparse, clean dormitories and private rooms are on offer in this massive building. **$-$$**

Graham Court Apartments
15 Pirie Street, New Town, North Hobart
Tel: 03-6278 1333
www.grahamcourt.com.au
Helpful and friendly management makes this a favourite for families or groups. **$$-$$$**

The Henry Jones Art Hotel
25 Hunter Street
Tel: 03-6225 7016
www.thehenryjones.com
A stunning conversion of the old jam factory on the waterfront, with stylish room decor featuring contemporary art. Some of the suites have harbour views and spas. **$$$-$$$$**

Hobart Tower Motel
300 Park Street, New Town, North Hobart
Tel: 03-6228 0166
www.hobarttower.com.au
One of the best-value options in Hobart. The unassuming rooms are spacious and family units are available. **$$**

Islington Hotel
321 Davey Street
Tel: 03-6220 2123
www.islingtonhotel.com
This luxurious guesthouse is set in landscaped gardens overlooking Mt Wellington. Luxe rooms are decorated with art and antiques. **$$$$-$$$$$**

Lenna of Hobart
Corner Runnymede Street and Salamanca Place

Tel: 03-6232 3900
www.lenna.com.au
Ideally located in Battery Point, this modern hotel is adjacent to a landmark heritage building. It offers spacious, comfortable rooms and truly extraordinary modernist penthouses. **$$$-$$$$$**

Somerset on the Pier
Elizabeth Street Pier
Tel: 03-6220 6600
www.somerset.com/australia/hobart/somerset_on_the_pier
Well-equipped serviced apartments in this converted wharf building feature panoramic views of the Derwent and waterfront. **$$$**

Around Hobart

Tasman Peninsula
Stewarts Bay Lodge
6955 Arthur Highway, Port Arthur
Tel: 03-6250 2888
www.stewartsbaylodge.com.au

The Henry Jones Art Hotel

Self-contained one-, -two- and three-bedroom log cabins overlooking Stewarts Bay, a short walk from the Port Arthur Historic Site. **$$$**

The Tree House
Bruney Island
Tel: 0405-192 892
www.thetreehouse.com.au
This fully equipped wooden house overlooking the water comfortably sleeps four people. **$$$**

East Coast and Freycinet Peninsula
Freycinet Lodge
Tel: 03-6257 0101
www.freycinetlodge.com.au
This environmentally sensitive resort development is set inside the boundary of the magnificent Freycinet National Park. Comfortable private bush cabins lead down to tiny beach areas. **$$$–$$$$**

Launceston and the North Coast
@VDL Stanley
16 Wharf Road, Stanley
Tel: 03-6458 2032
www.atvdlstanley.com.au
Located in the Van Diemen's Land Company Store *(see p.251)*, the two utterly gorgeous rooms on offer here are as hip as they are historic. **$$$**

Arthouse Backpacker Hostel
20 Lindsay Street, Launceston
Tel: 03-6333 0222

Freycinet Lodge

www.arthousehostel.com.au
Dorm beds and private rooms in a heritage building located near the converted railway workshops at Inveresk. Friendly and full of amenities. **$–$$**

Devonport Historic Cottages
66 Wenvoe Street, Devonport
Tel: 03-6424 1560
www.devonportcottages.com
Three refurbished 19th-century cottages on offer, all with two bedrooms and fully equipped kitchen. **$$$**

The Pier Hotel
5 Elizabeth Street, George Town
Tel: 03-6382 1300
www.pierhotel.com.au
Pleasant rooms and apartments overlooking the river. Well served by the pub's accomplished bistro and kids-friendly games room. **$$$**

Werona
33 Trevallyn Road, Launceston
Tel: 03-6334 2272
www.werona.com
Up-market B&B in a 1908 house set in well-tended gardens and enjoying marvellous views of the Tamar River and Valley. **$$$**

West Coast
Cradle Mountain Lodge
4038 Cradle Mountain Road,
Cradle Mountain
Tel: 03-6492 2103
www.cradlemountainlodge.com.au
Wilderness retreat at the entrance to the Cradle Mountain–Lake St Clair National Park with secluded cabins, alpine spa and excellent restaurant. **$$$–$$$$$**

Franklin Manor
The Esplanade, Strahan
Tel: 03-6471 7311
www.franklinmanor.com.au
Situated at the edge of Macquarie Harbour with a restaurant and range of accommodation, including rooms within the historic mansion and in the old stables. **$$$**

RESTAURANTS

Inspired by seasonal – often organic – produce and wholeheartedly embracing the locavore philosophy, Tasmania's chefs are among the best in the country.

Hobart

Cargo Bar Pizza Lounge
47–51 Salamanca Place
Tel: 03-6223 7788
Enjoying an early-evening beer and wood-fired pizza at the outdoor tables here is a popular local pastime. **$**

Jackman & McRoss
57–59 Hampden Road, Battery Point
Tel: 03-6223 3186
The best café in Hobart, famed for its freshly baked breads and pastries. There's another branch at 4 Victoria Street. **$**

Marque VI
Elizabeth Street Pier
Tel: 03-6224 4428
www.marqueiv.com.au
The stunning waterfront views are complemented by sleek decor and Italian-accented food. Vegetarians are well catered for. **$$$**

Smolt
2 Salamanca Square
Tel: 03-6224 2554
This hugely popular place is known for its delectable breakfasts, Italian/Spanish-influenced menu and casual vibe. **$$**

Lebrina
155 New Town Road, New Town,
North Hobart
Tel: 03-6228 7775
Housed in an 1840s cottage, Scott Minervini's elegant restaurant utilises local produce to excellent effect. **$$$**

Restaurant 373
373 Elizabeth Street, North Hobart
Tel: 03-6231 9031
www.restaurant373.com.au

Stylish, innovative 373 is known for great service and top-notch wine list. **$$$**

The Source
Moorilla Estate, 655 Main Road, Berriedale
Tel: 03-6277 9900
www.moorilla.com.au
A delectable menu, impressive house wines and stunning surrounds make lunch at Moorilla a memorable eating experience. **$$$**

Around Hobart

Meadowbank
699 Richmond Road, Cambridge
Tel: 03-6248 4484
www.meadowbankwines.com.au
Located near Richmond, this vineyard restaurant serves delectable French cuisine. **$$**

East Coast and Freycinet Peninsula

Angasi
64a Main Road, Binalong Bay
Tel: 03-6376 8222
www.angasi.com.au
Bold flavours, excellent wine matching and a superlative view of the Bay of Fires are the hallmarks of this impressive restaurant. **$$$**

Piermont
Tasman Highway, Swansea
Tel: 03-6257 8131
www.piermont.com.au
In a small resort overlooking Great Oyster Bay, Piermont's menu is dominated by locally caught and utterly delicious seafood. **$$$**

Launceston and the North Coast

Stillwater
Ritchies Mill, Paterson Street
Tel: 03-6331 4153

Listings

www.stillwater.net.au
Drawing on global cuisines, Stillwater's menu is as pleasing as its waterfront setting. The same management runs the **Black Cow Bistro** (corner George and Patterson Streets; tel: 03-6331 9333; $$$) in the city centre. **$$–$$$$**

Tant Pour Tant
226 Charles Street
Tel: 03-6334 9884
The delicious breads, cakes and pastries here could hold their heads high in Paris. **$**

Daniel Alps at Strathlynn
95 Rosevears Drive, Rosevears
Tel: 03-6330 2388
This lunchtime-only venue has views over the Tamar River and a menu featuring simple, perfectly executed dishes. **$$$**

NIGHTLIFE AND ENTERTAINMENT

This isn't really a destination to visit in search of a party. Entertainment here comes courtesy of food and wine, with the occasional outing to a pub or cultural event.

Hobart
City Centre
Grape Bar & Bottleshop
55 Salamanca Place, Hobart
Tel: 03-6224 0611
In the thick of the Salamanca action, with over 600 wines available by the bottle and over 30 available by the glass.

Lizbon
217 Elizabeth Street, North Hobart
Tel: 03-6234 9133

In the city's main food and entertainment strip, this popular wine bar hosts occasional live jazz music.

Launceston and the North Coast
Royal Oak Hotel
14 Brisbane Street, Launceston
Tel: 03-6331 5345
Gravitate here for a friendly front bar, good pub grub and regular live acoustic rock music from Wed–Sun.

SPORTS AND ACTIVITIES

Those who enjoy outdoor activities will be spoilt for choice here.

Hollybank Treetops Adventure
Hollybank Road, Underwood
Tel: 03-6395 1390
www.treetopsadventure.com.au
A two- to three-hour aerial circuit through the Hollybank forest canopy culminating in a 371m (405yd) run above the Piper River.

The Tasmania Parks and Wildlife Service
www.parks.tas.gov.au

Kids love Hollybanks Treetops Adventure

The TPWS website has information on bushwalking in all of its national parks and reserves. Look on the 'Great Bushwalks' and '60 Great Short Walks' pages.

Listings

TOURS

Innumerable companies offer tours and organised activities around the island.

Fish Wild Tasmania
115A King Street, Sandy Bay, Hobart
Tel: 03-0418 348 223
www.fishwildtasmania.com
This outfit conducts trout-fishing tours, with or without fly-fishing tuition.

Freycinet Adventures
2 Freycinet Drive, Coles Bay
Tel: 03-6257 0500
www.freycinetadventures.com.au
Sea kayaking tours on the Derwent Estuary or Freycinet Peninsula.

Inala Nature Tours
320 Cloudy Bay Road, Bruny Island
Tel: 03-6293 1217
www.inalabruny.com.au
Personalised birding and wildlife tours of Bruny Island with specialist nature guides.

Rafting Tasmania
Tel: 03-6239 1080
www.raftingtasmania.com
Rafting tours on the Derwent and Picton Rivers, as well as tours on the Franklin River.

Tasmanian Expeditions
Tel: 03-6339 3999
www.tas-ex.com
This Launceston-based outfit operates a large range of active and adventure holidays.

FESTIVALS AND EVENTS

There are many festivals on offer, most of which are held in the first half of the year.

January
The Taste Festival
www.tastefestival.com.au
Local food and drink is celebrated on the Hobart waterfront for one week over new year.

February
Australian Wooden Boat Festival
www.australianwoodenboatfestival.com.au
Wooden boat-builders and -lovers head to Hobart in odd-numbered years.

Royal Hobart Regatta
www.royalhobartregatta.com
For one weekend the Derwent River is given over to a long-running maritime regatta.

March/April
Ten Days on the Island
http://tendaysontheisland.org
In late March and April in odd-numbered years, island-dwellers from around the world celebrate with art, music and drama.

May/June
Savour Tasmania
www.savourtasmania.com.au
Epicurean festival in Hobart, Burnie and Launceston, showcasing the best Tasmanian food in degustation lunches and dinners.

May–August
Lumina
http://lumina.discovertasmania.com
A four-month festival featuring the Tasmanian Symphony Orchestra's mid-year season, AFL football matches and arts events.

December
Yacht Races
http://rolexsydneyhobart.com
www.orcv.org.au
The biggest event in Tasmania is the arrival of boats competing in the annual Sydney to Hobart/Melbourne to Hobart yacht races. Welcoming celebrations occur at Constitution Dock between Christmas and New Year.

PRACTICAL ADVICE

Accommodation

Australia welcomes travellers with a wide range of accommodation options, offering everything from luxurious five-star hotels and resorts to well-appointed budget-priced hotels, hostels and motels.

Accommodation can be difficult to find during Australian school holidays and the high season (December to February everywhere except the Top End). During these times it may be necessary to book a few months in advance for tourist hotspots (especially coastal locations). The Christmas/summer holidays are from Christmas to the beginning of February. School holidays can vary, but most states have adopted a four-term school year with two-week breaks in April, June/July and September/October. For actual dates, go to http://australia.gov.au/topics/australian-facts-and-figures/school-term-dates.

During the low season, hotels may offer substantial discounts and last-minute deals.

HOTELS

The luxury end of the accommodation spectrum matches the most sumptuous world standards in rooms and suites, as well as in associated restaurants, lounges, saunas and spas. But even in budget-priced hotel and motel rooms you can expect a private shower or bath and toilet, a telephone, TV, small refrigerator and coffee- and tea-making equipment (and free coffee, tea and milk). In most regions, air conditioning, or at least a ceiling fan, is provided.

Overseas offices of Tourism Australia have listings of hotels and motels – see www.australia.com. You can reserve accommodation through your travel agent, the nearest offices

Sails in The Desert Hotel, near Uluru

The Base Backpackers hostel chain provides quality accommodation

of the international and Australian hotel chains, or your airline. Within Australia, many visitor information centres, domestic airlines and hotel chains offer instant free bookings. If you arrive out of the blue, local tourist offices have desks for last-minute reservations.

During the low season, luxury and mid-range hotels offer a range of discounts and special packages. Check out hotel websites before you arrive or during your visit for last-minute deals.

BUDGET ACCOMMODATION

There are two main types of budget accommodation: privately owned backpacker hostels and YHA (Youth Hostels Association) hostels. Both provide a range of dormitory accommodation with self-catering facilities, a communal area with TV and a laundry. Some also offer twin/double rooms (generally with shared toilet facilities).

Prices range from A$25–35 per night for a dorm room and A$70–90 per night for a twin/double room with shared facilities. Some hostels also have job centres and travel offices on-site.

Base Backpackers (tel: 02-8268 6000; www.stayatbase.com) is a hostel chain focusing on quality budget accommodation; it offers a wide range of options.

The Australian **YHA** (422 Kent Street, Sydney, NSW 2001; tel: 02-9261 1111; www.yha.com.au) is Australia's largest budget accommodation network, with more than 140 hostels in a wide range of locations. These are open to all ages and offer sleeping, self-catering kitchens and common rooms where you'll meet fellow travellers. You can join the YHA in your own country or in Australia. Contact the YHA for a free information pack giving membership details and a list of hostels.

OTHER ACCOMMODATION

In addition to hotels, motels and hostels, Australia offers a wide range of bed and breakfast, guesthouse, serviced apartment and homestay options.

Accommodation

Camping is a much-loved
pastime in Australia

The B&B scene is very popular in Australia, and is no longer confined to nestling down for the night in the not-so-private setting of someone else's home. Options vary from cosy cottages, restored farmhouses and churches to luxurious beach getaways and heritage-listed houses.

The best source of current information is the Bed and Breakfast Farmstay and Accommodation Australia (BBFAA) website (www.australian-bedandbreakfast.com.au). Farmstays include everything from small dairy farms in the hills to vast grain farming and sheep- and cattle-grazing properties. Staying here is a great way to learn about how a farm runs and how Australia's food is produced. Prices for B&Bs and farmstays run upwards from A$120 a night per double.

CAMPING

Australians are huge fans of camping, campervan and caravan holidays, and you'll find campsites and holiday parks dotted all over the areas frequented by tourists. Campsites tend to be jam-packed during the school holidays, with coastal areas being particularly popular over the summer months. Outside of bush-camping in national parks, most commercially run campsites have at least the basic amenities, and in some cases much more in the way of comfort, including roomy tents with lights and floors.

Most have powered sites for caravans (trailers) and a range of cabins for rent. Showers, toilets, laundry facilities and barbecue grills are commonly available.

You'll expect to pay around A$20–30 per night for two at a basic campsite, with powered sights a little more expensive. Cabins can range in price from around A$80 for a basic cabin with kitchenette up to A$175 for a two-bedroom cabin with kitchen and living area.

The national parks generally have well-organised camping facilities; to bush camp beyond the designated zones you must ask the rangers for permission. Some national parks close seasonally and on days of total fire ban.

You can rent a campervan or motor home by the day or week. Campervan rental companies include **Apollo** (tel: 1800 777 779; www.apollocamper. com), **Britz** (tel: 1800 331 454; www. britz.com.au), **Kea Campers** (tel: 1800 252 555; http://au.keacampers. com) and **Maui** (tel: 800 200 80 801; www.maui.com.au).

Transport

GETTING TO AUSTRALIA

By Air

Most foreign visitors travel to Australia by air. Brisbane, Melbourne and Sydney are the major international gateways, with daily flights arriving from Asia, Europe and North America. Less frequent direct flights also arrive in Adelaide, Darwin and Perth.

More than 40 international airlines fly to and from Australia. Direct flights from the US depart from Los Angeles and San Francisco (flight time around 15 hours); from the UK they depart from London, Manchester and Glasgow (flight time around 23 hours).

Getting to Australia can be expensive. Fares vary widely (as do flight times; a cheap ticket can mean hours of extra flight and transit time), so seek advice from a knowledgeable travel agent before buying a ticket.

Since the launch of budget carriers Virgin Blue, Jetstar and Tiger (see Getting Around Australia, p.264), competition has lowered domestic fares considerably. The early birds often secure the best deals.

Major Airlines Flying to Australia

Air Canada www.aircanada.com
Air New Zealand www.air newzealand.com
American Airlines www.aa.com
British Airways www.ba.com
Cathay Pacific Airways www.cathaypacific.com
Emirates Airlines www.emirates.com
Etihad Airways www.etihad airways.com
Japan Airlines (JAL) www.jal.co.jp.en
Malaysia Airlines www.malaysia airlines.com
Qantas www.qantas.com.au
Singapore Airlines www.singapore air.com
South African Airways www.flysaa.com

Qantas is Australia's main carrier

Virgin Blue is the country's second-largest airline

GETTING AROUND AUSTRALIA

Australia lacks a unified national transport network, and due to its size, flying is the best option when it comes to getting around the country.

Bus is the least expensive option, but you'll be spending a lot of time travelling. Train travel isn't cheap, or fast, but it's a lovely way to see the country and worth consideration.

Domestic Flights

Australia's national airline is Qantas, which also runs its own budget domestic airline, Jetstar (tel: 131 538; www.jetstar.com). Its main competitors are Virgin Blue (tel: 136 789; www.virgin-blue.com.au) and Tiger Airways (tel: 03-9335 3033; www.tigerairways.com). Competition can be fierce between the budget carriers, resulting in discount offers. Keep an eye on airline websites and newspapers for deals.

The main carriers fly between all major cities and some regional destinations. There are also several smaller airlines that fly to regional and more remote locations; many of these airlines are subsidiaries of Qantas.

Thai Airways International www.thaiair.com
United Airlines www.united.com
Virgin Atlantic www.virgin-atlantic.com

International Airports within Australia

Adelaide (ADL) 6km (4 miles) west of the city; www.aal.com.au
Brisbane (BNE) 13km (8 miles) northeast of the city; www.bne.com.au
Cairns (CNS) 7km (4 miles) north of the city; www.cairnsairport.com
Darwin (DIA) 13km (8 miles) northeast of the city; www.darwinairport.com.au
Melbourne (MEL) 23km (14 miles) northwest of the city; www.melbourneairport.com.au
Perth (PER) 15km (7 miles) northeast of the city; www.perthairport.net.au
Sydney (SYD) 12km (7 miles) southwest of the city; www.sydneyairport.com.au

Approximate Flying Times

Sydney–Melbourne 1 hour
Sydney–Perth 4 hours 55 minutes
Melbourne–Adelaide 1 hour 20 minutes
Melbourne–Canberra 1 hour
Brisbane–Sydney 1 hour 25 minutes
Brisbane–Melbourne 2 hours 20 minutes
Adelaide–Alice Springs 2 hours
Perth–Adelaide 3 hours
Canberra–Sydney 50 minutes

Trains

A limited network of modern railways operates in Australia. The principal lines follow the east and south coasts, linking Cairns, Brisbane, Sydney, Melbourne, Adelaide and Alice Springs. Check Rail Australia (www.rail australia.com.au) for routes and fares.

The line between Sydney and Perth via Adelaide is the famous *Indian–Pacific* run (linking the Indian Ocean to the Pacific Ocean). On its 4,352km (2,700-mile) journey, taking 65 hours (three nights), the train crosses the Nullarbor Plain, the longest stretch of straight track in the world.

Other popular scenic rail journeys run by Great Southern Railway (tel: 132 147 or 08-8213 4592; www.train ways.com.au) include the *Overland*, an overnight journey between Melbourne and Adelaide; the *Southern Spirit*, which follows the Great Dividing Range through Victoria, NSW and South Australia; and the recently extended *Ghan*, which runs from Adelaide through Alice Springs and on to Darwin. The two-night, 3,000km (1,864-mile) trip can be broken in Katherine for short sightseeing tours by boat or helicopter, and Alice Springs for longer stopovers.

For travel in Western Australia you can take a bus or train to the southern and southwest regions in the area bounded by Kalbarri, Meekathara, Kalgoorlie, Esperance, Albany and Augusta. Contact Transwa (tel: 1300 662 205; www.transwa.wa.gov.au).

Tickets

Train travel in first, holiday and economy class is available. First-class passengers have sleeping berths with showers in their cabin, and a first-class restaurant and lounge. Other classes have reclining seats and a buffet car.

Countrylink (tel: 132 232; www.countrylink.info), operated by Rail Corporation NSW, offers a range of rail passes for international travellers. The Austrail Pass entitles international visitors to unlimited travel on Countrylink, Queensland Rail and Great Southern Railway services. It is valid for six months from the first day of travel. Prices are A$890 if purchased in Australia, A$800 if pre-purchased overseas.

The Backtracker Rail Pass is available in four price ranges, from a 14-day pass (A$232) up to six months (A$420), and allows unlimited economy-class travel on the Countrylink network.

The East Coast Discovery Pass allows six months' travel one way up or down the east coast. The full Melbourne to Cairns trip costs A$450, while a shorter trip such as Melbourne to Brisbane costs A$220.

Boarding the iconic *Ghan* train

Transport

Intercity Coaches

Many bargains are available when travelling by bus in Australia. The biggest company, with the most services, is Greyhound Australia (tel: 131 499; www.greyhound.com.au). Other companies operating state-wide and inter-state services include: Firefly Express (tel: 1300 730 740; www.fireflyexpress.com.au), running between Sydney, Melbourne and Adelaide; V/Line (tel: 136 196; www.vline.com.au) connecting major towns in Victoria; Crisps Coaches (tel: 07-4661 8333; www.crisps.com.au), serving all of Queensland; and Premier Motor Service (tel: 133 410; www.premierms.com.au), running along the east coast from Melbourne to Cairns. Book online, at capital city bus stations or through travel agents.

Bus routes cover all major cities and stop off at most towns en route. In general, the greater the distance between cities, the less frequent the timetable will be.

Australian buses are single class and the standard is generally high. Most have reclining seats, seating for the disabled, washrooms and air conditioning. Bus terminals are well equipped with toilets, showers and shops, and are generally very clean.

Greyhound has various money-saving passes including the Explorer pass, which offers a range of preset hop-on hop-off itinerary passes, including an East Coast Pass, West Coast Pass and Australia Pass.

To make the most of Australia's impressive size, Greyhound has come up with a Kilometre Pass. This pass starts at 500km (311 miles) and ranges up to a whopping 20,000km (12,427 miles), which you'd need if you wanted to see the entire country. You can backtrack using this pass, and travel in any direction.

Cycling

Australia has plenty of options for both the long-distance and leisure-seeking cyclist. There's an endless choice of country roads and scenic routes to explore, and most Australian cities are well set up for cyclists, with bicycle paths and routes. Cycling in Canberra in particular is excellent, and the flatness of Melbourne and Adelaide makes those cities very popular with cyclists. Throughout Australia, cyclists must wear helmets at all times by law.

Organised cycle tours of varying lengths are available, including transport to and from a scenic area (bikes provided), food and accommodation. Tasmania is a particularly popular bike-touring destination. You can also rent touring bikes. For details, look in the Yellow Pages phone book of the relevant city

Greyhound buses can be an economical way to get around Australia

(www.yellowpages.com.au). Local cycling organisations are a good source of information (*see box, below*).

Driving

The size of Australia means much of it isn't serviced by public transport, and other than taking tours your only real alternative is to drive. Away from the main cities and populated areas traffic can be light, with the open road stretching out endlessly ahead.

Road Conditions

Australian roads are good, considering the size of the country and the challenges of distance, terrain and climate. Freeways link populous regions, but most country roads are two-lane highways. Remote roads are often unsealed and if you want to get really off the beaten track you'll need a four-wheel drive. In the tropical north, roads can be impassable during the Wet season.

Australian drivers generally adhere to road rules, although speeding and drunk drivers pose problems on Australian roads. Finding fuel

Australia is ideal for exploration by bike

shouldn't pose any problems unless you are heading to remote areas, where it's best to carry extra fuel. Some filling stations are open only during normal shopping hours, so you may have to ask where after-hours service is available. Petrol (gasoline) in Australia comes in regular and premium grades, leaded and unleaded, and is sold by the litre.

Regulations

Australians drive on the left – which means you overtake on the right. Drivers and passengers must wear seat belts (the exception is buses, although many of them feature seat belts as an option). Car-hire companies can supply suitable child restraints, boosters and baby seats at an extra charge.

A tourist may drive in Australia on a valid overseas licence for the same class of vehicle. Licences must always

State Cycling Organisations

- **Pedal Power ACT** (Canberra; tel: 02-6248 7995; www.pedalpower.org.au)
- **Bicycle New South Wales** (tel: 02-9218 5400; www.bicyclensw.org.au)
- **Bicycle Queensland** (tel: 07-3844 1144; www.bq.org.au)
- **Bicycle South Australia** (tel: 08-8232 2644; www.bikesa.asn.au)
- **Bicycle Tasmania** (tel: 03-6266 4582; www.biketas.org.au)
- **Bicycle Victoria** (tel: 03-8636 8888; www.bv.com.au)

Driving past a termite mound

be carried when driving. If the licence is in a language other than English, the visitor must carry a translation with the licence. An International Driver's Permit must be accompanied by a valid national driver's licence.

The speed limit in cities and towns is generally 60kph (about 35mph), but many local and suburban roads have a 50kph (about 40mph) and 40kph (about 30mph) speed limit. Outside built-up areas the speed limit is generally either 100kph or 110kph (about 70mph). Speed limits are rigorously enforced by the police.

Throughout Australia, police make random checks for drugs or alcohol, using breath tests. The limit on alcohol in the blood is 0.05, meaning in practice that two standard glasses of wine or beer in the first hour for men and one standard glass for women and one standard drink per hour after that will take you to the limit. In New South Wales, if you are under 25 and in your first three years of driving, the limit must be under 0.02, which doesn't allow you to drink at all. In any state, being over the limit means an automatic hefty fine.

Motoring Associations

The Australian Automobile Association (www.aaa.asn.au) maintains links with similar organisations worldwide. Many state automobile associations have reciprocal arrangements with similar organisations overseas, so bring proof of your membership.

New South Wales NMRA (tel: 02-8741 6000; www.mynrma.com.au)

Northern Territory AANT (tel: 08-8925 5901; www.aant.com.au)

Queensland RACQ (tel: 07-3361 2140; www.racq.com.au)

South Australia RAA (tel: 08-8202 4600; www.raa.net)

Tasmania RACT (tel: 132 722; www.ract.com.au)

Victoria RACV (tel: 03-9790 2211; www.racv.com.au)

Western Australia RACWA (tel: 08-9436 4444; www.rac.com.au)

Vehicle Hire

By international standards, renting a car in Australia is expensive. The major companies are:

Avis (tel: 136 333; www.avis.com.au)

Budget (tel: 1300 362 848; www.budget.com.au)

Europcar (tel: 1300 131 390; www.europcar.com.au)

Hertz (tel: 133 039; www.hertz.com.au)

Redspot (tel: 1300 668 810; http://redspotcars.com.au)

Thrifty (tel: 1300 367 227; www.thrifty.com.au)

Smaller outfits are usually much cheaper and offer special deals, but they may not offer all the services of the major companies. These include discounts for pre-booking overseas, and the ability to return the car to another city at no extra charge.

The main companies have offices in almost every large city, as well as at airports and rail terminals. They offer unlimited kilometre rates in the city, but, when travelling in the Outback, rates are usually per kilometre. Compulsory third-party insurance is included in car rentals but collision damage waiver is an add-on. More comprehensive insurance plans are available for an additional fee, or your travel insurance may cover them. Most companies have 25 as their minimum driver age, or will charge a premium for drivers aged between 21 and 25. An intermediate-sized car with basic cover will cost around A$80 per day to hire.

Since driving a conventional vehicle off sealed roads may invalidate your insurance, four-wheel-drive (4WD) cars are expensive but worth considering

Be on the lookout for kangaroos while on the road in Australia

for Outback touring. The cost of hiring a 4WD could be anything from A$100 to A$250 per day. Though popular, campervans aren't cheap – it might work out cheaper to rent a regular car and stay at budget hotels.

If you're getting around the Outback independently, remember you're in seriously frontier country. Do plenty of planning before you head off. Carry adequate water, notify people of your intentions, use reliable vehicles and protect yourself from sunburn. Picking up hitchhikers is, in general, a bad idea.

Significant tracts of the Outback are designated as Aboriginal land, and a permit may be required to enter them.

Accessibility

Most new buildings, public transport and tourist attractions have wheel-chair access and other facilities for the disabled. Major rental car companies have a small number of cars with hand controls, which need to be reserved at least a week in advance. Advance notice will facilitate the best assistance from airlines, hotels or railway offices. Taxi fleets in state capitals have cars that can carry wheelchairs. Tourism Australia has further details (www.australia.com).

The National Information Communication Awareness Network (NICAN; tel: 1800 806 769; www.nican.com.au) keeps an online database of facilities and services with access for disabled, including accommodation and tourist sites.

Other useful organisations are the Disability Information and Resource Centre (DIRC; tel 08-8236 0555; www.dircsa.org.au) and e-bility (www.e-bility.com/travel).

Health and Safety

It's vital to protect yourself from the sun by wearing a hat

MEDICAL CARE

Australian doctors, dentists and hospitals all provide a high standard of care. New Zealand, Finland, Italy, Malta, the Netherlands, Norway, Sweden, the UK and Ireland have reciprocal health-care agreements with Australia. The agreement provides urgent treatment but doesn't cover elective surgery, dental care, ambulance services or illness arising en route to Australia. The agreements do not cover repatriation in the case of illness or injury. For information visit www.medicareaustralia.gov.au/public/migrants/visitors. Take out a travel insurance policy covering health before you leave home.

Vaccinations are not required if you are flying directly to Australia and have not passed through an epidemic zone or a yellow fever, cholera or typhoid-infected area in the six days prior to your arrival. If you need to see a medical practitioner, look in the Yellow Pages (www.yellowpages.com.au) or ask at your hotel. All major cities have a hospital with a casualty department operating outside working hours (www.health.vic.gov.au/related/hosps.htm). Pharmacies – some 24-hour – are numerous. To find a pharmacy in your particular area, use the Pharmacy Guild of Australia's online search tool (www.findapharmacy.com.au).

NATURAL HAZARDS

Australia is renowned for its sunshine, but be cautious as the southern hemisphere sun has extremely strong ultraviolet rays. Extended exposure is not recommended, especially between 11am and 4pm. A wide-brimmed hat and adequate-strength sunscreen are essential, even when it's overcast. Drink plenty of fluids and keep your salt intake up if you're not accustomed to hot conditions.

The dark, bulbous Sydney funnel web is one of the world's most lethal and aggressive types of spiders. Although its bites are rare (about 10 victims a year), immediate medical attention is required to stave off coma and death. Catch the spider for identification if you can. Other venomous spiders include the redback, the eastern mouse spider and the white-tail.

Shark attacks are also rare, but swim between the flags at patrolled beaches, and heed shark alarms.

In certain seasons and areas, the bluebottle jellyfish (also called a Portuguese-man-of-war) may be encountered. Its sting is painful but can be treated. Far more dangerous are the box jellyfish (seawasp) and the irukandji jellyish, which are found in tropical waters from about October to April. A sting from either species can be fatal. Never disregard warning signs on beaches. In the north of Australia, saltwater crocodiles can be a menace to swimmers. Again, obey the signs.

Several of the world's deadliest snakes, including the brown snake, tiger snake, taipan and death adder, are indigenous to Australia. You are unlikely to encounter them in built-up areas. If you are bitten by any snake, seek immediate medical attention.

Bushfire is a threat throughout the country. If you are visiting national parks or other bushland in summer, check conditions before you leave.

WATER

You can drink water from taps anywhere unless specifically marked otherwise. In the Outback, warnings may read 'Bore water', 'Non-potable' or 'Not for drinking'.

Jellyfish are one of the biggest beach hazards in Australia

CRIME

Australia is a relatively safe country, but employ the same common sense and precautions you would use elsewhere. Issues surrounding prostitution, drugs and alcohol occur in all cities but are unlikely to affect travellers. If an incident occurs, report it to the police or, for urgent attention, call 000.

EMBASSIES AND CONSULATES

If you need help with matters such as legal advice or a stolen passport while in Australia, most countries have diplomatic representations, with embassies in major cities.

Canada (Commonwealth Avenue, Yarralumla; tel: 02-6270 4000; www.canadainternational.gc.ca/australia-australie)

Ireland (20 Arkana Street, Yarralumla; tel: 02-6273 3022; www.embassyofireland.au.com)

New Zealand (Commonwealth Avenue, Yarralumla; tel: 02-6270 4211; www.nzembassy.com/australia)

South Africa (Corner State Circle and Rhodes Place, Yarralumla; tel: 02-6272 7300; www.sahc.org.au)

UK (Commonwealth Avenue, Yarralumla; tel: 02-6270 6666; http://ukinaustralia.fco.gov.uk/en)

USA (21 Moonah Place, Yarralumla; tel: 02-6214 5600; http://canberra.usembassy.gov)

Health and Safety

Money and Budgeting

CURRENCY

Australia's currency is the Australian dollar (A$). Notes come in denominations of A$5, A$10, A$20, A$50 and A$100. Coins are 5c, 10c, 20c, 50c, A$1 and A$2. Prices are rounded off to the nearest 5c.

At the time of print, exchange rates are: US$1 = A$0.94; £1 = A$1.52; €1 = A$1.34.

All currency that exceeds A$10,000 must be declared on arrival or departure.

CASH AND CARDS

Banks and their ATMs are the best places to get currency. Major Australian banks offer 24-hour ATMs throughout cities and larger towns, but these are less common in more remote areas. You are able to use an international PIN to access money from international bank accounts using these machines.

MasterCard and Visa are widely accepted (Diners Club and American Express less so). Bear in mind that some shops impose a small surcharge for credit card purchases.

Traveller's cheques are rarely used in Australia. If you are travelling with these you can exchange them at bureau de change outlets and most major banks.

ATM-related scams using skimming machines to collect credit card numbers are becoming more prevalent in Australia. Try to use an ATM that is located in a well-lit bank branch vestibule, rather than outside a convenience store. Be sure to keep your pin details concealed when entering them on the ATM keyboard.

TIPPING

It is not required, to tip in restaurants and cafés in Australia but a gratuity of up to about 10 percent of the bill is always welcome if you have been happy with the service. In taxis, rounding up fares to the nearest dollar is also standard practice. Bellboys are usually tipped A$1 or A$2 per bag.

TAX

A goods and services tax (GST) of 10 percent is applied to the cost of all goods and services and is generally included in all prices. GST is not charged on duty-free goods.

BUDGETING FOR YOUR TRIP

Before exchange rates became as volatile as Iceland's volcanoes, Australia was a reasonably cheap destination for visitors from the UK and US. The increasing strength of the Australian dollar has seen the cycle turn, with travel becoming cheaper for Australians holidaying overseas.

A cheap return flight from the UK to Australia costs around £580; a standard flight costs around £800 and a first-class return flight £4,650.

A cheap return flight from the US to Australia costs around US$785; a standard flight costs around US$1,850 and a first-class flight US$16,500.

If the service was good, a tip is welcome but not essential Down Under

For a budget, backpacker-style holiday you will need to set aside A$800 (£485/US$720) per person per week. A standard family holiday for four will cost around A$3,500 (£2,200/US$3,200) per week. A luxury, no-expense-spared break can cost over A$3,500 (£2,200/US$3,200) per person per week.

TIPS FOR BUDGET-CONSCIOUS TRAVELLERS

People over the age of 65 are often eligible for seniors' discounts; you'll need to show official ID. Holders of the International Student Identity Card (ISIC) are entitled to discounts at many attractions.

Budgeting Costs

Top-class/boutique hotel: A$250–550 for a double
Standard-class hotel: A$125–200 for a double
Bed & breakfast: A$100–250 for a double
Motel: A$90–180 for a double
Youth hostel: A$30–80 per person
Motor camp: A$20–35 per caravan
Campsite: A$15–30 per tent

Domestic flight: A$99–350 (Melbourne–Sydney)
Intercity coach ticket: A$88–150 (Sydney–Brisbane)
Intercity train ticket: A$59–140 (Adelaide–Melbourne)
Car hire: A$60–100 per day
Petrol: A$1.30 a litre
10-minute taxi ride: A$15–25
Airport shuttle bus: A$16–25
Short bus ride: A$4
One-day travel pass: A$12

Breakfast: A$8–20
Lunch in a café: A$10–25
Coffee/tea in a café: A$2.50–4
Main course, budget restaurant: A$10–15
Main course, moderate restaurant: A$15–25
Main course, expensive restaurant: A$25–45
Bottle of wine in a restaurant: A$20–75
Beer in a pub: A$5–10

Museum admission: A$5–30
Day trip from Melbourne to Castlemaine: A$60–100 (travel and food)
Football match: A$30–45
Hot-air balloon ride: A$200–350
Cycle hire: A$20–40 per day
Theatre/concert ticket: A$50–350
Australian wildlife soft toy from a shop: A$15–50
Nightclub entry: A$5–25

Responsible Travel

GETTING THERE

Travellers concerned about climate change may want to offset the greenhouse gases they create as a result of their long-haul flight to Australia. Organisations within Australia that will help you reduce your carbon footprint by donating to a variety of initiatives include: www.carbonneutral.com.au, www.greenfleet.com.au and www.jpmorganclimatecare.com.

ECOTOURISM

Ecologically sustainable tourism is the most direct way visitors to Australia can reduce their environmental impact. Ecotourism Australia (www.ecotourism.org.au) is a great resource where travellers to Australia can make informed choices on accommodation, tours and attractions that have all been accredited under the ECO certification programme.

ETHICAL TOURISM

If you are visiting Aboriginal land, sites or attractions in the Northern Territory, you will need a permit. For information, visit the Northern Land Council website: www.nlc.org.au.

When buying authentic Aboriginal art, try to buy your artwork from an Aboriginal art gallery or Aboriginal community arts centre. This will guarantee authenticity and ensure that the artist and community will receive the money. Aboriginal art pieces should all have a certificate of authenticity. For further information on buying Aboriginal art, visit www.arttrade.com.au.

Buying artwork from an Aboriginal art gallery helps support Indigenous communities

VOLUNTEERING

The popular **Willing Workers on Organic Farms** (WWOOF; tel: 03-5155 0218; www.wwoof.com.au) scheme offers bed and board in return for a few hours' work each day on an organic farm. **Conservation Volunteers Australia** (CVA; tel: 1800 032 501; www.conservationvolunteers.com.au) is a non-profit organisation that lets travellers participate in conservation projects. If the project includes an overnight stay, a contribution of A$40 covers accommodation and food. Longer projects start from A$208 per week and include food and board.

For more information about volunteering while in Australia, contact **Go Volunteer** (tel: 03-9820 4100; www.govolunteer.com.au).

THINGS TO AVOID

When travelling in the Outback, bush and all national parks, dispose of your rubbish responsibly.

Family Holidays

PRACTICALITIES
Australian cities and towns are well serviced for travellers with children and all major car hire companies supply and fit baby car seats. Bring pushchairs and carrier backpacks with you as they are not readily offered for hire.

ACCOMMODATION
Caravan parks offer plenty of distractions for kids. Motels and budget hotels may offer some child-friendly options; some mid-range and top-end hotels can offer accommodation that is suitable for families. Resorts occasionally offer kids' clubs. B&B and boutique accommodation may not be as child friendly.

FOOD & DRINK
Australia offers a wide range of eating options for families. Many cafés and restaurants will cater to children's needs; you have a 50/50 chance of scoring a highchair.

ATTRACTIONS & ACTIVITIES
The following highlights from each major city are guaranteed to keep kids amused. Alternatively, Australia's beaches and national parks provide stunningly diverse playgrounds.

Sydney The 'Search and Discover' section of the Australian Museum *(see p.70)* lets children get their hands on exciting exhibits, and the Powerhouse Museum *(see p.71)* also has stimulating Kids' Interactive Discovery Spaces.

Canberra Sights with appeal to kids are the National Zoo and Aquarium, the National Museum of Australia *(see p.112)* and the Questacon (National Science and Technology Centre, *see p.111)*.

Melbourne As well as the Royal Melbourne Zoo *(see p.173)*, the Melbourne Museum *(see p.173)* has an excellent children's section and the complex now features an Imax cinema.

Adelaide Adelaide Zoo *(see p.199)* is noted for its Australian birds; or head to the Beachouse (www.thebeachouse.com.au) in Glenelg, with its waterslides, rides, mini golf and a bouncy castle.

Brisbane Theme parks on the Gold Coast *(see p.123)* range from Wet'n' Wild Water World to Warner Brothers Movie World. Smaller kids love Sea World, while Dreamworld caters to older children. The Lone Pine Koala Sanctuary *(see p.122)* near Brisbane, and Australia Zoo *(see p.128)* north of the city, are bound to please.

Darwin Kids will enjoy the diverse wildlife at the Territory Wildlife Park. To see crocodiles, take them to Crocosaurus Cove and Crocodylus Park *(see p.161)*.

Perth Some of the best activities include the Aquarium of Western Australia *(see p.221)* and the Perth Zoo (www.perthzoo.wa.gov.au), where kids can stay overnight in summer.

Hobart The Discovery Space at the Tasmanian Museum and Art Gallery *(see p.242)* offers hands-on activities. Terrapin Puppet Theatre (www.terrapin.org.au) introduces under-12s to the magic of performance.

SETTING THE SCENE

History

Australia may have been populated for longer than Western Europe – possibly twice as long. Experts are divided about the dates, with some scientists suggesting Australia's first inhabitants arrived from Asia 50,000 or 60,000 years ago; others argue that it was far earlier.

The first migrations to Australia were most likely spurred by a period of glacial advance that encouraged the cave-dwellers of the northern hemisphere to head for the sun belt. This move set off a chain reaction, forcing more southerly folk out of their way. As ice caps accumulated, sea levels dropped drastically. So, in a search for greener pastures or more space, or perhaps blown off course, the original immigrants arrived here by boat from the north. The first Australians had little difficulty adapting to the new environment. As Stone Age hunter-gatherers, they were used to foraging, and the takings in the new continent were good: plenty of fish, berries and roots.

NAVIGATORS ARRIVE

For many millennia the Aborigines had Australia to themselves. Eventually, the rest of the world began closing in. Like the search for El Dorado, everybody seemed to be looking for Terra Australis Incognita, the 'Unknown Land of the South.' Throughout the 16th century, explorers from Europe kept their eyes peeled for the legendary continent and its presumed riches. Some may have come close, but the first known landing was by a Dutch captain, Willem Jansz, in 1606. It was

an anticlimax. 'There was no good to be done there,' was Jansz's conclusion as he weighed anchor.

However, the merchant adventurers of the Dutch East India Company were not to be discouraged. In 1642 the company dispatched one of its ace seafarers, Abel Tasman, to track down the farthest continent. On his first expedition, Tasman discovered an island that he called Van Diemen's Land – now known as Tasmania. A couple of years later he was sent back to cover much of the coast of northern Australia, but he still found no gold, silver or spices. Like Jansz before him, Tasman had nothing good to say about the indigenous people. The Dutch named Australia New Holland, but they believed the land so unpromising that they never bothered to claim it.

BOTANY BAY

Almost by accident, Captain James Cook, the great British navigator, landed on the east coast of Australia in 1770 on a very roundabout trip back to England from Tahiti. Aboard his ship *Endeavour* were the skilled naturalists Joseph Banks and Daniel Solander. They found so many fascinating specimens that Cook was moved to name the place Botany Bay.

Cook claimed all the territory he charted for George III, coining the name New South Wales. He returned to London with glowing reports of Australia: a vast, sunny, fertile land, inhabited by a native people who were 'far more happier than we Europeans.'

Captain Cook arriving at Botany Bay

In 1779 Joseph Banks, by now president of the Royal Society, had a novel idea. He proposed colonising Australia, but instead of conventional settlers, he would send out convicts as pioneers. This plan, he contended, would solve the crisis in Britain's overflowing jails. In May 1787 the British government began the transportation of criminals to Australia. The programme was to endure for 80 years. In that time more than 160,000 convicts were shipped to begin a new life 'Down Under'.

THE FIRST FLEET

A retired naval officer, Captain Arthur Phillip, was put in command of the first fleet of 11 sailing vessels carrying nearly 1,500 people – more than half of them convicts – on an eight-month voyage from Portsmouth to New South Wales. Against the odds, the convoy was a success.

Captain Phillip (now with the title Governor) came ashore in full ceremonial dress, unarmed, to meet the unwelcoming committee of spear-toting Aborigines. A lieutenant on the flagship wrote: 'I think it is very easy to conceive the ridiculous figure we must appear to these poor creatures, who were perfectly naked'.

The fleet's arrival unveiled the truth about Botany Bay, and Captain Cook's rosy claims faded to bleak. The expedition's officers discovered that there was no shelter from east winds, much of the alleged meadowland was actually swamp and there was not enough fresh water to go around. Luckily, the next best thing to paradise was waiting just around the corner. Governor Phillip and a reconnaissance party sailed 20km (12 miles) up the coast and discovered what Fleet Surgeon John White called 'the finest and most extensive harbour in the universe'. It could, he determined, provide 'safe anchorage for all the navies of Europe'. It was also strikingly beautiful. The fleet reassembled at Sydney Cove on 26 January 1788 (the date is marked every year as the

ENTER CAPTAIN BLIGH

When Governor Phillip retired, the colony's top army officer, Major Francis Grose, took over. His army subordinates fared very well under the new regime, which encouraged free enterprise. The officers soon found profitable sidelines, usually at the expense of the British taxpayers. The army's monopoly on the sale of rum made quick fortunes; under some tipsy economic law, rum began to replace money as Australia's medium of exchange. Even prisoners were paid in alcohol for their extracurricular jobs.

As news of disorder reached London, the government sent out a well-known disciplinarian to shake up the militia. He was Captain William Bligh, target of the notorious mutiny on HMS *Bounty* seven years earlier. Bligh's explosive temper was beyond control and his New South Wales victims nicknamed the new governor Caligula and plotted treason. Bligh was deposed by a group of insurgent officers on 26 January 1808, as the colony toasted its 20th anniversary. The Rum Rebellion, as the mutiny was dubbed, led to a radical reorganisation of personnel.

OPENING A CONTINENT

New South Wales, under Bligh's successor Lachlan Macquarie, gradually overcame the stigma of a penal colony and became a land of opportunity. The idealistic army officer organised the building of schools, a hospital and a courthouse, and roads to link them. To inspire exiles to go straight and win emancipation, Macquarie appointed an ex-convict as Justice of the Peace. One of the criminals Macquarie pardoned,

Captain Bligh's governorship of New South Wales did not last long

Australian national holiday), and the British flag was raised over the colony.

London's great expectations took for granted that New South Wales would be instantly self-sufficient, but the reality fell dangerously short. The Sydney summer was too hot for exertion, the soil was unpromising and most of the convicts were city-bred and didn't know the difference between a hoe and a sickle. Livestock died or disappeared in the bush. Shipwrecks and delays in London meant that relief supplies were delayed for nearly two years of increasing desperation. As food supplies dwindled, rations were cut and prisoners caught stealing food were flogged. Finally, to set an example, the Governor ordered a food looter to be hanged.

In June 1790, to all-round jubilation, the supply ship *Lady Juliana* reached Sydney Harbour and the long fast ended. As agriculture finally blossomed, many thousands of new prisoners were shipped out and even voluntary settlers chose Australia as the land of their future.

Francis Greenway, became the colony's prolific official architect.

Some of the ex-convicts fared so well under Macquarie's policies that he was accused of pampering criminals. London ordered tougher punishment, and the separation of prisoners from the rest of the population. This led to conflict between reformed criminals and their children on one side and privileged immigrants on the other. Nowadays, the shoe is on the other foot: descendants of First Fleet convicts often express the same kind of pride as Americans of *Mayflower* ancestry.

The biggest problem for Governor Macquarie and his immediate successors was the colony's position on the edge of the sea. There was not enough land to provide food for the expanding population, and the Blue Mountains, which boxed in Sydney Cove, seemed a hopeless barrier. Every attempt to break through the labyrinth of steep valleys failed. Then, in 1813, explorers Blaxland, Wentworth and Lawson had the idea of crossing the peaks rather than the valleys. It worked. Beyond the Blue Mountains they discovered a land of plenty – endless plains that would support a great new society.

Other adventurers opened new territories. Land was either confiscated or bought from the indigenous tribesmen: for 400 sq km (150 sq miles) of what is now Melbourne, the entrepreneurs gave the Aborigines a wagonload of clothing and blankets plus 30 knives, 12 tomahawks, 10 mirrors, 12 pairs of scissors and 23kg (50lb) of flour. By the mid-19th century, thousands of settlers had poured into Australia and all of the present state capitals were on the map.

AGE OF GOLD

Prospector Edward Hargraves slightly overstated the case when he declared: 'This is a memorable day in the history of New South Wales. I shall be a baronet.' The year was 1851. The place was near Bathurst, approximately 210km (130 miles) west of Sydney. Hargraves' audience consisted of one speechless colleague. The occasion was the discovery of gold in Australia.

No sooner had the news of the Bathurst find reached the farthest corner of the land than prospectors from Melbourne struck gold at Ballarat. With two colonies – New South Wales and Victoria – sharing in the boom, adventurers streamed in from both Europe and America. By 1860 Australia's population had reached 1 million. Thirty-three years later the bonanza became a coast-to-coast celebration when gold was discovered in Kalgoorlie in Western Australia.

The Australian gold rush

Life in the gold fields was rugged, aggravated by climate, flies and tax collectors. Whether big winners or small losers, all the diggers had to pay the same licence fee. Enforcement and fines were needlessly strict. Justice, the miners felt, was tilted against them, so they burned their licences and demonstrated for voting rights and other reforms. In the subsequent siege of the Eureka Stockade in Ballarat in 1854, troops were ordered to attack the demonstrators. There was heavy loss of life, and the licence fee was abandoned.

Another riot, in 1861, pitted the white prospectors against Chinese miners, who were resented for their foreignness, strong work ethic and frugality. At Lambing Flat, New South Wales, thousands of whites whipped and clubbed a community of Chinese. Police, troops and finally the courts were lenient on the attackers. It was the worst of several race riots. With the tensions of the gold rush, the notion of the 'yellow peril' was embedded in Australia's national consciousness.

ROGUES ON THE RANGE

Transportation of convicts finally ended in 1868, when London had to admit the threat of exile in Australia was no deterrent to crime. In Australia itself, crime was always a problem. Several wily characters, some escaped convicts, became bushrangers, the local version of highwaymen. They tended to rob the rich and flout authority. As the crimes grew more ambitious or outrageous, their fame was frozen into legend.

The saga of Ned Kelly (1854–80) reads like Robin Hood gone sour. The Kelly Gang preyed on bankers rather

Ned Kelly is Australia's most infamous outlaw

than humble farmers, but he killed his fair share of policemen. Wounded in a shoot-out, Kelly tried to escape in a suit of home-made armour; this contraption deflected most of the bullets, and he was captured alive. Sentenced to death, he invited the judge to meet him in the hereafter. Two weeks after Kelly was hanged, the judge, indeed, died.

AN INDEPENDENT NATION

Having received Queen Victoria's blessing, the colonies of Australia formed a new nation, the Commonwealth of Australia, on New Year's Day 1901. This federation retained the Queen as head of state, and also bowed to the parliament and Privy Council in London.

Loyalty to the British Empire was tested twice in the world wars. The Allied defeat at Gallipoli in 1915 was the first and most memorable single disaster for the Australian troops. In

World War I, over 200,000 Australians were killed or wounded.

Combat came closer to home in World War II, when Japanese planes repeatedly bombed Darwin, enemy submarines penetrated Sydney Harbour and sank a ferry (the torpedo had been fired at an American warship), ships were sunk off the Australian coast and a couple of shells hit Sydney's suburbs. American forces under General MacArthur arrived in Australia in 1942 and a US force supported by Australia defeated the Japanese decisively in the Battle of the Coral Sea in May of that year. Around 27,000 Australian servicemen died in action on the European and Asian fronts, and nearly 8,000 more died as prisoners of Japan. Almost one in three Australians taken prisoner by the Japanese died in captivity.

After the war, as Britain's regional power declined, Australia boosted its alliance with the US. More than 40,000 Australian troops fought alongside Americans in Vietnam, sparking vehement anti-war protests. Australian Prime Minister Harold Holt introduced conscription and promised US President Lyndon B. Johnson that Australia would go 'all the way with LBJ.'

CULTURAL CHANGES

Before World War II, 98 percent of Australia's population was of British or Irish descent. As for immigrants, 81 percent of Australia's overseas-born population came from the main English-speaking countries (Britain, Ireland, New Zealand, South Africa, Canada and the USA). Since then, the fortress walls of the infamous 'White Australia' immigration policy, enacted in 1901 to maintain racial purity, have been torn down under the slogan 'Populate or Perish.' Australia has seen immigration from countries including Italy, Greece, Malta, former Yugoslavia, Vietnam, Germany, the Netherlands, the Philippines, Malaysia, Lebanon, Turkey, Hong Kong, China, South Africa, Sudan, Afghanistan and Iraq.

Since 1945, Australia has accepted 6.5 million people as new settlers – about 660,000 of whom arrived under humanitarian programmes – creating a culturally diverse nation. Nearly a quarter of Australia's population is overseas-born. By 2006, only 34 percent of the overseas-born population had been born in English-speaking countries.

Australia has had an uncomfortable relationship with its own indigenous peoples, the Aborigines and Torres Strait Islanders. Together, they make up around 2.7 percent of the population, about 90 percent of whom are Aborigines. Aborigines could not vote in national elections until 1962, and were

US and Australian forces defeated the Japanese in the Battle of the Coral Sea

Thousands gathered to watch Kevin Rudd's apology to the Stolen Generations

Support continues to grow for a treaty with the Aboriginal people to foster national unity. In 2000, in cities across Australia, many thousands of citizens marched to demand that John Howard's Liberal government formally apologise to the Stolen Generations; Howard refused. No progress on the issue was made until February 2008, when Labor prime minister Kevin Rudd apologised. It remains to be seen what further steps will be taken.

REPUBLICAN LEANINGS

In the 1990s, Labor prime minister Paul Keating argued that Australia should become a republic, and engage strongly with Asia. His Liberal Party successor, John Howard, who won the 1996 election, was cut from very different political cloth. Under his stewardship Australia looked less towards Asia and more to traditional alliances with Europe and the US. In a 1999 referendum, a prototype republic was put to the vote – and rejected. Opinion polls show that Australians do, in fact, favour a republic, but they disliked the model put forward, which proposed that politicians, rather than the people, should elect the president. Britain's monarch remains Australia's head of state (represented by a governor-general), and the Union Jack still adorns its flag.

Australia entered the 21st century in an upbeat mood and with a booming economic outlook. Australia's economy was far less affected by the 2009 global financial crisis than other countries, but environmental issues abound. Scientists predict climate change will affect the country severely in coming years, causing more severe droughts and bushfires.

not included in the census until 1967. From the late 19th century until about 1970, governments forcibly removed as many as 100,000 Aboriginal children, mainly of mixed race, from their families. The children, dubbed the Stolen Generations, were taken to church missions, orphanages and foster homes.

In 1990, a government commission gave indigenous peoples the power to make decisions on social and other matters. In 1993, there were further moves towards reconciliation, with legislation effectively nullifying the doctrine of terra nullius ('uninhabited land'), which had deemed Australia to be empty at the time of European settlement and, by default, the property of the Crown. The court ruling recognised that Aborigines may hold common law rights or 'native title' to land.

Historical Landmarks

50,000BC
The Aborigines arrive on the Australian continent.

1642
Abel Tasman discovers Tasmania and New Zealand.

1770
Captain James Cook explores the east coast of Australia, which he calls New South Wales.

1788
Britain establishes a penal colony in Sydney Cove.

1808
The 'Rum Rebellion' overthrows Captain William Bligh.

1851
Gold is discovered in New South Wales.

1854
Battle of the Eureka Stockade, Ballarat.

1895
South Australian women gain voting rights; by 1901 most Australian women can vote.

1901
Six colonies federated into the Commonwealth of Australia.

1914–18
World War I: 330,000 Australians serve; 60,000 are killed, 165,000 wounded.

1917
Opening of the Trans-Australian railway.

1927
Federal parliament moves from Melbourne to Canberra.

1939–45
World War II: Australian Air Force active in Britain; navy operates in Mediterranean; soldiers fight in North Africa and the Pacific.

1956
Olympic Games held in Melbourne.

1960
Australia grants citizenship to Aborigines.

1962
Aborigines can vote in federal elections.

1972
'White Australia' immigration policy is abandoned.

1973
Sydney Opera House is finally completed.

1985
Uluru (Ayers Rock) and Kata Tjuta (The Olgas) are returned to Aboriginal owners.

1993
The Aborigines' land rights are recognised.

1999
Referendum rejects prototype republic.

2000
Olympic Games held in Sydney.

2003
Australian government supports US military action in Iraq.

2008
Prime Minister Rudd apologises to the Stolen Generations.

2009
173 people killed by bushfires in Victoria.

2010
Julia Gillard becomes prime minister after ousting Kevin Rudd as the parliamentary leader of the Australian Labor Party.

2011
Floods inundate southern Queensland, northern New South Wales and northern Victoria. Cyclone Yasi devastates coastal areas between Cairns and Townsville.

Culture

LIFESTYLE AND THE LOCALS

According to myth, the 'true Aussie' is a sun-bronzed stockman or jillaroo, riding the Outback range with a trusty sheepdog. In reality, Australia is the most urbanised country on earth, with 80 percent of the population living in cities (66 percent in the state capitals). More precisely, it's the most suburbanised country on earth, where the Great Australian Dream, still enjoyed by a huge proportion of the population, is to live on your own quarter-acre block of land.

Most Australians now work in office jobs, and wouldn't recognise a trough of sheep dip if they fell into it. And although many still see the Outback as somehow embodying the most distinctive part of the country, relatively few have visited it, let alone considered living there. The fact is that Australians have clung to the coast rather naturally, shrugging off the priggish, cramped and tight-lipped spirit of the first British settlers and openly embracing the more sensual and hedonistic spirit of their Mediterranean environment. In the 21st century, the coast – and specifically the beach – has a far more powerful claim on Australian souls than the Outback.

Leisure has become crucial to the Australian way of life – while working nine to five provides the means, it is at the weekends when Aussies truly come into their own.

And few other places give people such opportunities to use their leisure well. Nature is close in Australia as nowhere else: in Sydney with its 70 metropolitan beaches, in Melbourne with one-third of its area devoted to parkland.

MULTICULTURALISM

When a survey in 1939 showed that 98 percent of the Australian population was comprised of Anglo-Celtic stock, local newspapers proudly proclaimed that Australia was the most 'British' country on earth.

All that changed after 1945, when Australia embarked on one of the most ambitious immigration programmes of the modern era. The migrants were drawn first from the Mediterranean and Baltic countries of Europe, then –from the 1970s onwards – from around the world.

Migration from Britain to Australia was commonplace in the 1940s

Since the programme began, more than 6 million settlers from almost 200 countries have made Australia their home.

Almost one-quarter of the population was born overseas; 15 percent speak a language other than English at home. The humanitarian programme is gradually adding even more diversity to the population. In the 1990s, most of these arrivals came from the Balkans; lately African, Sri Lankan and Afghan arrivals have topped the list, and the guiding principle of Australia's immigration policy, and of society in general, has generally become 'multiculturalism' – tolerance and respect for all cultures and races.

Although the multicultural society is a *fait accompli*, balancing the demands of such a heterogeneous population can be a delicate task. Ethnic loyalties are encouraged, but the first loyalty must be to the Australian legal and parliamentary system; multiple languages are promoted, but English is the official tongue; and any coercive cultural practices, such as arranged marriages, are illegal.

Overall, the Australian experience of immigration has been one of the most successful in history, and it has been widely accepted as the key to the country's vitality.

RELIGION
Outwardly, Australia doesn't appear to have a strong religious element in its overall culture, though 64 percent of Australians call themselves Christian. The 5 percent of the population

The Moomba parade is held annually in Melbourne

that make up non-Christian religious groups include Buddhism (2 percent), Islam (1.7 percent) and Jewish (0.4 percent). Nearly 19 percent of Australians claim to have no religious beliefs.

The Dreamtime is central to Aboriginal religious beliefs. *See p.54* for more information.

EARLY ARTS
In music, drama, literature, film and the visual arts, Australia has absorbed influences from around the world – and now has its own distinctive voice.

The first century of Australian European culture was, unsurprisingly, entirely derivative. The white convicts and their white jailers took little notice of the Aboriginal culture that had been in existence in Australia for at least 50,000 years before their arrival. Georgian English art was transplanted to Australian soil at the same time as European crops.

The first great turning point in Australian cultural history was the

Culture

1890s, which saw a tremendous upsurge in Australian nationalism. This was reflected in the arts, especially in literature, and it was during this period that *The Bulletin* magazine's school of balladists and short-story writers got under way. Balladists such as Banjo Paterson, who wrote *The Man from Snowy River*, and Henry Lawson, Australia's finest short-story writer, celebrated the bush and its male traditions such as mateship, Aussie nationalism and the underdog, at the expense of the ruling Anglophile 'bunyip aristocracy'. Joseph Furphy wrote his novel *Such is Life* (said to be the last words of Ned Kelly, the bushranger and folk hero, before he was hanged) at this time.

AUSTRALIAN NATIONALISM

At a more popular level, Steele Rudd began writing his *On Our Selection* series, about life on poverty-stricken bush properties. A little later, C.J. Dennis started celebrating city larrikins in his poems about Ginger Mick and The Sentimental Bloke.

This creative leap was the start of a distinctive Australian literature, which continued strongly in the 20th century through the novels of Henry Handel Richardson, Miles Franklin, Christina Stead and Eve Langley, the short stories of Barbara Baynton, Gavin Casey and Peter Cowan, and the poetry of Christopher Brennan, Kenneth Slessor, R.D. Fitzgerald, Douglas Stewart and Judith Wright.

A similar nationalistic burst could be seen in the other arts of the 1890s. A recognisable Australian school of landscape painting emerged and crystallised in the work of Sir Arthur Streeton, Tom Roberts and the Heidelberg School (named after the Melbourne suburb). Dame Nellie Melba, the first of a line of Australian opera divas, made an international name singing French arias in Italian in British concert halls and gave her name to an ice-cream dessert, the Peach Melba.

Australians made *Soldiers of the Cross*, which is said to be the world's first feature film, and the film industry flourished.

In the late 1920s and early 1930s, an important change took place. At the very time that Australia was beginning to break free politically

C.J. Dennis' writing helped kick-start a distinctive brand of Australian literature

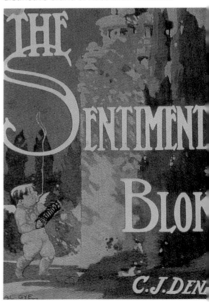

and culturally of British domination, it came under the influence of the United States. In doing this, Australia was taking part in the internationalisation of an immensely influential American culture, the influence of which is still felt today.

Despite this, a vernacular Australian culture continued to develop and strengthen itself. In a sense, it had merely added the American to the British, European and Asian ingredients already stirred into the local mix. There was considerable resistance to some of the American input: the traditional arts kept very close to their British and European sources, and American culture, though glamorous, was regarded as inferior.

CULTURAL GROWTH

The late 1960s and 1970s were the next great period of Australian cultural growth. The perils of World War II gave a boost to Australian nationalism, and the 1960s and early 1970s were a time of economic growth and growing self-confidence. Meanwhile, the nation's isolation seemed to have come to an end, as a massive immigration programme brought millions of migrants from Britain and Europe.

There was a sense of the old, stale moulds, which had contained Australian life for so long, being broken open, and the time was ripe for a cultural take-off. The traditional connection with British high culture was weakening, and the American input seemed to have been partly absorbed. The poets led the way. At first they were dominated by

academics such as A.D. Hope and James McAuley. These were followed by a loose collection of poets, such as David Malouf, Tom Shapcott, Bruce Dawe, Les Murray, Gwen Harwood, John Tranter and Robert Adamson, who adopted a freer, more vernacular approach to their verse and concentrated more on specifically Australian themes.

In the novel, progress was steadier, perhaps because it was dominated for so long by the late Patrick White. The 1974 Nobel Laureate influenced younger novelists, especially through his poetic prose style. A new generation of writers, including Shirley Hazzard, Helen Garner, Tim Winton, Murray Bail, Alex Miller, Peter Carey and David Malouf, has well and truly arrived on the world stage over recent decades, as have David Foster, Kate Grenville, Murray Bail, Joanna Murray-Smith, Geraldine Brooks and Richard Flanagan and a string of Aboriginal writers. Nobel Laureate J.M. Coetzee also lives and writes here.

FILM

With a burst of dramatic talent and new government incentives, the film industry became Australia's biggest cultural export, and the business generated A$1.5 billion in 2000.

The most celebrated films range from the brutal post-apocalpytic *Mad Max* series starring Mel Gibson to period pieces (Gillian Armstrong's 1979 version of the Miles Franklin classic, *My Brilliant Career*; Peter Weir's atmospheric *Picnic at Hanging Rock* in 1975); from George Miller's 1996 talking pig, *Babe*, to Baz Luhrmann's

Mad Max is still one of the most celebrated Australian films

dazzling dance comedy *Strictly Ballroom*, the drag-queen frenzy of *Priscilla, Queen of the Desert* and the kitschy vision of *Muriel's Wedding*.

Australian actors such as Nicole Kidman, Cate Blanchett, Toni Collette, Geoffrey Rush, Eric Bana, Guy Pearce and Hugh Jackman have become big names in Hollywood, following in the footsteps of Judy Davis and Mel Gibson; Russell Crowe, though born in New Zealand, has spent most of his life in Australia.

There are also actors and directors who prefer to create work that reflects the realities of modern Australia. In the early noughties, for instance, a spate of indigenous-themed films was released, including *Rabbit-Proof Fence* (Philip Noyce's 2002 tale of three Aboriginal girls trekking across the Outback to escape from menial jobs), *The Tracker*, *Yolngu Boy*, *Beneath Clouds* and *Australian Rules*. In 2006, Rolf de

Heer, the director of *The Tracker*, won international praise for *Ten Canoes*, the first Australian film to feature an entirely indigenous cast and to be spoken entirely in indigenous languages. In 2009, *Samson and Delilah* was filmed in Alice Springs with an Aboriginal cast and crew, winning international acclaim and an award at Cannes.

ART

Painting and sculpture enjoyed such popularity in the mid-1970s that it was commonplace to talk of an art boom, with buyers and business investors paying very high prices for local works.

Melbourne was the early focus; after World War II, a group of figurative painters emerged as 'the Australian School'. Its practitioners included Sidney Nolan, whose series on Ned Kelly, the outlaw bushranger, became national icons; Albert Tucker, whose cover illustration helped make Donald Horne's *The Lucky Country* a bestseller; Arthur Boyd, Lloyd Rees and Clifton Pugh.

In the early 1970s Sydney became the centre for an abstract expressionist movement that drew upon earlier painters such as Ian Fairweather, Mike Brown and Godfrey Miller, and was soon experimenting with hard edge, colour field and lyrical expressionist modes. Eric Smith, William Rose, John Coburn and Stanislaus Rapotec were followed by a new breed of younger painters such as Brett Whiteley, Jeffrey Smart, David Aspden, Michael Johnson, Peter Booth and Tim Storrier.

In Melbourne, Fred Williams established himself as the most important landscape painter of the post-war years – possibly in the history of Australian painting – with his haunting, semi-abstract depictions of the Outback.

Pop diva Kylie Minogue is one of the country's most famous exports

Contemporary visual artists of note include Tracey Moffatt, Ricky Swallow, Callum Morton, Bill Henson, Adam Cullen, Tim Maguire and Judy Watson.

MUSIC

Classical music in Australia has always been a matter of performance rather than composition. The nation has several well-established symphony orchestras, chamber groups and opera companies, including The Australian Opera. Despite the limited opportunities, contemporary composers such as Richard Meale, Peter Sculthorpe, Nigel Butterley, George Dreyfus, Anne Boyd and Moya Henderson frequently have their work performed here and in other countries. Ballet has shared in the recent growth in the 'high' arts, helped by the work of such dancer-choreographers as Graeme Murphy and Kai Tai Chan.

In recent years, Australia has become as well known for its rock bands as its films, and the local pub music scene, especially in Melbourne and Sydney, is extraordinarily healthy. Performers such as Nick Cave, Dave Graney, Powderfinger, The Cruel Sea, Jet and Wolfmother started off on the pub circuit and now enjoy international success. Other groups that made it big overseas include the Easybeats, the Seekers, the BeeGees, Skyhooks, the Go-Betweens, Mental as Anything, AC/DC, INXS and Men at Work. One of Australia's best-known exports is Kylie Minogue, a former teenage soap star and now pop icon.

Food and Drink

NATIONAL CUISINE

Not so long ago, the term 'Australian cuisine' conjured up grisly images of meat pies, Vegemite sandwiches and sausage rolls. Then, almost out of the blue, Australia transformed itself into a paradise for foodies. Few places in the world have restaurants that can compare with the variety, quality and sheer inventiveness of Australia's.

The starting point for the Australian food revolution was the massive migration from Mediterranean countries after World War II. Italians in particular helped revolutionise cooking, introducing wary Aussies to the wonders of pasta, garlic and olive oil. Today, each capital city has its concentration of Italian restaurants – Melbourne's Lygon Street and Sydney's Leichhardt being the most famous – serving authentic,

well-priced food. Meanwhile, classic French methods became the undisputed basis of fine cooking.

This was only the beginning. The extension of immigration in the 1970s added myriad new cuisines. The great 'melting pot' – or perhaps more appropriately 'salad bowl' – of Australian society meant that restaurants were suddenly opened by Lebanese, Turkish, Balkan, Hungarian and Spanish chefs. More recently, the biggest impact by far has been Asian cuisine.

The acknowledged basis of Australia's great cuisine is the quality of its ingredients. Aussies were slow to recognise the wealth of seafood swimming in their waters, but now a range of fresh fish is on every menu, and the local fish and chippery serves quality grilled or battered fish.

Toto's is one of many Italian restaurants on Lygon Street in Melbourne

Small farms devote themselves to gourmet beef and poultry, while the quality of everyday vegetables tends to be better than anything grown on organic farms in Europe or the United States. And far from pining for imports of French cheese, Greek olives or Italian wine, Australians are now producing their own – often of a superior standard.

Like Italy and France, Australia can be divided into regions that are known for particular produce: King Island cream, Sydney rock oysters, Bowen mangoes, Coffin Bay scallops, Tasmanian salmon, Illabo milk-fed lamb. Each state has its acknowledged specialities, which travellers should take advantage of. Tropical Queensland produces a wealth of exotic fruits (try Bowen mangoes and papaya in season), succulent reef fish, mudcrabs and Moreton Bay bugs (shellfish, not insects). The Northern Territory can add the white-fleshed barramundi and Mangrove Jack to the list of tropical fish, while in Darwin, buffalo and crocodile are regularly served as steaks and burgers.

New South Wales has Hunter Valley wines, buffalo mozzarella, Balmain bugs and perfect Sydney rock oysters. Victoria produces some of the most tender meats, such as Gippsland beef and Meredith lamb, Mallee squab and corn-fed chicken. Tasmania is one of the least-polluted corners of the globe, and has gained national attention for its salmon, trout, cheeses, Pacific oysters and raspberries. South Australia is home to the Barossa Valley wine industry,

Many Australians won't go without their Vegemite

cold-pressed virgin olive oil, Coffin Bay scallops, olive oils, tuna and cultivated native foods. Finally, Western Australia has received rave reviews for its superb new wines from the southwest and for its goat's and washed rind cheeses.

This abundance of superlative local produce – including native foods – and the plethora of international cuisines brought to Australia by its immigrants has prompted an astonishing flurry of innovation over the past few decades. The result is a Modern Australian cuisine, sometimes referred to as 'Pacific Rim'. Basically, it involves adding Asian flavours such as lemon grass, coriander, chilli and cardamom to essentially European dishes.

A Modern Asian cuisine has also emerged, as Asian chefs substitute traditional ingredients for unusual local ones: Cantonese stir-fried kangaroo meat, perhaps, or barramundi in a Thai green curry. And with the added options from the

Food and Drink

Mediterranean, young Australian chefs are currently afire with their own powers of invention.

Some Australian chefs have acquired celebrity status, and restaurants' fortunes rise and fall depending on which name is currently in the kitchen. Celebrity chefs with award-winning restaurants and/ or bestselling cookbooks include Stephanie Alexander, Maggie Beer, Shannon Bennett, Guillaume Brahimi, George Calombaris, Bill Granger, Kylie Kwong, Andrew McConnell, Christine Manfield, Karen Martini, Matt Moran, Justin North, Ben O'Donoghue, Neil Perry, Stefano di Pieri, David Thompson and Tetsuya Wakuda.

Recent innovations by Australian chefs have included greater use of indigenous foods in fine dining. Lemon aspen, bush tomatoes, Illawarra plums, lemon myrtle, lilli pillies, muntari berries and other

Luckily, bugs are shellfish, not insects

mysterious ingredients are appearing on menus, often blended with traditional dishes of meat and fish. Kangaroo and emu are commercially farmed and processed (both meats are low in fat and high in protein). Collectively known as native food

Seasonal Eating

Australia is a huge country with a vast range of climatic zones, all producing products at different times of the year. This means that many products are cross-seasonal, but the following provides a very basic guide (note that meat is generally multi-seasonal):

Summer: apricot, asparagus, Atlantic salmon, aubergine, barramundi (Nov–Dec), berries, capsicum, cherry, courgette, cucumber, mango, nectarine, peach, peas, pineapple, rockmelon, salmon, tomato, watermelon
Autumn: apple, Asian greens, banana, beetroot, broccoli, Brussels sprouts,

cauliflower, fennel, fig, grapes, lemon, lime, mandarin, mushrooms, parsnip, pear, plum, pomegranate, potato, pumpkin, quince, silverbeet, spinach
Winter: blood orange, horseradish, Jerusalem artichoke, kale, kohlrabi, nuts, okra, olives, snapper, warehou, whiting, spring lamb (end of winter)
Spring: artichoke, asparagus, Atlantic salmon, blood orange, coral trout, papaya, Seville orange, tangelo

To check the seasonality of many more products, go to www.marketfresh.com.au and www.sydneyfishmarket.com.au

– or sometimes bush tucker – these are just some of the fruits, seeds, nuts, fungi, mammals, reptiles, fish and birds that sustained Australia's indigenous inhabitants for up to 100,000 years before white settlers came to the region.

Other bush-tucker ingredients include quandongs (similar to a peach with a touch of rhubarb), wattle seeds (sometimes used in ice cream), Kakadu plums (less sweet than the usual variety) and bunya bunya nuts (delicious in satays). Even wilder Aboriginal ingredients, very rarely seen in restaurants, include the Bogong moth (a hefty moth roasted in a fire and eaten like a peanut) and the witchetty grub (a puffy, white grub found in the trunks and roots of certain wattle trees), which tastes like a cross between prawns, peanuts, pork crackling and chicken skin, and has been shown to be a virtual powerhouse of protein.

WHERE TO EAT

If you enjoy dining out at down-to-earth prices, with a wide choice of menus reflecting varied ethnic influences, you're going to enjoy mealtimes in Australia's cities.

Eating well here doesn't carry an inflated price tag, either, as the whole country is well stocked with inexpensive bistros, cafés and food markets where diverse and wholesome cuisines can be enjoyed at moderate prices.

Italian, French, Regional Chinese, Thai, Vietnamese, Japanese and Indian restaurants are ubiquitous, with the Korean, Sri Lankan, Singaporean, Malaysian, Lebanese, Greek, Ethiopian, Spanish, Turkish and Indonesian cuisines also popular. Singapore-style 'food courts' have sprung up in cities, with several fast-food stalls offering meals from different Asian cuisines. Favourite snacks for busy Australians are Japanese sushi,

Food and Drink

Doyles on the Beach is a Sydney favourite

Lebanese falafel, Malaysian laksa and Indian samosas. Supermarkets stock the required pastes and condiments for everyone's favourite Thai, Malaysian or Indian dish.

Fine-dining options are generally restricted to inner-city areas and some wine-producing regions, but most suburbs and country towns have at least one decent Thai or Chinese restaurant. There are, however, culinary black holes, especially in remote rural areas, where café menus will probably include nothing more exotic than spaghetti bolognese. The traditional Aussie meat pie, doused liberally with tomato sauce, rules supreme in these outposts, as does the hamburger. Outside the standardised US chains, Australian hamburgers tend to include beetroot, lettuce, egg, onion and occasionally pineapple; pickles are strictly for American-style burgers.

Don't miss a chance to visit Australia's wine-growing areas

DRINKS

Drinking is one of Australia's great pastimes, whether it be downing a beer in a classic Aussie pub, sipping an Australian red in a European-style wine bar or having your daily caffeine fix in a busy city café. In fact, there are many European-style wine bars where you can indulge in all three types of refreshment – a few will also offer the opportunity to snack on tapas or dine in full. Australian cities like Melbourne and Sydney pride themselves on the quality of their caffeine brew and café culture.

The wines of Australia are among the world's best – a judgement consistently confirmed at international wine shows. Not only are the country's finest wines world-beaters, but even the humble cask wine is the worthy equivalent of any *vin de table* served in a bistro in France.

Australians drink more than twice as much wine per capita as Americans, and anything that's left over (800 million litres of it) is exported to over 100 countries. Wine is one of the country's most important export industries and the range sold in liquor stores is extensive and usually moderately priced.

Most of Australia's European grape varieties are grown by some 2,400 producers on 158,000 hectares (390,000 acres) of vineyards.

Riesling, Chardonnay and Semillon are the most favoured white varieties, while popular reds include Cabernet Sauvignon, Pinot Noir, Merlot and Shiraz (also known in Europe as Syrah). Climatic conditions ranging from warm to hot provide excellent ripening, with an abundance of flavour (and often high alcohol levels). Australia's vintage (harvest) occurs between January and May each year.

If you're interested in seeing where the wine comes from, every state capital has wine-growing areas nearby, and the chance to sample wines at the cellar door is one of their most interesting features. As most wineries are concentrated in a relatively small area, they make ideal touring for a day or – better still – two days, either independently or on a guided tour. *See p.28* for more about the country's major food and wine trails.

Of course, wine isn't the only tipple of choice. During the 19th century, most Australian beer was made in the style of English ales. Just over 100 years ago, German immigrants began to brew lighter Continental-style lagers in Melbourne, and nowadays lager is the dominant style. It's a hugely popular drop throughout the country.

Beer in Australia is served very cold. Low temperature is considered so important that beer-lovers will insist on glasses that have been chilled, or will keep their 'tinnie' (beer can) or 'stubbie' (small bottle) in an insulating jacket (often decorated in football team colours).

The best-known beer is probably Foster's lager, but that's only one of many varieties. Reschs, Tooheys, Victoria Bitter, Castlemaine XXXX, Swan, Cascade and Boag's are also popular brands. Some beers are sold in 'new' and 'old' types, the first being lager and the latter darker in colour. Coopers beer, made in South Australia, is a favourite among connoisseurs – it's rich and strong, similar to the best British real ales. Cascade, made in Tasmania, regularly wins international competitions and has a devoted following around the country.

Australia's standard alcoholic strength for canned beer is 4.9 percent – pretty strong by international standards. A word of advice for weight watchers from Europe or America: the word 'light' or 'lite' applied to beer in Australia means lighter in alcohol, not lighter in calories; it has exactly the same calorific content as the regular type. The alcoholic strength of beer is displayed on the can or bottle.

Food and Drink

Beer is the nation's other favourite tipple – best served cold

Index

Accommodation Index

Credits for Berlitz Handbook Australia

Written by: Virginia Maxwell and David McClymont
Series Editor: Tom Stainer
Cartography Editor: Zoë Goodwin
Map Production: Stephen Ramsay
Production: Linton Donaldson, Rebeka Ellam
Picture Manager: Steven Lawrence
Art Editors: Richard Cooke and Ian Spick
Photography: Sarah Ackerman 143; Androuk 87; Avlyx 5BL, 6MR, 142, 187; AWL Images 8BR, 46, 72, 81, 222, 223; Bidgee 265; Andrew Braithwaite 196; Brett Boardman/Mona 9ML; J Brew 9BR, 51, 60/61, 131; Chris Burchill 262; Gonzalo Carles 12; Courtesy Coral Princess Cruises 147; Rob Dasha 5CL; APA Jerry Dennis 14, 40, 42, 169/T, 170, 172, 173, 174, 177, 178, 179, 180, 182, 183, 184, 185, 241, 244, 245, 246, 247, 248, 249, 250, 251, 252, 261, 287, 296, 297; Du Re Mi 15B; Eli Duke 7TL; Electric Images 22; Sheila Ellen 217T, 235; Love In Elgin 33; Eli Fan 192; Thin Boy Fatter 88; Fotolia 186; Marc Fueg 130; G4Glenno 58; Hector Garcia 86; Helen Genevere 206; Getty Images 107, 210, 284; APA Glyn Genin 2TL, 3TL, 4TL, 5BR/TL, 6TR, 8T, 9TL/TR, 12, 16, 17, 31, 34, 35, 47, 50, 54, 55, 56, 65BL, 67, 68, 70, 71, 74, 75, 76, 77, 98, 99, 101, 102, 103, 149/T, 151, 152, 153, 154, 155/T, 156, 168, 159, 160, 161, 199/T, 201, 203, 204, 217B, 219, 220, 225, 229, 330, 258/259, 263, 264, 265, 273, 274, 293, 294, 295; MD111 69, 90; Miles Goodhew 208; Jimmy Harris 141; iStockphoto 4B, 5TR, 7TR, 23, 24, 27, 32, 48, 49, 79, 91, 92, 128, 132, 133, 157, 142T, 268, 269, 270, 271; Mark Johnson 93; Aiden Jones 134, 135, 138; Atsushi Kase 256; Tim Keegan 96; Jiaren Lau 125; Robyn Lawrence 15T; Mike Lawton 212; Tina Li 140; Loloieg 73, 89, 334 Pail London 146; Stefan M 195; Mela Louise 144; Glen McClarty 30B; Macro2000 43; Ann Oliver 214; Pat Ong 226, 236; PA Photos 291; Courtesy Penitentiary Chapel 242; Photolibrary 6bBL/TL, 7B/MR, 8BL, 25, 39, 52, 57, 59, 190, 207, 228, 332, 333; Pro Dive Cairns 3TR, 4TR; APA Peter Quinn 106; Redvers 18; Rex Features 290; Peter Ross 167; Scott Sandars 111; Paul Sayer 243; Andrea Schaffer 104; Shiny Things 189; Harry Watson Smith 87T; APA Virginia Starr 175, 194, 267, 292; APA Peter Stuckings 9BL, 10/11, 13, 20/21, 44, 45, 53, 119/T, 121, 122, 123, 126, 127, 134, 135, 136, 137, 276/277; Amanda Slater 95, 100, 139, 202, 221, 338; Superstock 109BL, 209; Malcolm Tredinnick 117; Topfoto 279, 280, 281, 282, 283, 286; Tourism Australia 28, 29, 36, 37, 80, 84, 85, 94, 109T, 112, 113, 31; Werner Forman Archive 2TR; Robert Young 227; ZoomZoom 188

Cover: front: photolibrary.com; back: iStockphoto
Printed by: CTPS-China
© 2011 APA Publications GmbH & Co. Verlag KG (Singapore branch)
7030 Ang Mo Kio Ave 5
08-65 Northstar @ AMK
Singapore 569880
apasin@singnet.com.sg

First Edition 2011
Reprinted 2011

Contact Us: We strive to keep our guides as accurate and up to date as possible, but if you find anything that has changed, or if you have any suggestions on ways to improve this guide, please write to Berlitz Publishing, PO Box 7910, London SE1 1WE, UK, or email: berlitz@apaguide.co.uk;
Worldwide: APA Publications GmbH & Co. Verlag KG (Singapore branch), 7030 Ang Mo Kio Ave 5, 08-65 Northstar @ AMK, Singapore 569880; tel: (65) 570 1051; email: apasin@singnet.com.sg
UK and Ireland: GeoCenter International Ltd, Meridian House, Churchill Way West, Basingstoke, Hampshire, RG21 6YR; tel: (44) 01256-817 987; email: sales@geocenter.co.uk
United States: Ingram Publisher Services, 1 Ingram Boulevard, PO Box 3006, La Vergne, TN 37086-1986; email: customer.service@ingrampublisherservices.com
Australia: Universal Publishers, 1 Waterloo Road, Macquarie Park, NSW 2113; tel: (61) 2-9857 3700; email: sales@universalpublishers.com.au

www.berlitzpublishing.com